POLITICAL PHILOSOPH

Chief Editor of the Series:
Howard Williams, University of Wales, Aberystwyth

Associate Editors:
Wolfgang Kersting, University of Kiel, Germany
Steven B. Smith, Yale University, USA
Peter Nicholson, University of York, England

Political Philosophy Now is a series which deals with authors, topics and periods in political philosophy from the perspective of their relevance to current debates. The series presents a spread of subjects and points of view from various traditions which include European and New World debates in political philosophy.

POLITICAL PHILOSOPHY NOW

Hegel and Marx after the Fall of Communism

David MacGregor

UNIVERSITY OF WALES PRESS • CARDIFF • 1998

© David MacGregor, 1998

British Library Cataloguing-in-Publication Data
A catalogue record for this book is available from the British Library.

ISBN 0–7083–1429–5 cased
     0–7083–1430–9 paperback

All rights reserved. No part of this book may be reproduced, stored in a retrieval system, or transmitted, in any form or by any means, electronic, mechanical, photocopying, recording or otherwise, without clearance from the University of Wales Press, 6 Gwennyth Street, Cardiff, CF2 4YD.

The right of David MacGregor to be identified as author of this work has been asserted by him in accordance with the Copyright, Designs and Patents Act, 1988.

Typeset by The Midlands Book Typesetting Company, Loughborough.
Printed in Great Britain by Dinefwr Press, Llandybïe.

For Ethan, Rachael and Patricia

Contents

Acknowledgements — viii

Introduction — ix

1 Marx's Relationship with Hegel — 1

2 Dialectics of Youth and Maturity — 31

3 Hegel's Development, 1770–1801 — 48

4 Hegel and Tom Paine in the Age of Revolution — 63

5 Revolution, Despotism and Censorship, 1801–1831 — 89

6 Property and the Corporation — 112

7 Labour and Civil Society — 141

8 The State in Time — 174

Notes — 209

Index — 237

Acknowledgements

Howard Williams generously invited me to contribute this volume to the Political Philosophy Now series, and even suggested the title. Many friends and colleagues have read and criticized parts or all of it, including Joe Hermer, Kathy Kopinak, Sandy Aylward, Paul Werstine, Jacques Goutor, Jim Kow, Jane Borecky, Ted Winslow, Norma Jo Baker and Ken Westhues. My friend Gillian Watts prepared the index for the book. The Research Grants Committee of King's College extended helpful financial assistance. During the writing of this book my young son became a junior athlete, and I plunged into the strange world inhabited by soccer and hockey parents, where discussions about Hegel and Marx, surprisingly, were not out of place! I want to acknowledge the support and comfort I have received from Matthew Delean, and parents at Toronto's West End United Soccer Club, and from parents of players in the Ted Reeve Thunder Novice A (1996–7) and Minor Atom A (1997–8) teams of the Metro Toronto Hockey League, especially John and Sue Stewart and Brett Lye. I must also express gratitude for the painstaking work of the editorial staff of the University of Wales Press. My family has borne the trials of this book with extraordinary cheerfulness. I owe everything to my spouse Patricia Bishop, and to my children, Ethan and Rachael.

Introduction

Hegel and Marx

Decisively opened to Western capitalism in the 1990s, the former communist republics have been baptized with blood and soaked in Pepsi-Cola. As I started to write this book, in the summer of 1994, the Canadian Harvey's burger chain and USA's McDonald's were fighting for space on Prague's Wenceslas Square in the infant Czech Republic. Kellogg's announced a Corn Flakes plant opening in Latvia. In the summer of 1996, the great newspaper *Pravda*, founded by Lenin before the Russian Revolution, disappeared. It was closed by its two Greek owners who complained that the newspaper's staff had become lazy and unmanageable. In January 1997, as this book neared completion, the boss of a notorious Moscow gang was shot to death in his BMW 525 sedan a few metres away from Moscow police headquarters. Two bodyguards waited in a small Russian Zhiguli car just behind him. Mr Naumov's brazen slaying was followed by a startling disclosure. His bodyguards were themselves members of an élite paramilitary police unit who were protecting the gang leader under a contract for cash signed by their superior officers.[1]

Once Moscow printing presses flooded Europe and North America with bargain copies of Lenin, Engels and Marx. Today they are run by apostles of the Harvard Business School. Jobless ex-Soviet rocket scientists hawk nuclear secrets of the FSU (former Soviet Union) to Western news correspondents and Third World dictators. Where previously their greatest concern may have been with the secret police, foreigners in Moscow risk being mobbed by beggars or murdered by the Russian Mafia. Wealth looted from the FSU by former commissars and industrial *apparatchiks* is laundered in the West and reappears in Russia and the other republics as respectable 'foreign investment'. An expert on the Italian Mafia warns that unless the Russian state learns 'to produce the basic goods and services which are associated with the definition, enforcement and protection of property rights . . . Sicily is a reminder to Russians of the path they are likely to go down'.[2]

The Soviet superpower has all but become a US client state, and its erstwhile fealty to Marx has evolved into a cruel joke, as illustrated by US investigative reporter Seymour Hersh:

> A former senior State Department official provides a graphic description of his visit to a former Soviet republic: 'My image is Harpo Marx. You go to discuss foreign affairs with the Foreign Minister. As you get up to leave, he opens his coat. He's got a bottle of aspirin and a $3.95 watch for sale.'[3]

In the United States a fashionable auction house reports there is no longer much demand for artefacts associated with early twentieth-century Marxist revolutionaries. A document autographed by Trotsky went for a song. Marxism has lost its former market value.

Now that the West has less need to compete ideologically with world communism the façade of equality and freedom – never very convincing in any event – is being lifted entirely from social relations. Race riots are common in big European cities. In the USA and Canada equal opportunity legislation is abandoned. The poor are to be jettisoned and the rich allowed to pollute at will. Similar movements are at work in the nations of the European community, and in Australia and New Zealand. Any notion that government should be independent of the business system has been discredited, in theory as well as in practice. In 1995, to cite an instructive example, the world-famed Royal Canadian Mounted Police sold its name and product rights to the Walt Disney Corporation.

In this age of triumphant capitalism can there be any room for the alternative vision of G. W. F. Hegel and Karl Marx? I will argue in this book that the two thinkers are even more vital now that commissars have become free-marketeers and the Mounties have joined the Mickey Mouse Club. To grasp Hegel's and Marx's continued importance, however, means interpreting their work afresh, and settling accounts with standard assessments of the two thinkers.

Most interpreters suggest Marx (1818–83) is the more important of the two. Apart from the rarefied world of Hegel scholarship, Hegel (1770–1831) is often seen as a strange conservative philosopher who played an ambiguous role in the young Marx's development. Let us look briefly at some of the ways in which their relationship has been portrayed.

Even before 1917 the ideal of Marx's communism inspired many in the West who rejected the capitalist order. Initially the Soviet experiment seemed to confirm this ideal, and helped to anchor radical movements which grew in the Hungry Thirties. The giant war effort mounted

INTRODUCTION

by the Soviets against Hitler attested to communism's strength and relevance. Communist theory and literature thrived. Hegel belonged on every diligent party member's reading list. The Hegelian dialectic, as interpreted by Friedrich Engels and V. I. Lenin, was a staple of debate in party conferences. Orthodox communism took for granted Marx's own account of his relationship with Hegel. In Marx's famous words, he turned Hegel's idealism upside down, and rescued the 'rational kernel from the mystical shell'.[4]

A left opposition to Soviet 'Marxism-Leninism' rooted in Hegelian thought began in the 1920s. Here Hegel appeared more an autonomous thinker than second fiddle to Marx. Hegelian Marxism provided a haven for communists disillusioned with Stalinist betrayal. In the post-Stalinist period the Hegelian influence dwindled among orthodox communists. This ceded to Hegelian Marxists such as Alexandre Kojève, Georg Lukács and Herbert Marcuse a near-monopoly on left-wing Hegel studies. In the 1960s and 1970s Hegelianized 'Western Marxism' flourished on university campuses and on the left wing of the social democratic movement. 'The Marx-Hegel relationship', noted the French Marxist Louis Althusser in 1970, 'is a currently decisive theoretical and political question.'[5]

Hegelian Marxism apparently went into eclipse by the early 1980s. The varieties of socialist theory that multiplied in the West during the 1980s and early 1990s generally took pride in rejecting much of Hegel's message. The Italian theorist, Gramsci, was a favourite of many Marxists. He filled the void in anti-capitalist cultural and intellectual theory created by Hegel's absence. Another powerful stream of radical theory, analytical Marxism, abandoned much of Marxism's former terrain, and Hegel as well. Led by thinkers like Eric Roemer and Jon Elster, this current of Marxism concentrated on subtle and complex logico-mathematical models loosely based on certain Marxian formulas.[6]

Feminists, I would argue, have done some of the most exciting theoretical work of the last two decades. Many feminist theorists have some sympathy for Marx, finding his categories useful in their own analysis. Few can tolerate Hegel, however. Although earlier twentieth-century feminist writers like Simone de Beauvoir acknowledged their debt to him, ambivalence about Hegel predominates in recent feminist literature. Hegel is seen as a 'phallogocentric or "male rationalist"' philosopher whose writings dwell primarily 'on the white European Christian bourgeois woman, the wife of the male citizen, and ignore[] all differences between women'.[7]

Strangely, the retreat from Hegel made Marxism dependent on a brittle form of millenarianism. Most writers presented no coherent alternative to capitalism, relying instead on an inchoate notion of total revolution, in which few truly believed. Some Marxists fled, opting for the siren call of postmodernism. Indeed, the postmodernist outlook – featuring a blanket rejection of universal or totalizing schemes associated with Hegel – was invented in the 1970s by disillusioned Parisian Marxists, perhaps as a form of consolation for a failed left movement, as Terry Eagleton speculates.[8]

While Marxism lurched away from Hegel, he was embraced fervently by neo-conservatives in the United States. They adopted a modified form of the Hegelian End of History thesis, as set forth by Francis Fukuyama, according to which liberal capitalism is the last, best form of society on earth. From this standpoint, the agenda of history would be the privatization of the entire globe, until nothing remained except what can be itemized on a corporate balance sheet.

Paradoxically, the success of the neo-conservative swing to Hegel brought renewed interest among Marxists. A revival of Hegel among radical theorists may now be under way. I want to suggest that a new generation of thinkers is likely to find Hegel much more conducive to the project for progressive change than anyone could have imagined two decades ago. My argument resembles one put forward by the Hegel scholar, Errol E. Harris: 'My contention', he writes, 'is that had Marx understood Hegel aright he would have found in him much that he (Marx) was seeking, including a basis for socialism that would not have led his followers astray into totalitarian repression of human liberty.'[9]

Life courses

Hegel created his dialectical philosophy in response to a stormy period of reaction resembling our own. He and old friends like the poet Friedrich Hölderlin (1770–1843) and the political activist Isaac von Sinclair (1775–1815) watched in shock as Napoleon betrayed the ideals of the 1789 French Revolution and established in 1799 what Hölderlin called 'a species of dictator[ship]'.[10] After 1815 even the compromised liberal achievements of the Napoleonic era were smashed by an axis of reactionary European regimes led by the chief aristocratic-capitalist power, England.

Hölderlin, the first of the great modernist poets, was thrown into a mental asylum, and condemned to live out his days in a wooden tower. Hegel, too, was stung by the icy breath of reaction. Like his friend he retired from active politics, but he did not forfeit his sanity. Rather, as we shall see in this book, he created a political philosophy that could penetrate the terrible twists and ironies of history.

Similar circumstances shaped Marx's world-view. Raised and educated in the fires of a rising continental bourgeois-liberal revolt, Marx took an active part in the 1848 revolutions. In 1849, Marx escaped to England where he lived for the rest of his life. After staying for a period in working-class Soho, he spent some of his most productive years in a quiet suburb of London. The communist revolutionary must have resembled many other middle-class fathers as he watched his children gambol on the green hills of London's serene Hampstead Heath.

Marx's portrait once dominated May Day Parades on Moscow's Red Square, and politicians in the East European Communist republics paid lip-service to his philosophy. Yet Marx was born in Trier, the western-most city of Germany. When the Caesars ruled, Trier was a Roman centre. In modern times, Marx's hometown leap-frogged between Germany and France. Today, road signs around the town are bilingual: German and French. A thoroughly Western figure, Marx was well prepared for the comfortable bourgeois English life. In the mid-nineteenth century Great Britain was scarcely touched by armed dissent. The factories of the great nation were in full swing. When the bearded revolutionary reached his seat in the newly founded British Museum, English goods flooded world markets and London was the centre of global commerce.

In a delightful little tour book entitled *Marx in London*, the historian Asa Briggs repeats the standard line that Marx was relatively unaffected by his quarter-century stay in the mushrooming metropolis. 'He never became so preoccupied with London – or England – that the English connection changed his attitudes and feelings.'[11] There are in many large cities small immigrant communities some of whose denizens live entirely separated from the homogenizing city. London was famous as a haven for German exiles, and had its own Little Germany. Was Marx one of those immigrants who remained untouched by their stay in a foreign land?

Indeed he was not. Marx wrote and rewrote *Capital* while he and his wife Jenny Marx (née von Westphalen) raised three daughters and saw them imbricated in the solid upper middle-class milieu of Hampstead. He prowled London as the city was transformed by population flows and building booms. He witnessed the familiar topography of Little Germany disappear in the upheavals. True, he did not ride to hounds or keep a world-class wine cellar as did his friend and partner Friedrich Engels, who lived a few blocks away in upper-class Regent's Park. However, Marx's eventful years in London gave his thinking an unmistakably English cast. S. S. Prawer recounts that Marx's language was filled with English allusions and literary references. The whole Marx family 'professed its admiration for the works of Charlotte and Emily Bronté and ranged them above those of George Eliot'.[12] Marx certainly did not end up speaking German with an English accent; but his writings bore the unmistakable imprint of his long residence in London. Perhaps the most striking result of Marx's English sojourn was his abandonment of the philosophical themes that occupied Hegel, and his near-total immersion in political economy.

In a sense Marx lived Robert Louis Stephenson's tale of Dr Jekyll and Mr Hyde. He was the quiet scholar who spent his days at a reserved seat in the British Museum, and the family man who helped raise three girls in the proper manner of the English bourgeoisie. He was also the Hegelian dialectician whose fiery texts transmogrified the workaday English industrial scene into a catechism of revolution.

US historian Jerrold Seigel's magnificent biography *Marx's Fate* contends that Marx spent his final years obsessively revising a system that could not possibly account for the amazing success of Victorian capitalism.[13] None of his finely constructed models offered an outcome that conformed with hopes for a ground-up transformation of capitalist society. Yet under Hegel's influence, Marx drafted an exploratory blueprint of the new society in the first volume of *Capital*. Perhaps this explains why Marx, in the decade following its publication in 1867, gave priority to new editions of volume 1 of *Capital* rather than to completing the other two volumes of his *magnum opus* (which were put together after his death by Engels). A major argument of this book is that Marx did not go far enough in his Hegelian exploration of a rational society. Marx's ideal of communism offers only a ghostly outline of a system that Hegel had already constructed in detail.

Themes and structure of this book

Terrell Carver offers a useful reminder of the difficulties involved in the relationship of Hegel and Marx. 'Hegel and Marx', he says, 'did not just happen. They are not like Gilbert and Sullivan ... or even Marx and Engels. They never met and they never corresponded (Hegel died when Marx was 13).' The pairing of the two is necessarily 'a construct or narrative, not a conceptual reflection of a "fact" that cannot be otherwise than it has come down to us through the literature'. The difficulty is compounded by a great contrast in the political environment in which the two men wrote. After moving permanently to London Marx became an independent scholar largely supported by his benefactor and partner, Friedrich Engels. It was almost as though Marx occupied a research chair in some large university, but Marx's was funded by his wealthy friend rather than Exxon or Microsoft. Like Hegel, Marx lived in a climate of reaction, yet, secure in London, he had relatively little to fear from censorship or the secret police. Marx was not compelled to disguise his writings, or to cast ideas in an abstract dimension. Here is another instance in which England made Marx. Hegel's case was quite different. He was an educator without independent means living in an authoritarian state. Hegel and his family relied on income from his jobs in publicly supported schools and universities. A noose of censorship and terror lay around his neck, and around the necks of his colleagues and students. 'Hegelian language', declares Carver,

> is deliberately difficult to interpret, for political reasons, not just philosophical ones. Moreover, it is a philosophy, not just because the thinkers were that way inclined, but because any critical consideration of society would have to take place in a suitably circumscribed and abstract frame.[14]

I have tried to surmount the problem of censorship by focusing in the latter chapters of this book on Hegel's *Lectures on Natural Right and Political Science*, delivered at Heidelberg in 1818–19, but only discovered in the 1980s. Hegel could never speak freely in public; still, for a brief period at Heidelberg and Berlin he was able to outline his political theory in relatively open terms. A few months later, while Hegel was preparing the *Philosophy of Right* for publication, writes Shlomo Avineri, radical student agitation broke out, Kotzebue was assassinated by the student Carl Sand, the student *Burschenschaften* were suppressed by the authorities, and the Carlsbad Decrees introduced an unprecedented system for the surveillance of publishing and academic life in all German states and primarily in Prussia. There are numerous indications in Hegel's correspondence that because of this atmosphere of intimidation and fear from the intervention of Prussian censorship, Hegel rewrote many passages in the *Rechtsphilosophie* so as to make them more acceptable to the authorities.

Avineri explains that the Heidelberg and Berlin lectures 'provide a key to a reading of some of the more esoteric passages in the published version . . . There appears also a greater degree of continuity between Hegel's early criticism of modern society . . . and his later system'.[15]

In chapters 1 and 2, I address the issue of narrative in the relationship between Hegel and Marx. Though Engels was the first to compare Marx with Hegel in his 1859 book review of Marx's *A Contribution to the Critique of Political Economy*, Marx himself broached the problem in the 1873 Postface to the second edition of *Capital*. Chapter 1 takes a critical look at Marx's account of his connection with Hegel. Then I move to Engels's influential rendering of the relationship in *Ludwig Feuerbach and the End of Classical German Philosophy*. Contrary to the prevailing view that Engels's *Ludwig Feuerbach* offers a distorted perspective, I profess with some reservations that Engels's essay stands as a valuable guide to the two theorists. In the concluding sections of chapter 1, I apply Hegel's dialectic of history, as understood by Engels, to the fall of communism, and the August 1945 atomic bombing of Hiroshima and Nagasaki.

Engels's *Ludwig Feuerbach* points to a consistent line of development linking Hegel and Marx. According to Engels, the mature Hegel retained faith in the radical conceptions of his younger years, and Marx never abandoned the Hegelian themes that marked his earliest writings. Chapter 2 considers a double challenge to Engels's view of the Hegel–Marx relationship. On one hand, Georg Lukács's *The Young Hegel*, written in 1930s Moscow, pioneered the concept of 'reconciliation', a staple of modern-day Hegel commentary. For Lukács, Hegel drifted from the radical liberalism of his early days, ultimately becoming an apologist for Prussian tyranny. On the other hand, Louis Althusser declared that Hegel had little impact on Marx, who weaned himself from Hegelianism very early in his career. Both of these readings hang on a psychology of the human life cycle that Hegel opposed.

INTRODUCTION xvii

The final section of chapter 2 examines Hegel's dialectical account of the stages of life.

The next chapter briefly surveys Hegel's early career as well as some oppositional themes in his writings. Hegel's friendship with the troubled poet Hölderlin throws light, I think, on the young philosopher's intellectual growth. My intention is to show how Hegel's youthful discussion of Christ and Christianity presaged the democratic politics of his maturity. The chapter concludes with an examination of Hegel's thorny concept of the 'external state'.

The fall of communism has renewed interest in the democratic conceptions of Tom Paine (1737–1809) as well as in Hegel's theory of the constitutional liberal state. In chapter 4 I try to show that Hegel may have been influenced by the epoch-making texts of the radical visionary. Tom Paine was one of the most controversial personalities of the age, and it is virtually certain that Hegel was aware of him. We know, for example, that Hölderlin and Sinclair associated with followers of Paine's leading German disciple, Georg Forster. While Paine receives not a single mention in any of Hegel's writings and lectures, I think there are strong parallels between his concerns and those of Hegel. The most striking of these are the separation of civil society and the state, the nature of democratic politics and the fate of the United States of America.

If Hegel's aim was to construct a thoroughly democratic politics, as I think it was, he had to do so under extremely adverse conditions. Chapter 5 chronicles the trials of censorship and persecution that Hegel and his students endured in Berlin, as well as the terrible destiny of Hegel's dearest friend, Hölderlin. Along with his close colleague Eduard Gans, Hegel searched in Berlin for an answer to capitalism's most urgent problem, the scourge of poverty. I look at the solutions the two men offer, and consider the final political disagreement between them that some commentators believe is an indicator of Hegel's conservative politics.

One of the students who sat in Eduard Gans's packed lecture halls in Berlin at the end of the 1830s was a young man from Trier named Karl Marx. The final three chapters of this book consider the conflicted Hegelian legacy Gans may have bequeathed to his eager student. Admittedly, my exegesis of Hegel in these concluding chapters is contentious. Even in the Heidelberg lectures Hegel kept his cards fairly close to his chest, and no single interpretation, least of all mine, can clear the field of all competitors. What Leon Craig says in regard to Plato is equally true for Hegel:

[T]he art of political writing, or rather the political act of writing, entails more than a mastery of the various rational and passionate means of persuasion, more than a talent for crafting beautiful speech, or amusing informative speech. Its paramount requirement is a mastery of equivocal speech.[16]

Chapter 6 introduces the key issue separating Marx and Hegel – the concept of private property. This is no dry theoretical dispute, for it involves the contested borderline between civil society and government that is convulsing politics in the West and the former communist world. The second part of chapter 6 surveys what I believe is Hegel's solution to the problem of poverty, the democratic corporation.

A widely held notion about Hegel is that he had no interest in the future, or in what ought to be. Marx, by contrast, had a noble plan in mind for the human race. In chapter 7, I compare Marx's ideal of communism with Hegel's concept of a developing order of liberal democracy. Starting from Fukuyama's End of History thesis, the chapter places the democratic corporation within the overall framework of Hegel's radical political project. The chapter also features perhaps the most disputable element of my perspective on Hegel, the labour theory of property. I confront Jürgen Habermas's model of civil society with Hegel's in the last section of chapter 7.

Every existing state, said Hegel, is a state in time. In the final chapter I apply my interpretation of Hegel's political theory to the conditions of governance in our own period of transition after the fall of communism.

1 • Marx's Relationship with Hegel

Introduction

This chapter will look at the ways Marx's relationship with Hegel has been characterized, starting with Marx's own assessment. We shall also learn how antagonism towards Hegel has affected the presentation of Marx's connection with him.

First, I survey Marx's own version of his relationship with Hegel, and then examine the distrust and hostility of many writers, including contemporary Marxists, toward Hegel. Two of the most influential accounts of the Hegel–Marx relationship – those provided by Georg Lukács and Friedrich Engels – are discussed. We shall discover that the presumed disparity between Hegel's writings as a young man and his mature work has created difficulties for commentators. The young Hegel is seen virtually as a proto-Marx; while the mature philosopher is viewed as a betrayer of the principles of his youth and a supporter of the Restoration. By contrast, Marx's lifelong partner, Friedrich Engels, did not regard Hegel as a toady of the Prussian state. Although its argument has been widely disputed, Engels's *Ludwig Feuerbach and the End of Classical German Philosophy* remains a classic statement on the Marx–Hegel problem. His piece offers a valuable viewpoint on some substantive areas in Hegelian theory.

The second half of this chapter applies Hegel's dialectic of history, as interpreted by Engels, to the fall of communism in Eastern Europe and the former Soviet Union. I use the beginning of the nuclear era with the bombing of Japan to illustrate Engels's (flawed) rendering of Hegel's concept of truth. My key argument throughout this chapter is that the differences between Hegel and Marx have been exaggerated – not least by Marx and Engels. I hope to show that a reconstruction of the relationship between Hegel and Marx can shed light on the world-shaking events after the fall of the Berlin Wall in 1989.

Unlikely testimony

The problem of Marx's relationship with Hegel has sparked extensive debate. The difficulty is compounded by the fact that we have the testimony of only one of the persons involved. Marx was just thirteen years old when Hegel died in 1831. In a sense Marx's entire intellectual life was spent in the shadow cast by Hegel, perhaps the greatest member of the German idealist tradition, one of history's most challenging philosophical dynasties.

Marx's unsuccessful struggle to escape the mesmerizing influence of Hegel forms part of the puzzling legacy he left to his followers. During the crucial years following the outbreak of the First World War, V. I. Lenin, the founder of Soviet communism, also fell under Hegel's spell. While building the communist movement that would capture power in the 1917 October Revolution, Lenin secretly grappled with the nature of the Hegelian heritage to Marxism. As Kevin Anderson points out, 'Lenin was the first Marxist leader or theorist since Marx to undertake the type of serious Hegel studies exemplified in the work he did on Hegel's *Science of Logic* from September to December 1914, studies he expanded in 1915 to include other works of Hegel.'[1]

Most interpreters have taken at face value Marx's legendary gloss on his connection with Hegel, which appears in the 1873 Postface to the second edition of volume 1 of *Capital*. Phrases from this famous three-paragraph assessment, written when Marx was fifty-four years old, appear again and again in every commentary on the Hegel-Marx problem. It is worth looking at these paragraphs in detail, keeping in mind the context within which they were written.

In the 1873 Postface Marx was seeking to deflect criticism – including his own *self-criticism*[2] – that he relied too heavily on Hegelian methodology. The ruling empiricism of the mid-nineteenth century put under a cloud any social investigator foolish enough to make a direct appeal to idealist forms of thought. Fourteen years earlier in the Preface to *A Contribution to the Critique of Political Economy*[3] – where he talked about his intellectual growth – Marx concealed his massive late 1850s return to Hegel in the *Grundrisse*, a work left unpublished in his lifetime that provided the foundations for *Capital*. As Marx's biographer, Jerrold Seigel, points out, the three-paragraph account in the 1873 Postface also contains 'strange and unrealistic' testimony.[4]

Marx characterizes his 'dialectical method' as 'not only different from the Hegelian, but exactly opposite to it'. Hegel, says Marx, believes that the 'process of thinking, which he even transforms into an independent subject, under the name of "the Idea",' creates the world, 'and the real world is only the external appearance of the idea'. For Marx, on the other hand, 'the ideal is nothing but the material world reflected in the mind of man, and translated into forms of thought'.[5]

Omitted in this passage is an account of how the material world itself is constructed. Marx seems to be subscribing to a pre-Kantian description of the mind as a passive receptor of sense impressions, a view he decisively rejects elsewhere. Marx must have known that calling his method the 'opposite' of Hegel's led him onto treacherous ground. Dialectic is all about the interaction and union and supersession of opposites.

Marx wants to make it clear that he has escaped the clutches of Hegel's idealism. 'I criticized the mystificatory side of the Hegelian dialectic nearly thirty years ago, at a time when it was still the fashion.' Marx finds much to appreciate in Hegel, whose reputation, he points out, was being slandered in Germany during the period that 'I was working at the first volume of *Capital*'. Marx claims that his outrage at 'the ill-humoured, arrogant and mediocre epigones who now talk large in educated German circles', and who treated Hegel 'as a "dead dog,"' led him to 'openly avow[] myself the pupil of that mighty thinker, and even, here and there . . . [to] coquette[] with the mode of expression peculiar to him'.[6]

At the very least this is an odd reason to adopt the views of a thinker: because everyone else rejects him. Moreover, as many observers have noted, Marx does more than 'coquette' with Hegelianism in *Capital*. In the past twenty-five years scholars have mined a whole new area on the Hegelian resonances in Marx's *magnum opus*. Even a casual glance through volume 1 of *Capital* confirms that Hegel is indeed a presence. There are allusions to, and direct quotations from, Hegel's mature writings, including the *Encyclopaedia Logic*, the *Philosophy of Right*, and the *Science of Logic*. Remarkably, all of the references are in a positive, even laudatory vein; none mention a quarrel with Hegel's idealism. Except for one or two on dialectic method, and another on natural science, the quotations concern relations of property, social class and the labour process. These selections from the corpus of Hegel's work are of great significance for our study. I want to show that Hegel's influence on Marx rests precisely on the more solid, materialist relations of property, class and labour.

In his 1873 confessional, Marx contrasts the 'mystified form' of Hegel's dialectic, 'which seemed to disfigure and glorify what exists', with the 'rational form' it takes in Marx's own hands. Nevertheless, he blames the 'mystified' use of dialectic more on followers of philosophical 'fashion in Germany' than on Hegel himself. Hegel is 'the first to present its general forms of motion in a comprehensive and conscious manner. With him, it is standing on its head. It must be inverted, in order to discover the rational kernel within the mystical shell.' Obviously for Marx something akin to his own rational dialectic was practised as well by Hegel. 'In its rational form', says Marx,

> [i]t is a scandal and an abomination to the bourgeoisie and its doctrinaire spokesmen, because it includes in its positive understanding of what exists a simultaneous recognition of its negation, its inevitable destruction; because it regards every historically developed form as being in a fluid state, in motion, and therefore grasps its transient aspects as well; and because it does not let itself be impressed by anything, being in its very essence critical and revolutionary.[7]

The view that I will develop in this book is that Hegel's method is very much the same as Marx's 'rational dialectic'.[8] By approaching the two thinkers in this way we can better understand our own situation after the fall of Soviet communism, and maybe peer into the future.

Guess who's coming to dinner?

Resolving the complex relationship between Hegel and Marx is certainly made difficult by the unreliable character of Marx's own statements on the subject. Another obstacle is the distrust and hostility of many toward Hegelian thought. The great German writer Goethe liked to have guests over without informing his family of their identity. One day in 1827 he invited the famous philosopher Hegel to dine. After Hegel's departure Goethe asked the sister of his daughter-in-law what she thought of the mystery guest. 'Strange,' she replied. 'I cannot tell whether he is brilliant or mad. He seems to me to be an unclear thinker.'[9]

She was not alone in her negative opinion. After Hegel's death, the philosopher Schopenhauer – who taught along with Hegel at the University of Berlin in the 1820s – accused him of 'the greatest effrontery in serving up sheer nonsense, in scrabbling together senseless and maddening webs of words, such as had previously been heard only in madhouses'. Hegel's philosophy, fumed Schopenhauer, 'became the instrument of the most ponderous and general mystification that has ever existed, with a result that will seem incredible to posterity, and be a lasting monument of German stupidity'.[10]

Countless writers have shared Schopenhauer's opinion, from the noted English philosopher Bertrand Russell to the logical positivist, Karl Popper. The Frankfurt School philosopher Theodor Adorno put it this way:

> In the realm of great philosophy, Hegel is no doubt the only one with whom at times one literally does not know and cannot conclusively determine what is being talked about, and with whom there is no guarantee that such a judgement is even possible.[11]

Among the majority of Marx's followers today feelings about Hegel range from incomprehension to outright rejection. Terrell Carver complains that 'the analytical character of Marx's thought was derived from German idealism, a philosophical tradition alien to most English readers and arguably to the English language itself'.[12] For the analytical Marxist school, 'the idea that [Hegel's] *dialectics* constitutes a sound way of reasoning, superior to formal logic for purposes of elaborating social theory, is . . . false and pernicious'.[13] In the opening essay of a recent collection on the future of Marxism Douglas Kellner argues that Hegel is Soviet totalitarianism's 'spiritual ancestor'. Like Stalin, Hegel believes 'that the overcoming of alienation requires total submission to the community, whereby individuals gain their liberty'. Kellner submits that 'For Hegel, the state was the incarnation of reason and freedom, and it was the citizen's duty to recognize this and to submit to the dictates of the state.'[14]

The day after Hegel's surprise appearance at Goethe's household, he was invited again for tea. The celebrated philosopher entertained his host with an attractively simple explanation of dialectic as the 'methodically cultivated spirit of contradiction which lies within everyone as an innate gift and which is especially valuable for discerning truth from falsehood'. Anticipating analytical Marxism, Goethe worried that such expertise might actually be used to 'turn falsehood into truth and truth into falsehood'.[15] Hegel, however, always contended that his method was only common sense. 'Genuine common sense', he had remarked thirty years before, 'is not peasant coarseness, but something in the educated world which freely and forcefully confronts the fetishes of culture with the truth.'[16]

As we have seen, Marx's own attitude to Hegel actually grew from intense doubt about Hegel's version of dialectic. Such distrust characterized the radical German intellectual environment of his youth. While Hegel was alive, competing factions retailed entirely different versions of his philosophy. These solidified into Old Hegelians and Young Hegelians a few years after Hegel's death. Old Hegelians saw Hegel's ideas as a form of theology; Young Hegelians pursued the radical elements they thought they found in his philosophy. By the 1840s, however, a new form of Young Hegelianism emerged that rejected the teachings of the master.

This new Young Hegelian movement originated the idea that Hegel had to be stood on his head 'in order to discover the rational kernel within the mystical shell', as Marx put it three decades later.[17] Marx eagerly embraced the new movement's leading thinker, Ludwig Feuerbach. Once a student and ardent disciple of Hegel, Feuerbach reacted against the master in the late 1830s. He produced a series of works in the 1840s that badly damaged Hegel's reputation among intellectuals of the period. According to Feuerbach, the only way to find truth in Hegel's philosophy was to invert subject and predicate. The idea did not create the world, the material world created the idea.

Hegel as a 'Young Hegelian'

A troubling complication in the job of untangling the Hegel–Marx connection is the change many writers have traced in Hegel's own development. The Canadian philosopher Charles Taylor's influential *Hegel* claims that around 1800, when he was thirty years old, Hegel shifted his emphasis from the human individual to a cosmic *Geist* or Spirit. He switched from primarily human-centred concerns to ones that were clearly idealist. This transformation in Hegel's thinking was especially significant because his pre-1800 work was deeply reminiscent of the humanist writings of Feuerbach and the early Marx. For Marx and the other Young Hegelians, what Hegel called *Geist* is identical with the human individual. 'If I am right,' Taylor speculates, 'the young Hegel had some affinities with the later Young Hegelians, which the mature Hegel had shed.'[18]

Taylor argues that before 1800 Hegel believed in transforming the world through social and political action. By the turn of the century, however, Hegel was presenting a view in which women and men had no real active part in history. Their function comes to be seen by Hegel as merely carrying out the purposes of *Geist*. The enigmatic ends of *Geist* that human beings unconsciously carry out can only be truly comprehended by philosophy (namely Hegel's), and then only long after these purposes have been achieved.

Taylor's account of Hegel's intellectual turn is now part of the conventional wisdom. It conforms in large part to the much earlier, and equally influential, assessments of Georg Lukács and Herbert Marcuse. However, Lukács and Marcuse placed Hegel's transformation later than 1800, for they saw the themes of Hegel's *Phenomenology of Spirit* (published in 1806-7) as more or less consistent with his youthful writings.

How was it, though, that Marx in the 1840s, using only the *Phenomenology* and Hegel's later texts, was able to reproduce with astonishing accuracy (though without wilful intention) some of the key patterns in Hegel's writings before 1800? As we shall see later, the pre-1800 Hegel is very close to the young Marx in his elaboration of the concepts of love, property, labour, religion and the state – concepts which are often only implicit in Hegel's mature writings. Yet Marx was wholly unaware of Hegel's early writings, which were not published until the twentieth century. Had they been available, these writings might have convinced the young Marx that he was actually the rightful heir to the Hegelian legacy.

This is the main theme of Georg Lukács's *The Young Hegel*, written in 1938 and published after the Second World War. In his 1923 work, *History and Class Consciousness*, Lukács – a Hungarian communist who died in 1971 at the age of eighty-six – had 'elevat[ed] Hegel for the first time to an absolutely dominant position in the prehistory of Marx's thought'.[19] Lukács's return to Hegel in *History and Class Consciousness* had an important influence on the Frankfurt School's critique of the culture of capitalism, and on other forms of neo-Marxism that flourished in the 1960s and 1970s. Arguably, however, *The Young Hegel* may be Lukács's most significant contribution to an understanding of the relationship between Marx and Hegel. Lukács, says his biographer, 'utilized . . . Hegelian ideas in order to legitimate Marxism by discovering its radical continuity with, rather than its reversal of, Hegelianism'.[20] Working in 1930s Moscow, with its rich collection of Marx's writings, Lukács was among the first to appreciate the importance of Marx's *Economic and Philosophical Manuscripts of 1844*, published in 1932. Reading the young Marx together with the young Hegel sparked Lukács's entirely original reassessment of Hegel's development.

The Young Hegel contends that its subject, at least until the publication of the *Phenomenology of Spirit* in 1807, was a republican, a democrat, and a supporter of the classless ideal of the ancient Greeks, and of the Jacobins under Robespierre. Unlike many of his contemporaries, who at first praised the French Revolution but later turned away in despair, Hegel never lost his enthusiasm for the Great Revolution. Other Germans in love with ancient Greece saw the classical ideal as part of an unrecoverable past. For Hegel, however, '[a]ntiquity survives as an actual, living example to mankind. It may have passed away but we must revive it; in fact, this revival constitutes the central practical, cultural and religious task of the age.'[21]

Lukács brilliantly assembles the elements in Hegel's early writings that foreshadow not only the young, humanist Marx but also the mature Marx of *Capital*. He also set the pattern for what is now the dominant interpretation of the Hegel–Marx relationship, an interpretation that I want to challenge. According to Lukács, Hegel was a radical in his youth – virtually a proto-Marx – but he eventually reconciled himself with the established order in Restoration Prussia.

In Lukács's view, Hegel was trapped by his own historical period. Hegel 'could only choose between utopian illusions and resigned acceptance of the miserable reality of Germany as it then was'. The young philosopher studied the two great transformations of his time – the French Revolution and the English Industrial Revolution – yet he never reached as deep an understanding of capitalism as Marx achieved. Hegel's 'knowledge of the conflict between capital and labour', Lukács suggests, 'only comes to him from reading . . . not from his own experience, from a real insight into capitalism in ordinary life'. Marx's critique of capitalist economics, by contrast, 'was much more entrenched and more solidly based scientifically, his condemnation of capitalist culture was much more profound, more comprehensive, and annihilating than Hegel's could ever be'. Throughout his life Marx remained a fiery revolutionary while the later Hegel preached 'resigned acceptance of the actual state of human culture'.[22]

It is worth taking Lukács's argument with a grain of salt. His discussion of Hegel's inferiority to Marx was written in exile in Moscow at the height of the Great Purge, when thousands of communists were executed by Stalin. Too sharp a departure from the Stalinist line on Hegel – which at the time painted him as a lackey of the German aristocracy – would surely have involved its author in a dangerous controversy. There are pregnant moments in *The Young Hegel* when Lukács, seemingly almost overwhelmed with enthusiasm for Hegel's social theory, has to draw himself back to sobriety. Lukács fails to follow obvious leads that might have brought him directly to Hegel's mature theory in the *Philosophy of Right* and the *Science of Logic*. He repeats so often the caveat about Marx's superiority to Hegel that one wonders if, like Shakespeare's lady, he protests too much. When Lukács suggests that Hegel's outlook was determined by the limitations of 'the most developed form of manufacturing in Germany . . . linen weaving which was still organized as a cottage industry',[23] the effect is almost risible.

Yet Lukács puts his finger on a point that is central to our study. Hegel is convinced that capitalism is not destined to disappear. There is no attempt by Hegel to create a utopia, or – as in Marx – to construct a form of communism completely at odds with the market. Instead of providing a socio-political resolution, says Lukács, 'the idealist dialectic transforms the entire history of man into a great philosophical utopia: into the philosophical dream that "externalization" can be overcome in the subject, that substance can be transformed into subject'.[24]

Lukács's work was in the tradition of Friedrich Engels (1820–95), who for half a century provided the sole interpretation of the relation between Hegel and Marx. Like Engels, Lukács insisted on the 'contradiction' between Hegel's fruitful dialectic 'method' and his deadening philosophical 'system'.[25] According to Engels and Lukács, conservative thinkers are drawn to Hegel's systematic philosophy, while radicals eschew the system and embrace Hegelian dialectics.

Engels was unaware of the writings of the young Hegel. Only the *Phenomenology of Spirit* and Hegel's later writings were available in Engels's lifetime. Nevertheless, Engels had a unique vantage point. As Marx's lifelong partner and benefactor, he played a crucial role in the unfolding of Marx's thought. He introduced Marx to political economy in 1844 while his friend was still absorbed in philosophy, and together with Marx started a Communist Correspondence Committee two years later. *The German Ideology* and *The Holy Family* – which settled accounts with Hegelianism and outlined the methodological principles for the study of history and society – were written jointly by the two men in 1845–6. The famed *Communist Manifesto* of 1848 was also a product of their intellectual partnership. As Engels put it in 1885, two years after his friend's death, 'Marx and I were pretty well the only people to rescue conscious dialectics from German idealist philosophy and apply it to the materialist conception of history and society.'[26]

The most learned man in Europe

Engels was in a position to resolve the problem of Marx's relation to Hegel, but instead his writings added to the mystery. Since the 1960s scholars have claimed Hegel had a greater impact on Engels than on Marx. Many blame what they see as Marxism's mistakes on the obvious Hegelianisms that show up in Engels's work, especially his *Dialectics of Nature* and *Anti-Dühring*, which make direct claims on Hegel's method. Engels's strange brew of positivism and Hegelianism, on this account, helped create 'dialectical materialism', the official philosophy of the Soviet state.

These scholars see Marx as relatively innocent of Hegel's perverse influence. Engels's position as the founder of the Marxist political movement, and one of the central stars in the firmament of world communism, meant that his 'Hegelianized' version of Marx's social theory became the paramount interpretation at least until the middle of the twentieth century. 'Anything further [than Engels's work] from Marx's investigative, rigorous and independent approach to the politics of capitalist society', claims Terrell Carver, 'is difficult to imagine.'[27]

Historian Dillard Hunley convincingly argues that the line drawn between Marx and Engels is arbitrary and untenable. The two may not have been intellectual twins, but there is very little evidence of a huge gap dividing them. Hunley points out that supporters of the 'dichotomist' position, as he calls it, present self-cancelling arguments.[28] Thus, writers who claim that Engels was the Hegelian while Marx was the sober scientist are contradicted by scholars making the opposite argument. For example, the American social theorist, Randall Collins, suggests that Engels's clear superiority to Marx with regard to social history, and the sociology of the family, the state, and social class resulted from his rejection of Hegel. According to Collins, Marx was the one misled by Hegelian dialectics.

> Marx's own personal [Hegelian] labyrinth is not a place that sociology should be trapped. It is Engels who breathed sociology into

the vision, and it is Engels's own writings – and those of Marx that were collaborative with, or inspired by, joint work with Engels – that delivers what sociology can learn from this 'Marxian' view.[29]

Tom Rockmore, by contrast, questions Engels's ability to comment on German idealism, finding fault with his academic credentials. Marx had 'a solid philosophical background' and a 'doctorate in philosophy', Rockmore writes, but Engels's education 'stopped with the German *Gymnasium*, which roughly corresponds to completion of the first two years of an American college'.[30]

Marx would have had trouble accepting Rockmore's evaluation of Engels, however. For Marx, Engels was 'the most learned man in Europe'.[31] Unlike his partner, Engels actually attended the University of Berlin lectures of one of the legendary German idealists, Schelling. At the age of twenty-one, before he graduated from the *Gymnasium*, Engels wrote a critical pamphlet on Schelling under the pen-name of Friedrich Oswald that received wide attention. Arnold Ruge, the founder of the Young Hegelian journal, the *Hallische Jahrbücher,* thought the pamphlet was actually written by Michael Bakhunin, the founder of anarchism. 'This promising young man', wrote Ruge, 'is outstripping all the old donkeys in Berlin.'[32]

Except for his writings of the mid-1840s, which are briefly discussed in chapter 2, Marx never attempted a paper or book on Hegel. Engels, however, wrote a remarkable essay in 1886, entitled *Ludwig Feuerbach and the End of Classical German Philosophy*. This was the last major contribution Engels made to the development of Marxist theory. The remaining nine years of his life were mainly devoted to editing the second and third volumes of Marx's *Capital*. *Ludwig Feuerbach* affords a fascinating look at the Marx–Hegel relationship and also a preliminary glimpse of some substantive areas in Hegel's philosophy. Perhaps more than any other single work, *Ludwig Feuerbach* illustrates Engels's remarkable ability to convey complex ideas in an entertaining and lucid style. Whatever else may be said about the two men, Engels was perhaps a better teacher than Marx.

Engels the legend-maker

The reliability of Engels's text has been controversial at least since George Lichtheim's highly influential piece, 'The concept of ideology', first published in 1965. Lichtheim – then a leading commentator on radical theory – dismissed 'Engels' platitudinous essay on Feuerbach', and accused him of forgetting the 'meaning [of] . . . the classical tradition'. Incidentally, Lichtheim also pilloried Lukács's 'dull tome' *The Young Hegel*, as the work 'of a pedestrian exponent of Marxist-Leninist scholasticism' – a shocking misjudgement.[33] Terrell Carver submits a more generous appraisal in his intellectual biography of Engels. *Ludwig Feuerbach*, says Carver, is 'a classic Young Hegelian reading of Hegel, finding in the great philosopher's most famous proposition – all that is real is rational, and all that is rational is real – a revolutionary message, once the Hegelian dialectic of change through contradiction had been correctly applied'.[34]

Pace critics such as Lichtheim, *Ludwig Feuerbach* is an insightful, probing and witty examination of Marx's intellectual roots in Hegel and the Young Hegelian movement. Like all of Engels's writings, the essay sparkles with clarity and effortless erudition. Yet, as British philosopher David Lamb reports, it is also a 'source of much confusion'.[35] Engels's piece has been taken from Lenin onwards as a call to arms against idealism, and an affirmation of the materialist worldview. Partly as a result of *Ludwig Feuerbach* entire generations of Marxists have mistakenly seen Hegelian idealism as their chief ideological foe. In fact, the essay shows considerable sympathy for Hegel and succeeds in illuminating many widely misunderstood Hegelian concepts. As we shall see later, Engels demonstrates the intimate connection between Marx's key concept of *revolutionizing practice* and the central notion of Hegel's philosophy, *ideality*.

Engels's essay also originated the legend of Hegel as merely a precursor of Marx, a hoary contributor to the latter's world-shaking outlook. Moreover, he created this fantasy by overlooking the critical role played in Hegel's system by the idea of freedom. This idea depends radically on what Hegel meant by absolute truth, the subject of the next section.

Absolute truth

In *Ludwig Feuerbach* Engels argues that the greatest difference between Marx and Hegel is the latter's belief in absolute truth. Marx could take over the dialectic method practically intact but he was never tempted by the siren call of Hegel's system. According to Engels, Hegel 'conceived of the end of history as follows: mankind arrives at the cognition of this self-same absolute idea, and declares that this cognition of the absolute idea is reached in Hegelian philosophy'. Since Hegel is able to discern absolute truth through his philosophy, this means that the absolute must also be carried out in reality, namely in the reforms 'vainly promised' by the Prussian monarch Frederick William III of 'a limited, moderate, indirect rule of the possessing classes suited to the petty-bourgeois German conditions of that time'. Thus, through the 'inner necessities of the system', Engels avers, 'a thoroughly revolutionary method of thinking produced an extremely tame political conclusion'.[36]

Engels's leap from the Hegelian absolute idea to the politics of early nineteenth-century Prussia is not entirely satisfactory. He furnishes no proof of this transition in Hegel's text. Still, the equivalence of Hegel's supposedly reactionary politics with a (poorly defined) absolute idea is accepted well beyond the borders of Marxism. Although Engels saw the Hegelian system as untenable, he had great respect for its achievements, an attitude shared by Marx. In fact, Engels provides one of the best outlines available of Hegel's mature work. Though Hegel never quite freed himself from 'German philistinism', writes Engels,

> this did not prevent the Hegelian system from covering an incomparably greater domain than any earlier system, nor from developing in this domain a wealth of thought which is astounding even today. The phenomenology of mind (which one may call a parallel of the embryonology and palaentology of the mind, a development of individual consciousness through its different stages, set in the form of an abbreviated reproduction of the stages through which the consciousness of man has passed in the course of history), logic, natural philosophy, philosophy of mind, and the latter worked out in its separate, historical subdivisions; philosophy of history, of right, of religion, history of philosophy, aesthetics, etc. – in all these different historical fields Hegel laboured to discover and demonstrate the pervading thread of development. And as he was not only a creative genius but also a man of encyclopaedic erudition, he played an epoch-making role in every sphere.

In Engels's view – and that of Marx – the time for 'absolute truth' discovered by a single individual, even one of outstanding genius, had long past. '[I]nstead one pursues attainable relative truths along the path of positive sciences, and the summation of their results by means of dialectical thinking.'[37]

Freedom

A strange lapse occurs in Engels's account of the Hegelian legacy in Marx. He treats Hegel's absolute idea as an ideological construct, as an abstraction without any correlate in grounded reality – 'the absolute idea', Engels jests, 'is absolute only in so far as [Hegel] has absolutely nothing to say about it'.[38] Hegel indeed had a lot to say about the absolute idea, as Engels must have known.

The leading concept in Hegel is the idea of freedom. This is the key to his philosophy from the earliest writings, and as much a part of his 'system', as it is of dialectic method. The absolute idea in the final analysis means freedom for the individual human being. Hegel's philosophy is an attempt to adumbrate this idea, to provide it with an institutional existence in the state, to discover it in the workings of human history, and show its development in the spheres of art, religion and philosophy. As he puts it in the *Philosophy of Mind*: 'When individuals and nations have once got in their heads the abstract concept of full-blown liberty, there is nothing like it in its uncontrollable strength, just because it is the very essence of mind, and that as its very actuality.'[39]

This idea is so powerful in Hegel that it has always attracted lovers of freedom to his philosophy. This accounts not only for Marx's attraction to Hegel, but also for that of many others – from his first disciple, the Jewish radical Gans, to the French feminist Simone de Beauvoir, who used Hegel's *Phenomenology* to define the position of women in her landmark *The Second Sex*; and to the leader of the 1960s American black freeedom movement, Martin Luther King, who said that he learned from Hegel 'a doctrine of growth through struggle'.[40] Reflecting on Hegel's concept of freedom, Francis Fukuyama observes that 'the "struggle for recognition" is evident everywhere around us and underlies contemporary movements for liberal rights, whether in the Soviet Union, Eastern Europe, Southern Africa, Asia, Latin America, or in the United States itself'.[41]

Freedom is hardly the 'relative truth' that Engels celebrates in *Ludwig Feuerbach*. Hegel finds transhistorical evidence for this idea, which he traces back to the ancient Greeks and the civilizations that preceded them. The struggle for recognition – the war between master and slave – forms the heart of progress in history.

> As regards the historical side of this relationship, it can be remarked that the ancient peoples, the Greeks and Romans, had not yet risen

to the notion of absolute freedom, since they did not know that man as such, man as the universal 'I', as rational self-consciousness, is entitled to freedom. On the contrary, with them, therefore, freedom still had the character of a natural state. That is why slavery existed in their free States and bloody wars developed in which the slaves tried to free themselves, to obtain recognition of their eternal human rights.[42]

Engels uses the term 'rationality' to explain Hegel's dialectic of history, but he offers no explanation of the term itself. Today rationality is often interpreted in the sense that Max Weber later gave to it. Weberian rationality means the historical process of finding the most efficient way for the structures of a mass society to be organized. It involves the development of a complex division of labour; double-entry bookkeeping; the growth of bureaucracies; formal codes of law – in other words, systems that ensure calculability, predictability, and control. Weber worried that modern society was headed toward an 'iron cage' of rationality that would stifle human warmth and creativity.

As George Ritzer argues, Weberian rationality is interestingly exemplified in the organization of McDonald's fast-food restaurants, which now cover much of the globe. This kind of rationality takes the form of what Hegel called, the understanding consciousness, the guiding intellect of market – or civil – society. On one hand, the understanding consciousness hinges on thought and reflection. In the case of McDonald's, for instance, endless contemplation has been invested in providing 'the best available means of getting us from a state of being hungry to a state of being full'.[43]

On the other hand, the understanding is capricious and unpredictable because it is aimed only at satisfying impulses and inclinations, and depends on objects which remain external and alien to it. Thus, the rationality of the understanding is also profoundly irrational. This is why Hegel refers to motivations and actions based on the understanding consciousness as the 'arbitrary will'. McDonald's is driven not by its affection for hamburgers alone, or by its desire to create balanced food for healthy citizen consumers, or a concern with the self-development of its employees. Its strict goal is profit, lots of it.

The understanding is an essential aspect of human consciousness, and must come into play in the struggle for freedom. For Hegel, however, the understanding's mode of rationality is subordinate to the real dialectic of history, which concerns the highest form of consciousness, reason. At this level, rationality means creating the maximum opportunity for the full development of each individual in society. Nothing is external to, or alienated from, rational consciousness because reason has only itself as its 'content, object . . . and end'.[44] Hegel calls intention and action based on reason, the 'rational will'.

As an instrument of the understanding, the free market stands for a certain limited form of rationality. But the requirements of reason, as opposed to the understanding, are more likely to be filled by the state than the market. Today these would include universal education, childcare and health care; protection of human rights; full employment and equal opportunity for jobs and careers; care of the environment; guarantee of mobility rights; national defence; an equitable distribution of income and wealth, and meaningful opportunity to participate in decision-making in the community and the nation. Now right-wing governments are trying to 'privatize' many of these functions – transfer them to the market – and abandon those that cannot be served by the private sector. Yet, as managerial theorist Henry Mintzberg suggests, this move is likely to be unsuccessful. Market rationality concerns the rights of customers and clients versus those of the providers of goods and services. The state revolves around the very different, and higher, rights of *citizens*. 'Most of the services provided by government,' Mintzberg argues,

> including highways, social security, and economic policy, involve complex trade-offs between competing interests. Tom Peters captures this idea perfectly with a story about getting a building permit to enlarge his house. 'I don't want some bureaucrat at City Hall giving me a hard time . . . I want proper, quick, businesslike treatment. But what if my neighbour wants to enlarge *his* house? Who's City Hall's customer then?'[45]

How does freedom develop in history? This is the question that animates Hegel's *Philosophy of History*, in which he traces the growth of freedom from the ancient Eastern civilizations, the Greek and Roman worlds and feudalism, to the Western European nations where individual freedom finally begins to take formal shape. Commentators associate Hegel's famed metaphor of the 'cunning of reason' with a divine agency outside and above human thought. But Hegel saw reason, the love of freedom, as an instinctive quality in human beings. This fundamental human characteristic is at first unrecognized by its bearers, but takes shape, and enters their consciousness, through their own actions and will in the movement of history.

Hegel is not proposing a vulgar idealist history, in which thought determines what happens in the real world. Like Marx, he is aware that ideas are bound to their material context. Engels is wrong, therefore, when he accuses Hegel of 'importing' the motives of historical actors 'from outside, from philosophical ideology, into history'.[46] Hegel is, I think, arguing something akin to modern chaos theory which suggests that determinate structures arise from entirely random events. For example, the beautiful patterns that make each individual snowflake unique emerge from billions of random collisions. Similarly, freedom results from the unintended consequence of the selfish actions of individuals, as well as from the mass struggles of those guided (whether they are entirely aware of it or not) by ideas of freedom.

Engels's occlusion of the idea of freedom allowed him to propound the originality of Marx's historical materialism on the basis of Hegel's 'ideological perversion'.[47] As we shall see, however, Marx's social theory owes much more to Hegel than Engels admitted.

The real and the rational

Ludwig Feuerbach begins with a discussion of one of the most disputed phrases in the Hegelian lexicon: 'What is real is rational and what is rational is actual.'[48] The phrase appears in the legendary Preface to Hegel's textbook on politics, the *Philosophy of Right*. For many, the phrase is the hallmark of Hegel's conservatism, his benediction of the Prussian state of his own day. As Engels puts it: 'That was tangibly a sanctification of things that be, a philosophical benediction bestowed upon despotism, police government, Star Chamber proceedings and censorship.'[49] But was it? Engels knew that Hegel's phrase posed an elementary problem in dialectics – though, as we have seen, by omitting the concept of freedom Engels's own solution is badly flawed.

The terms 'real' and 'actual' in Hegel's logic play on submerged meanings in ordinary language. What is 'real' is also something that contains the 'necessary'. The 'necessary', in turn, refers to rational development, the rationality of freedom. We may say, for example, that an advantageous circumstance is 'a real opportunity', meaning that it offers us a unique chance for self-fulfilment. The 'actual', for Hegel, is the core of reality that contains the possibility of freedom. We often use 'actual' in the sense of exposing an underlying reality. 'I said I was sick, but *actually* I just couldn't handle going to that sexist beer party.' In his Heidelberg and Berlin lectures on the philosophy of right – only discovered in the early 1980s – Hegel supplied the dialectical solution for his students: 'What is real *becomes* rational, and what is rational *becomes* actual.'[50]

For Hegel, the only 'real' aspects of a state are those that contribute to the growth of human freedom; the elements of a state that suppress freedom are 'unreal' and destined to disappear. The democratic gains of the American Revolution of 1776, for example, have been incorporated into the constitutions of many modern countries. But the Revolution's reliance on black slavery has been everywhere rejected. Engels uses the French Revolution to explicate the meaning of 'real' and 'unreal' (but Engels never refers to the term, freedom).

> In 1789 the French monarchy had become so unreal, that is to say, so robbed of all necessity, so irrational, that it had to be destroyed by the Great Revolution ... In this case, therefore, the monarchy was the unreal and the revolution the real.[51]

The fall of communism in our own era (ironically, at the bicentenary of the French Revolution) represents the same dialectic.[52] The Soviet Union became less and less 'real' with the passage of time; increasingly it strangled the possibilities for freedom of the Soviet peoples. Denial of freedom affected all areas of Soviet society, whether in economics, in politics or in the domain of culture. The demise of communism, in Hegel's terms, was 'necessary'.

Hegel and the fall of communism

In his *Lectures on the History of Philosophy* Hegel discusses the transformation and disappearance of states. This passage – which accords with Engels's dynamic interpretation in *Ludwig Feuerbach* – is hauntingly evocative of the revolutions that came in the aftermath of the fall of the Berlin Wall in 1989. Hegel writes that no constitution – no particular form of government – could possibly suit the needs of every nation. In order to be real or 'true', a constitution 'must relate itself to the common morality, and be filled with the living spirit of the people ... and it is quite the case that for men as they are – for instance, as they are Iroquois, Russians, French – not every constitution is adapted'. Forms of governance are in constant transformation to suit the changing requirements of the national consciousness. Every nation 'makes such alterations in its existing constitution as will bring it nearer its true constitution'. As with the Soviet Union in the 1980s, however, a country may come to reject 'what its constitution expresses to it as the truth'. If the nation's 'constitution or Notion and its actuality are not one', Hegel observes, 'then the nation's mind is torn asunder'.[53]

Canada in the 1990s provides a salient example of a nation with a divided mind. The narrowly defeated October 1995 Referendum in which Quebec citizens voted on separation from the rest of Canada very nearly split the country. Unlike the Soviet Union and the other communist states of Eastern Europe, however, Canada survived the crisis (so far).

Hegel suggests a variety of possibilities for a country at loggerheads with its own system of government. Interestingly, his analysis of the dynamics of revolution is strikingly reminiscent of that offered by Andrew G. Walder, an expert on post-communism in Eastern Europe. Walder contends that state socialism fell as a result of accumulating failures in the central planning system that undermined the authority of the Communist Party. Yet the political outcome differed sharply in each of the countries affected by this process. 'In Hungary', he writes,

> the end came through a fundamental division within the party leadership, a split, negotiated transition to free elections, and electoral defeat of the reform wing of the Hungarian Socialist Workers' party ... Yet other outcomes would be equally consistent with this quiet undermining of the traditional institutions of communist rule: a coup or revolution; fragmentation of the polity along regional lines, leading either to a new form of federalism that enshrines increased local autonomy or to national fragmentation and civil war; or gradual evolution into a more fluid and contested form of authoritarianism, which in the optimistic scenario will gradually evolve into multiparty competition.[54]

As in Walder's example of Hungary, Hegel suggests constitutional reform as one option for an embattled state. The nation could, he writes, 'through a supreme internal effort dash into fragments this law which no longer claims authority'.[55] Something like this happened in several East European nations in 1989. Responding to Soviet President Gorbachev's 1988 promise not to send troops to defend communist administrations, the Polish Solidarity movement with the support of the Catholic church successfully recast the government. Poland abandoned communism in favour of a radical free-market experiment. A short interregnum of reform communism persisted in Bulgaria and

Albania, but free elections in 1991 and 1992, respectively, toppled the communists.

Yet as Katherine Verdery argues, the verdict is not yet in on the final result of these attempts at internal reform. While post-socialist nations are unlikely to return to Soviet-style communism, they might well construct political systems that differ markedly from those in the West.

> The Soviet Union may be irretrievably gone, but the electoral victories of renamed Communist Parties in Poland, Hungary, Bulgaria, and elsewhere have shown that the party is far from over. Indeed, exposure to the rigors of primitive capitalism has made a number of people in the region think twice about their rejection of socialism and their embrace of 'the market'.[56]

Internal reform, notes Hegel, could also be achieved 'more quietly and slowly . . . on the as yet operative law, which is, however, no longer true morality, but which the mind has already passed beyond'.[57] Gorbachev's programme of *Perestroika*, begun after his election as General Secretary of the Communist Party of the Soviet Union in 1985, was an attempt at this kind of reform. Similar programmes were tried in the 1980s in Hungary and Bulgaria, and, so far successfully, in China, where – some scholars insist – the market-socialist model is being vindicated.[58]

Reform movements are open to failure, Hegel warned, since 'a nation's intelligence and strength may not suffice . . . and it may hold to the lower law'. This could have been the fate of the Soviet Union in August 1991 when a coup attempt against Gorbachev by old-line Communists almost succeeded in rescuing the old regime. Failed reform movements, says Hegel, can also result in a people 'giv[ing] up its nationality and becom[ing] subject' to 'another nation [that] has reached its higher constitution'.[59] The German Democratic Republic (East Germany) suffered this ignominious end.

An emigration crisis in the GDR began the cycle of events with led to the fall of the Berlin Wall. In conformity with its policy of opening to the West, the Hungarian Communist government opened its borders with Austria on the eve of a visit by President Bush. This allowed East German tourists to travel through Hungary into Austria and West Germany. When Gorbachev refused in the ensuing crisis to send Soviet troops to defend the borders of East Germany, the Wall collapsed.[60] Reform Communists expected to form a government in liberated East Germany. They were knocked out of contention by West Germany's Christian

Democratic Helmut Kohl in the March 1990 elections. The GDR disappeared into the maw of West German liberal democracy. The almost anticlimactic break-up of the Soviet Union a few months after the failed August 1991 coup illustrates another of the outcomes adumbrated by Hegel. The former superpower slid silently away as though it had never existed. 'Who could have foreseen', writes Verdery, 'that with Mikhail Gorbachev's resignation speech of 25 December 1991 so mighty an empire would simply vanish? Television cameras lingered on the final image: the small red table at which he sat.'[61] Hegel's account of the disappearance of states reads almost as if he were commenting on the surprising fate of the USSR:

> [I]t is of essential importance to know what the true constitution is; for what is in opposition to it has no stability, no truth, and passes away. It has a temporary existence, but cannot hold its ground; it has been accepted, but cannot secure permanent acceptance; that it must be cast aside, lies in the very nature of the constitution . . . Revolutions take place in a state without the slightest violence when the insight becomes universal; institutions, somehow or other, crumble and disappear, each man agrees to give up his right.[62]

For a peaceful transformation to succeed, 'a government must recognize that the time for this has come'. Should the regime 'cling to temporary institutions . . . that government will fall, along with its institutions, before the force of mind'. When Czechoslovakia's Communist leader Gustav Husák ordered police to shoot student demonstrators in 1989 public outrage swept him out of office. Under President Vaclav Havel and right-wing finance minister Vaclav Klaus, both elected in 1990, Czechoslovakia followed Poland along the free-market path. Later the country split in two, becoming the Czech Republic (under the two Vaclavs) and Slovakia. As Hegel puts it, 'the breaking up of a government breaks up the nation itself'.[63] Romanian dictator Nicolae Ceauşescu and his family were slaughtered when his government resisted a popular uprising. Nevertheless, Romania remained the one reform communist government to survive the débâcle of 1989 (until it was defeated in the autumn 1996 election).

Yugoslavia is the most tragic example of Hegel's dictum that destruction of a country's constitution often 'breaks up the nation itself'. Yugoslavia was in the grip of a reform movement well before 1989. As in other East European countries, the transition from socialism to free-market capitalism in the 1980s corroded the country's social infrastructure. An ensuing debt crisis opened Yugoslavia to cruel restructuring guided by foreign bankers. 'Under the impact of the IMF program in the first nine months of 1990,' write James Petras and Steve Vieux in their electrifying article on the Yugoslav crisis, '600,000 workers out of a workforce of 2.7 million had been laid off.' The cataclysmic events following 1989 fatally weakened the alliance of eight regional states. 'The economic policies promoted by the West in Yugoslavia during the 1980s helped create the social and psychological preconditions for war along with a ready pool of embittered potential combatants.'[64]

The struggling nation fell prey to power rivalry between the USA and the European Community led by Germany. '[I]nternal conflicts and territorial break-ups were in large part fuelled and fomented by Western European and U.S. politicians, intent on carving out spheres of influence in Central Europe.' Germany encouraged independence for Slovenia and Croatia. The Europeans offered no support for rights of the large Serbian population in Croatia, which had been subjected to genocidal massacres by pro-Nazi Croats during the Second World War. 'They thus handed Serbian chauvinists and extremists a powerful mobilizing issue.' The USA confirmed its own interests in the divided country by supporting the sovereignty claims of Bosnia and Macedonia. 'Yugoslavia was transformed into a region of warring ethnic entities occupying the same territory and dependent on external patrons. Each of the patrons sought the moral high ground, spot-lighting the victims of their particular ethnic clients.'[65]

The Yugoslav federal army, and its client force the Bosnian Serbs, became the mailed fist of Greater Serbian nationalism. Under former bank director and neo-liberal Slobodan Milošević the Serbs unleashed horrifying violence, on a scale not seen since the Second World War, against Bosnia. Yet the Western mass media ignored terrible war crimes committed by armed forces other than the Serbs. Co-operation between Croatia and Serbia in the carve-up of Bosnia was overlooked. Atrocities against Serbs by Croat and Muslim forces went unreported. The US version of events, in which the Serbs were the sole villains, was widely played in the media, and hampered efforts to negotiate an end to the conflict.

The final type of outcome discussed by Hegel does not fit the experience of any of the East European nations, though it may apply to non-European communist administrations. Here, 'the government and the unessential retain the upper hand'.[66] Arguably, the political earthquake of 1989 left 'unessential' communist governments in command in Cuba, China, Vietnam and North Korea. The same forces that brought down communism in Europe may make themselves felt in these states as well. 'The remaining Communist regimes walk the earth like condemned men,' writes US philosopher Richard Hudelson. 'It appears to be only a matter of time.'[67] Still, this prognosis may turn out to be incorrect. As we have seen, China better fits Hegel's model of internal reform. Cuba may also succeed in recasting the nature of communism. Despite the continuing efforts of the USA to destroy Cuban socialism 'by aggression, large-scale terror, and economic strangulation',[68] the vast majority of the people support the government of Fidel Castro, as shown, for example, by a 1994 Gallup poll.[69]

A problem for the dialectic

According to Hegel's dialectic of history, the communist governments in the former Soviet Union and Eastern Europe were – as Engels phrases it in *Ludwig Feuerbach* – 'justified for their time and circumstance'. The fall of communism, like the disappearance of other systems of government in history, reveals

> the true significance and revolutionary character of Hegelian philosophy . . . that it once for all dealt the death blow to the finality of all products of human thought and action . . . [A]ll successive historical systems are only transitory stages in the endless course of development of human society from the lower to the higher. Each stage is necessary, and therefore justified for the time and conditions to which it owed its origin. But in the face of new, higher conditions which gradually develop in its own womb, it loses its validity and justification. It must give way to a higher stage which also will in its turn decay and perish.[70]

Of course, Engels could not have dreamed that the dialectic would turn against communism itself. Like Marx, he was confident that communism was the higher stage toward which capitalism was advancing. Perhaps if he were alive today Engels would compare 1989 not to the Great French Revolution, but to 1814, the year of the Congress of Vienna, in which the leading states of Europe – Britain, France, Austria, Prussia and Russia – divided up the spoils left by the abdication of Napoleon. If that parallel has any truth, then communism is certain to rise again, just as liberalism recovered from the Bourbon Restoration in the revolutions of 1830 and 1848.

Yet communism in Eastern Europe and the former Soviet Union was the victim of world capitalism rather than military defeat. Katherine Verdery argues that socialism's collapse resulted from the intersection of the economic crisis of global capitalism with the need for communist countries to deal with problems of insufficient economic production. Starting in the early 1970s, capitalist countries began to feel the bite of an economic downturn that still continues today. One response to the crisis was to lend large amounts to Soviet sector states, which then used the money to avert structural reforms that might have endangered authoritarian rule. 'In this way, the internal cycles of the two contrasting systems suddenly meshed.' Socialist states could not pay off their debts with exports to the West because the world market was too weak to absorb them. Rising interest rates saddled the communist states with impossible debt. In 1979–80 Western bankers decided to stop lending to socialist countries, which fell into economic disarray. Chaos in socialist economies tipped the scales 'toward the faction in the Communist Party of the Soviet Union that had long argued for structural reforms, the introduction of market mechanisms, and profit incentives, even at the cost of the Party's "leading role".'[71] Reformers like Gorbachev attempted to blend selective privatization with collective ownership and party control. The result was the ruin of the Soviet Union and its member states.

Intriguingly, Verdery suggests that capital flows monopolized by communist governments may have made them special targets for international financial interests, eager to increase their opportunities by undermining socialist states. A factional split developed 'between the groups who managed socialism's interface with the outside world (such as those in foreign policy, counterintelligence, and foreign trade) and those who managed it internally (such as the Party's middle-level executive apparatus and the KGB)'. This suggests that communism's fall may have been speeded by secret collaboration between privatizers within the Soviet system and Western financial and political forces. 'The irony is', says Verdery

> that had debtor regimes refused the definitions imposed from without – had they united to default simultaneously on their Western loans (which in 1981 stood at $90 billion) – they might well have brought down the world financial system and realized Kruschev's threatening prophecy overnight. That this did not happen shows how vital a thing was capitalists' monopoly on the definition of social reality.[72]

There is not much hope for the recovery of Soviet-style communism, at least from the standpoint of Hegel's philosophy. In fact, Engels suggested that the Hegelian dialectic is really only the philosophical reflection of market dynamics: 'Just as the bourgeoisie by large-scale industry, competition and the world market dissolves in practice all stable time-honoured institutions, so this dialectical philosophy dissolves all conceptions of final, absolute truth and of absolute states of humanity corresponding to it.'[73] This passage reads as though it were Engels's prediction for the fate of any system constructed apart from global capitalism. But does this mean that capitalism is immortal? Have we reached what former US State Department official Francis Fukuyama has called 'the End of History'? As we shall see in the final chapter, if the dialectic is hostile to chances for a revival of communism, it is probably even more unfriendly to the notion of the free market as the final arbiter of human progress.

'Ideality' or 'revolutionizing practice'

Engels's account of the dynamics of Hegel's philosophy was a landmark contribution to the problem of the relationship between Marx and Hegel. At a stroke, he showed the close continuity between Marx's theory of history and Hegel's. His rejection of the supposed conservatism of Hegel's theory of the state is especially important. Yet Engels exaggerated the differences between the two thinkers by ignoring the social and economic factors underlying Hegel's theory, and by omitting the concept of freedom. There is a similar contradiction in Engels's portrait of Hegel's theory of truth. *Ludwig Feuerbach* pours scorn on Hegel's 'ideological' notion of the absolute, but, as David Lamb points out, Engels also proffers an illuminating interpretation of Hegel's theory.

Hegel's absolute idealism defined truth as the 'identity of thought with its object', a definition ever since mocked by his enemies as 'identity theory'. Hegel's concept, complains Theodor Adorno, one of Hegel's chief modern critics,

> connives at the prohibition of thought, cuts back the negative labour of the concept which his method itself claims to perform, and endorses on the highest peak of speculation the Protestant pastor urging his flock to remain one instead of relying on their own feeble light.[74]

Adorno had second thoughts about his attitude to Hegel's 'identity thesis', however. Two decades after *Minima Moralia*, where this passage appeared, he observed that in a time when 'conformity chains spirit . . . the now cheap critique of idealism . . . needs to be reminded that there is a moment of truth in the identity thesis itself'.[75]

Engels needed no such reminder. He pointed out that Hegel's theory of truth is based on practice, unlike the classical definition which simply refers to a correspondence between subject and object. For example, in the classical theory the following statement is true:

> On 6 August 1945 the United States dropped an atomic bomb on the Japanese city of Hiroshima.

Clearly this statement is correct, there is a correspondence between this sentence and the actual occurrence a half-century ago. Yet as a statement of truth this description of the event that heralded the beginning of the nuclear age is highly inadequate.

Hegel's theory of truth involves different shapes of consciousness. The classical definition belongs to the level of consciousness Hegel called the understanding. For this form of consciousness, notes Hegel, truth means the agreement of an object with our conception of it. For truth to be achieved, according to the understanding, our conception of the object is determined by the object itself. The truth about the atomic blast that destroyed Hiroshima is merely a passive reflection of that event. This is truth on the level of a newspaper report. For example, the headline on the 7 August 1945 issue of *The New York Times* read:

> FIRST ATOMIC BOMB DROPPED ON JAPAN;
> MISSILE IS EQUAL TO 20,000 TONS OF TNT;
> TRUMAN WARNS FOE OF A 'RAIN OF RUIN'

Hegel insisted that the classical theory of truth did not take its own premisses seriously enough. If truth means that the object should be identical with the thought-form of it, then much more is demanded than mere correctness. The classical view takes for granted the alienation of thought from its object, the basic externality of thinking. The object appears as an external phenomenon which the mind grasps by modelling itself in conformity to it.

As Engels contends, however, the Hegelian theory of truth involves a historical 'process of cognition' between the subject and object of knowledge. Because truth is a process, it 'is modified, even created by, the means of approaching it'.[76] The knower does not – cannot – remain external to the thing known. For the headline in the 7 August *New*

York *Times* to make sense – to be true – for example, its readers required some prior knowledge. They knew about the war between the USA and Japan; they had an elementary understanding about atomic bombs, how they are delivered, and what TNT is; they knew who President Harry Truman was, and what he meant by a 'rain of ruin'. As with any technical achievement, the 'truth' of the bombings, their possiblity and fulfilment, depended (to quote Engels's innocent celebration of science) on 'the long historical development of science, which mounts from the low to ever higher levels of knowledge without ever reaching . . . a point at which it can proceed no further'.[77]

The atomic-bomb attack on Japan resulted from a lengthy series of scientific and technical achievements and depended mightily on conditions within the society from which it originated. Thus in important ways the bombing of Japan was a creation of everyone in the United States and its allied countries who read the terrible headlines over breakfast on 7 August 1945. What was true of the three 'hidden cities' described on the *New York Times* front page was true universally of the societies that gave birth to the nuclear age. 'The War Department', wrote reporter Jay Walz,

> revealed today how three 'hidden cities' with a total population of 100,000 inhabitants sprang into being as a result of the $2,000,000,000 atomic bomb project, how they did their work without knowing what it was all about, and how they kept the biggest secret of the war.
>
> One of these, Oak Ridge, situated where only oak and pine trees had dotted small farms before, is today the fifth largest city in Tennessee. Its population of 75,000 persons has thirteen supermarkets, nine drug stores, and seven theatres.
>
> A second town of 7,000 was built for reasons of isolation and security on a New Mexico mesa. The third, named Richland Village, houses 17,000 men, women and children on remote banks of the Columbia River in the State of Washington.
>
> None of the people . . . had the slightest idea of what they were making . . .

The truth disclosed by the *Times* on the morning of 7 August was a complex result of human endeavour, of thought and practical action – of what Hegel called ideality and Marx labelled praxis. This activity not only destroyed two cities and the lives of hundreds of thousands of people (for another city, Nagasaki, was bombed three days later). It also severely modified the landscape around the target areas, and forever altered the global environment: it used and transformed nature, as well as society.

Hegel's great predecessor Immanuel Kant taught that the mind could only know external phenomena; mere human knowledge could never penetrate the absolute, what Kant called, 'the thing-in-itself'. As Engels noted, Hegel's concept of truth was a decisive reply to Kant.

> If we are able to prove the correctness of our conception of a natural process by making it ourselves, bringing it into being out of its conditions and making it serve our own purposes into the bargain, then there is an end to the Kantian ungraspable 'thing-in-itself'.[78]

In *History and Class Consciousness*, Lukács rebukes Engels, pointing out that industry and experiment under capitalism hardly 'constitute praxis in the dialectical, philosophical sense'. Bourgeois science is based on an 'artificial, abstract milieu', that removes the object of research from its origins and context.[79] Moreover, in so far as science merely serves external financial and political masters, it must be unconscious of the social and political forces that provide it with an object, shape its methodology and determine its results. Similarly, the bombing of Hiroshima is utterly inadequate to Hegel's concept of truth, even though it fulfils all the criteria for truth recommended by Engels. The atomic scientists made the bomb themselves; and they ensured that the natural processes triggered by the bomb would serve their own purposes (or the purposes of their political bosses).

At its highest level, Hegelian truth means the unity of the *rational* concept and reality through practice. It is not enough to conceive an idea and put it into action. The idea must also be rational. 'If mere existence be enough to make objectivity,' Hegel remarks, 'even a crime is objective; but it is existence which is nullity at the core, as is definitely made apparent when the day of judgement comes.'[80] The truth, in Hegel's sense, of Hiroshima is expressed in the poem by Galway Kinnel, which retains the tension between Hiroshima as an event and the real essence of human beings:

> ... a ring of skull-
> bone fused to the inside of a helmet; a
>   pair of eyeglasses
> taken off the eyes of a witness, without
>   glass,
> which vanished, when the white flash
>   sparkled.[81]

Truth, in Hegel's view, is a product of rational activity, of action that deepens freedom for the individual human being. Objectivity, then, is not achieved by eschewing values; rather, rational values are the core of truth.

Hiroshima, Nagasaki and the philosophy of history

Hegel observes that reason develops gradually in the lifetime of the human individual; and the slow development of the human being is paralleled by the tortoise-like growth of societies in history. In early childhood, the individual senses no disruption between herself and the outside world. Paradoxically, the growth of self-consciousness in the child depends on a feeling of estrangement. '[T]he child, in reaching a feeling of the actuality of the outer world, begins to become an *actual* human being himself and to feel himself as such.' Through speech the individual begins 'to apprehend things as universal, to attain to the consciousness of his own universality, to express himself as "I"'. The 'incipient self-dependence [of the child] expresses itself in the child's learning to play with tangible things. But the most rational thing that children can do with their toys is to break them.'[82]

Perhaps the bombing of Hiroshima belongs primarily to the childlike stage of development of our own civilization. Doubtless, the atom bomb and its far more powerful successors will be seen as the supreme technological achievement of the twentieth century. This grotesque weapon marked our final alienation from nature, our dawning awareness of being surrounded by a fragile and treacherous environment. We have learned to play with tangible things, as Hegel puts it, and destruction is the most rational activity of the child.

When Hegel acknowledges that the study of history 'forms a picture of most fearful aspect, and excites emotions of the profoundest and most hopeless sadness, counterbalanced by no consolatory result', he reflects our own feelings about 6 and 9 August 1945. But Hegel adds, 'even regarding History as the slaughter-bench at which the happiness of peoples, the wisdom of States, and the virtue of individuals have been victimized – the question involuntarily arises – to what priniciple, to what final aim these enormous sacrifices have been offered'.[83] Critics argue that decision-makers complicit in the atomic bombings were motivated by a desire to enhance the superpower ambitions of the USA, not by a concern to save the lives of American troops, allied

POWs, or Japanese civilians. Physicists and engineers rushed to complete the bombs ahead of schedule for fear the Japanese would surrender before the missiles could be dropped. Nagasaki was bombed in order for the second atomic development team to try out its version of the doomsday weapon. Nevertheless, the 'cunning of reason' Hegel claimed to operate in history may also have played a role at Hiroshima and Nagasaki. Almost fifty years of superpower confrontation between the United States and the Soviet Union – and the invention of bombs a thousand times more powerful than the two used in 1945 – have ended in the fall of communism, but without a nuclear holocaust. 'The bombing of Japan', argues E. L. Doctorow,

> can be seen in this light as a kind of inoculation. And, while this hypothetical benefit of the bombings cannot acquit those who ordered them of their moral responsibility for sufferings that were all too real, it does at least suggest the possibility that those sufferings were not in vain.[84]

Wouldn't 'the cunning of reason' have been happy with just Hiroshima as a sacrifice? Why was Nagasaki's tragedy necessary? Hegel said that

> in all periods of the world a political revolution is sanctioned in men's opinions when it repeats itself. Thus Napoleon was twice defeated, and the Bourbons twice expelled. By repetition that which at first appeared merely a matter of chance and contingency, becomes a real and ratified existence.[85]

Hiroshima opened the age of nuclear war; hopefully Nagasaki sealed it.

2 • Dialectics of Youth and Maturity

Introduction

According to Engels's *Ludwig Feuerbach and the End of Classical German Philosophy*, there is a direct line of development between the thought of Hegel and Marx. In Engels's account, Hegel never entirely abandoned his radical past, and Marx remained loyal to the Hegelian influences of his youth. Unaware of Hegel's writings before the *Phenomenology*, Engels had little reason to suspect a massive dislocation in the philosopher's intellectual growth. Similarly, Engels suggested no significant displacement between the writings of the young Marx, and those of Marx's maturity.

During the heyday of Hegel–Marx interpretation in the 1960s and 1970s, a large academic industry grew up around the supposed contrast between the early and the later Marx. A similar, though much smaller, scholarly enterprise developed on the subject of the young Hegel versus the old Hegel. This chapter examines the work of two significant twentieth-century theorists who seriously challenged Engels's view of the Hegel–Marx problem. Georg Lukács claimed that in his youth Hegel was much closer to Marx than anyone had ever realized. But Hegel's maturity was marked by an 'abject' reconciliation with the established order. Lukács's view remains highly influential today. Louis Althusser's version of the Hegel–Marx relationship created shock waves in the mid-1960s. The French theorist discounted Hegel's role in Marx's growth, and asserted that the mature Marx broke completely from his youthful philosophical ideals.

Both Lukács and Althusser took for granted the popular view that maturity is marked by a loss of ideals. This chapter concludes with a survey of Hegel's approach to the human life cycle – which he implicitly linked to his own intellectual development. Maturity's trademark, in Hegel's view, is not a loss of innocence. Rather, adulthood consists in putting youthful ideals into practice.

The fate of Engels's *Ludwig Feuerbach*

In retrospect, Engels's portrait of the connection between Hegel and Marx in *Ludwig Feuerbach* radiates a compelling simplicity. Engels's piece was written decades before the era of total war, when Germany was vilified in the eyes of the world as a militaristic power responsible for the deaths of many millions of people in two world wars, and for the Nazi attempt to eradicate the Jews of Europe. The shadow cast by Hitler on German culture was nowhere deeper than the gloom which covered Hegel.

Sir Karl Popper's highly successful *The Open Society and its Enemies*, written – in its author's words as a 'War effort' intended to 'fight collectivism'[1] – and published in London in November 1945, reflected the *Zeitgeist*. Popper, then an obscure Austrian exile teaching in New Zealand, ranked Hegel above Plato and Marx as history's top intellectual villain. As a result of the book, which has never since been out of print, Popper 'became the guru for a generation of young British centrist political intellectuals'.[2]

Plato and Marx soon eluded the corrosive reach of Popper's invective, but not Hegel – 'the first official philosopher of Prussianism,' as Popper called him[3] – whose reputation still suffers from the attack. Hegel's defenders have easily shown the crude defects in *The Open Society* which 'displayed all the the sins of amateur historical writing, where sources are merely quarries for quotes to buttress arguments advanced uncritically'.[4] Nevertheless, the myth of Hegel as the fawning servant of a totalitarian Prussian state survives, especially on the left.

In his eulogy for Popper, who died at the age of 92 in 1994, Robin Blackburn, editor of the *New Left Review*, reflects on the philosopher's 'formative influence on the New Left in Britain.' According to Blackburn, the 'conservative' Popper weaned the radicals of the 1960s away from 'the deterministic and positivist Marxism of the Second International'. The *NLR* editor adds disingenuously that '(o)ne soon discovered that the Hegel scholarship in [*The Open Society*] was open to serious question'.[5] But for many on the left, Popper's Hegel is still current, and the recent return of Blackburn's *New Left Review* colleague, Perry Anderson, to Hegel was inspired by another conservative, Francis Fukuyama, writing a quarter of a century after the ferment of the 1960s finally subsided.

Engels could not have anticipated Popper's proto-Nazi Hegel. Equally in an age when progress was a byword, he had little reason to question Hegel's dialectic of freedom in history. The stormy century that lay ahead, however, destroyed the kind of faith in the Hegelian prognosis that shines through *Ludwig Feuerbach*. Yet Engels was hardly an incurable optimist; if anything, this shows just how deep the moral cataclysms of the twentieth century actually were. From the 1880s onwards, documents Hunley, Engels warned of 'the dangers and potentially disastrous consequences of a European war'. He presciently outlined the factors that could bring about a 'world war' and the 'massacre of one and a half million men'. If war broke out, Engels thought there could only be 'one sure outcome: mass butchery on an unheard-of scale, the exhaustion of Europe, and the breakdown of the entire old system'.[6] Still, he believed the conflict could be averted, and his estimate of casualties proved to be grossly understated: about 12 million men in uniform died in the First World War; the civilian death toll brought this figure even higher.

Another engaging quality of *Ludwig Feuerbach* is its uncomplicated view of the intellectual development of Marx and Hegel. For Engels, Hegel eventually compromised with Prussian state power, certainly; but he retained the liberal orientation of his youth. Similarly, Marx may have started as a young Hegelian, but his shift to communism followed more or less logically from the Feuerbachian critique of Hegel. As we have seen, Engels's assumption that Hegel's growth registered a smooth upward trend was questioned in the late 1930s by Georg Lukács. Lukács's *The Young Hegel* argued that the mature Hegel veered away from his youthful concerns, a process that began after he suffered an intellectual crisis between the ages of twenty-seven and thirty, when he was a tutor in Frankfurt.

Lukács and 'reconciliation'

Lukács's account of Hegel's development, like that of other writers, is based on extremely fragmentary and confusing evidence of the young philosopher's writings. Hegel published very little of his early work, although he kept records of his writings, and preserved much of it. Unfortunately, many of these early contributions have been lost or destroyed since Hegel's death; and scholars are uncertain about the exact dating, and in some cases even authorship, of what remains. Therefore, speculation about Hegel's intentions, and rough reconstructions of the pattern and content of his writings, are necessary in any account of Hegel's intellectual growth.

Lukács based his conception of Hegel's mental crisis on the latter's own description of the difficult transition between youth and maturity in a discussion of the *Bildungsroman* of classical German literature: 'During his years of apprenticeship the hero is permitted to sow his wild oats; he learns to subordinate his wishes and views to the interests of society; he then enters that society's hierarchic scheme and finds in it a comfortable niche'.[7] Applying this schema to Hegel's development, Lukács contended that the young philosopher's initial radicalism was overtaken by the 'tortured, hypochondriacal crisis-ridden mood of the Frankfurt period [of 1797–1800] . . . [and] found a provisional solution [several years later] in Jena when he came to accept the existing social order in its specifically Napoleonic form'.[8]

Lukács used the concept of 'reconciliation' to explain the trajectory of Hegel's thought after 'unhappy Frankfurt'. The radical young philosopher, suggests Lukács, grew to accept the abhorred system. Perhaps Lukács went through a similar development. Lukács's critics, especially Theodor Adorno, suggest that 'reconciliation' aptly characterizes Lukács's own political adjustment from political firebrand in the 1920s to Stalinist apologist in the 1930s and beyond.[9] In his biography of Lukács, Kadarkay explicitly compares his subject's life with that of Hegel.

> Lukács['s] . . . similarities with Hegel are indeed noteworthy. Hegel did his most original work before he went to Berlin, where his growing conservatism went together with a lack of new ideas. Lukács, similarly, wrote his most important works, apart from *The Young Hegel* itself, before he went to Moscow. Like the young Hegel, the young Lukács placed great value on the power of cultural coherence and community to heal the wound of his estranged and wounded self. In Moscow, Lukács's power to fashion his youthful vision into lasting works was all but gone. In a sense, *The Young Hegel* was Lukács's valedictory to his own youth.[10]

For Lukács, the concept of reconciliation is the keystone of the mature Hegel's philosophical outlook. He perceives a growing reactionary tendency in Hegel on one side, and the development of a deep dialectical philosophy on the other. Lukács claims that these are dependent on one another. The reactionary in Hegel was needed to bring out the dialectician. Anticipating Charles Taylor's position (see chapter 1), Lukács contends that there is a striking difference between the early and late Hegel on the role of human action in history. After Frankfurt, where Hegel was a private tutor, the maturing philosopher comes to see 'the objective course of history (as) independent of the moral aspirations and evaluations of the men alive within it'. According to Lukács, this is an advance on the young Hegel's 'moral indignation' at the ways of the world because it 'achieve(s) such a profound and true insight into the necessity of the historical process and the methodology of history'. But it is also a profoundly 'retrograde' turn. 'The fact that this maturity could only be achieved at the cost of renouncing the goals of a democratic revolution is a grim indication of the tragic conflict imposed on Hegel by the backward socio-economic state of Germany.'[11]

For Lukács, the young Hegel saw history as 'a unified process of decline' from the golden age of the Greeks that could only be rescued by an abrupt transformation of the social world. During his time in Frankfurt, he comes to recognize that modern civil society is 'a fundamental, incontrovertible fact with whose existence and nature he has to come to terms both intellectually and practically'. Hegel's chief concern becomes the relationship of the individual with civil society, a concern which brings him to a revolutionary conception of dialectic – the contradictions that the individual must overcome to be at home in the world. Thus Hegel turns directly to the study of the supremely important categories of private property and labour.

> His effort to discover a philosophical reconciliation between the humanist ideals of the development of personality and the objective, immutable facts of society leads him to an increasingly profound understanding, firstly of the problems of private property and later of labour as the fundamental mode of interaction between individual and society.[12]

Variants of Lukács's 'reconciliation' thesis have cropped up in a number of important writings on Hegel and Marx over the last half-century. Herbert Marcuse claimed in *Reason and Revolution: Hegel and the Rise of Social Theory*, which first appeared in 1941, that Hegel's appointment at the University of Berlin in 1817 (when he was forty-seven years of age) coincided 'with the end of his philosophical development. He became the so-called official philosopher of the Prussian state and the philosophical dictator of Germany'.[13] From Marcuse's perspective, Hegel's 'reconciliation' with the existing order was a process that stretched over a period of almost twenty years.

Shlomo Avineri's *Hegel's Theory of the Modern State*, published in 1972, relies on the concept of reconciliation to explain why Hegel's social theory contains 'no radical call of action' despite a 'harsh analysis' of civil society reminiscent of Marx's. 'The nature of modern society is grasped with an amazing lucidity . . . ; but all is incorporated within the integrative functions of the state. There is neither rebellion nor deviation.'[14]

In his *Hegel: An Introduction* – published the same year as Avineri's text and revised in 1983 – Raymond Plant contends that Hegel's early critiques of religion and the state pointed toward far-reaching reform or overthrow of these institutions. After the crucial Frankfurt period, however, Hegel preaches 'resigned acceptance of the fate which faces man in a fragmented world, a resignation which is expressed by the quest of philosophy to come to reconciliation with the world as it is, rather than to attempt to transform it'.[15] According to Plant, Hegel believed that government represents the universal interests of society. In so far as the modern state falls short of this ideal – most obviously in its inability to eradicate poverty – Hegel's own theory must be declared a failure.[16]

It is worth noting that Plant's assessment of Hegel's theory seems to rely on a criticism of the welfare state led by F. A. Hayek and others that became increasingly popular in the late 1970s and early 1980s as the right-wing animus against government gathered force. In a sense, Hegel's state-centred solution to poverty was itself called into question by the supposed failure of Keynesianism, and the rise of market-oriented neo-conservatism and its ideologues. Hayek's *The Road to Serfdom* – a founding text of the new right – was published the same year (1945) as Popper's *Open Society*. Indeed, Hayek assisted Popper in finding a publisher, and both saw their efforts as contributions to the defeat of 'collectivism' and the revival of market economics.

Plant points to Hegel's contention that rich civil societies are driven outside their borders to solve their economic problems – a clear anticipation of the theory of imperialism propounded by Lenin, Rosa Luxemburg and J. A. Hobson. However, Plant contends that Hegel's contribution is 'irrelevant . . . because it is an explicit admission that the modern state cannot provide a home in the world within its frontiers for its citizens'. In other words, 'globalization' – the capture of the entire world within the web of market relationships and the subsequent weakening of national governments – is also viewed by Plant as a refutation of Hegel's political theory.

More recent versions of the reconciliation thesis appear in Michael O. Hardimon's 1994 book on Hegel[17] – which makes reconciliation a key feature of Hegel's thought – as well as in a series of illuminating articles by Joseph McCarney. Hegel's inability to find a solution for poverty, says McCarney, demonstrates

> the bourgeois horizons of his thought. What ultimately cramps and stultifies it is the fact that the true realm of freedom cannot be built on the foundation of the private accumulation of capital. This is, however, a truth which Hegel only partially and fitfully perceives and which he can never fully acknowledge, still less draw to the centre of his theoretical framework.[18]

Althusser's 'epistemological break'

If Lukács, Marcuse, Avineri and the rest tossed Engels's account of the relationship between Hegel and Marx into the air, the French Marxist Louis Althusser (1918–90) – like the proverbial movie gunfighter – shot it full of holes. His *For Marx* and *Reading Capital*, both published in the mid-1960s, transformed the way the relationship between Marx and Hegel was seen on the left. While Althusser's reputation has faded considerably, his legacy of anti-Hegelianism is still very strong.

Louis Althusser was a complex and enigmatic figure. A theorist with the French Communist Party (PCF), he was universally acknowledged as one of the leading Marxist writers of his generation. His reputation continued to soar in Europe and North America even after he began to lose favour in France, partly a result of the brisk decline of the fortunes of the PCF in the late 1970s. In 1980 Althusser strangled his wife of many years, Hélène Legotien, a prominent scholar. He was declared mentally unfit for trial and languished out of the limelight until his death a decade later. In 1992, his autobiography was published posthumously. This document scandalized Althusser's friends and enemies alike. Althusser recounted a lifetime of mental illness, suicide attempts and incredible ambivalence about his own achievements. A review of the book in *Lingua Franca* gives some of the flavour of Althusser's confessions.

> The man who taught philosophy to generations of students at the Ecole Normale admits to having read 'little' Hegel, 'scarcely any' Spinoza, Heidegger or Husserl, 'and not to have understood Freud'. The brilliant author of *For Marx* and *Reading Capital* . . . was 'an imaginary marxist . . . full of artifice and fakery'.[19]

Althusser's most sensational theoretical innovation was his conception of 'the epistemological break' in the intellectual development of Karl Marx, which – Althusser claimed – occured in 1845. For Althusser, the two works Marx produced in that year, *The German Ideology* (written jointly with Engels) and the famous *Theses on Feuerbach*, created a new science, historical materialism, and the accompanying philosophy of dialectical materialism.

Althusser by no means discovered the 'young Marx.' A huge literature on the young Marx grew after the Second World War, based on Marx's early writings, which were not published until the 1930s. Following Lukács's pioneering studies, many writers argued that the humanist currents in the young Marx – his concern for individual rights and the rule of law, as well as his criticism of human alienation – had important implications for his later writings. Seen in this light, Marx's mature theory was not a rejection of the bourgeois democratic heritage – as it was commonly portrayed by communist theorists – but an inclusive call for a widening and deepening of democracy. This view of Marx quickly became a rallying cry among opponents to Soviet authoritarianism, and for radical reformers within established Communist Parties.

Althusser's work was a response to the humanist critique of orthodox communism. By expelling Hegel and the young Marx from the pantheon, Althusser hoped to shore up the leadership of the Communist Party. He wrote in *For Marx*:

> The communism to which the Soviet Union is committed is a world without economic exploitation, without violence, without discrimination – a world opening up before the Soviets the infinite vistas of progress, of science, of culture, of bread and freedom, of free development – a world that can do without shadows or tragedies.

There were great challenges ahead for the Soviet system, Althusser acknowledged, but they could not be solved by the humanism of the early Marx.

> Why is it that these problems are posed by certain ideologues as a function of the concepts of a *philosophy of man* – instead of being openly, fully and rigorously posed in the economic, political and ideological terms of Marxist theory? Why do so many Marxist philosophers seem to feel the need to appeal to the pre-Marxist ideological concept of *alienation* in order supposedly to think and 'resolve' these concrete historical problems?[20]

Althusser postulated that just as Galileo 'opened up' 'the continent of Physics', Marx in 1845, 'opened up . . . the continent of History'. Althusser unselfconsciously employed terms drawn from European imperialism to describe Marx's achievement.

> A continent, in the sense of this metaphor, is never empty: it is already 'occupied' by many and varied more or less ideological disciplines which do not know that they belong to that 'continent'. For example, before Marx, the History continent was occupied by philosophies of history, by political economy, etc. The opening-up of a continent by a continental science not only disputes the rights and claims of the former occupants, it also completely restructures the old configuration of the 'continent'.[21]

As a consequence of the 'break', Althusser contended, Marx initiated a dialectic completely unlike Hegel's and put forward non-Hegelian conceptions of history and social structure.

Althusser's theory of the 'epistemological break' in Marx's writings formed an opposing image to Lukács's thesis on Hegel. Lukács found evidence that the young Hegel pursued ideas that anticipated Marx. In Lukács's account, it was almost as though a movie editor had spliced the youthful Hegel's growth into the early phases of Marx's career. According to Lukács, however, Hegel careened off the radical path at Frankfurt, while Marx transformed the mature Hegelian method into a revolutionary analysis of capitalism and history.

Althusser disagreed with Lukács on every point. The French theorist decried Lukács's portrait of the young Marx as a follower of Hegel, and transformed (without acknowledgement) Lukács's idea of Hegel's Frankfurt rupture into Marx's 'epistemological break' from Hegel. These moves were part of Althusser's general programme to expunge Hegelianism completely from the work of the mature Marx.

According to Althusser in *For Marx* (we shall see that Althusser later changed his position), Marx was never a Hegelian (except, perhaps, when he wrote *The Economic and Philosophical Manuscripts of 1844*). Instead, Marx developed along a series of positions that took him further and further away from Hegel. Starting as a follower of Fichte and Kant at the beginning of the 1840s, Marx progressed through Feuerbach and emerged free of Hegel in 1845. Althusser dismissed Engels's and Lukács's assertion that Marx applied the Hegelian method to history while eschewing Hegel's system – in fact, Marx used neither Hegel's method or his system. Althusser firmly resisted the notion that Marx applied Hegel's theory of alienation to the world of social relations. He mocked the famous inversion thesis, that Hegel was standing on his head and needed only to be set back on his feet. 'A man on his head is the same man when he is finally walking on his feet', Althusser sniffed.[22]

Althusser's theoretical 'interventions' created great excitement. His dramatic flair and stylistic elegance were unequalled, and had a profound effect on young scholars of the period. He originated a new era of precision and exactitude in Marxist scholarship, and encouraged writers to believe that 'theoretical practice' almost unaided could penetrate the defences of capitalism and bring forward the communist revolution. Nevertheless, as the English Marxist historian Edward Thompson complained in *The Poverty of Theory*, his famous 1978 rebuttal of Althusser, the French Marxist also pushed Marxism toward a barren form of structuralist abstraction, the zealous worship of empty formulae. Reflecting the mood of the time, Thompson refrained from a defence of Hegel's role in Marxism and declared that the debate about Hegel and Marx was exhausted.[23]

Althusser never offered much support for his claims about Marx's relationship to Hegel. These were mostly untested assertions despite Althusser's frequent gestures toward a rigorous 'reading of the text'. As intellectual historian Michael Kelly puts it, 'Althusser's remarks [on Hegel and Marx] largely constitute[d] a clearing of the ground'.[24] By getting Hegel out of the way, Althusser created a vast space in which to insert his own conceptions into Marxism. Yet the French philosopher's anti-Hegelian project was based on falsified and inadequate evidence, as he subsequently admitted. By the end of the 1960s, Althusser had moved the epistemological break from 1845 to much later in Marx's life – namely 1882, the year before he died! 'The *tendency* of Marx's thought', said Althusser, presumably tongue in cheek, 'drove him irresistibly to the *radical* abandonment of every shade of Hegelian influence, as can be seen by the 1875 *Critique of the Gotha Programme* and the 1882 *Notes on Wagner*.'[25]

The fate of Althusser's project suggests, I believe, the ultimate futility of any approach that would erase the Hegelian heritage in Marx. Moreover, it left the question of the real nature of the relationship between Marx and Hegel unexplored. The next section looks at Hegel's discussion of the break that characterizes human consciousness in the transition from youth to maturity.

Hegel's stages of life

The idea that a crisis in the form of an 'epistemological break' marked the development of both Marx and Hegel is based on the psychological argument that as people get older they turn away from their youthful ideals. Thus, the old Hegel was frightened by what Lukács called the 'revolutionary atheism' of his early years, and fled to the security of the strong state. Marx eschewed the romantic humanism of his young Hegelian past – 'this crushing layer of ideology' as Althusser described it[26] – and became the rigid social scientist enamoured of ineluctable socio-historical laws and mysterious economic formulae.

The notion that a sharp break in the growth of consciousness marks the transition from youth to adulthood was actually first put forward by Hegel in the *Philosophy of Mind*, the third section of his *Encyclopaedia of the Philosophical Sciences*, first published in 1817 and revised in 1830. His account of this transition recalls assessments by various commentators of the changes that took place in Hegel's own mind, and in that of Marx, as they grew older. Yet Hegel rejects the view that the mature individual discards the ideals of youth. Maturity means accepting the dialectical structure of the world – the interactive relationship between individual action and society – but it does not entail an abandonment of principles. Hegel's argument has deeply influenced major thinkers on the psychology of the human life cycle. It also offers a unique perspective on Hegel's conception of the relationship between individual action and social structure.

Hegel defines no age limits for his stages of life. It is likely, however, that he – in common with other writers in the early nineteenth century – subscribed to a modified version of the categorization first articulated by Isidore of Seville in the Middle Ages. 'According to him, up to six years constituted infancy; 7 to 13, childhood; 14 to 27, adolescence, 28 to 48, youth; 49 to 76, maturity (*senectus*); and 77 to death, old age'.[27] Hegel's notion of childhood includes two stages, which would correspond to Isidore's infancy and childhood. In the first stage, infancy, the child remains at home with parents or caregivers; in the second stage, the child begins the transition to life in civil society by going to school.

As I mentioned in chapter 1, Hegel saw childhood as the stage of unity between subject and object. The conflicts which may occur in this stage, Hegel writes, 'remain devoid of any serious interest. The child lives in innocence, without any lasting pain, in the love it has for its parents and in the feeling of being loved by them.' Even at birth, however, human infants may be distinguished from the lower animals, not only in their 'delicately organized, infinitely plastic body', but also their 'unruly and stormy and peremptory' nature. Where the animal is silent or expresses its pain by whimpering, the human infant makes its wants known by imperious screams. 'By this ideal activity', notes Hegel wryly, 'the child shows that it is straightway imbued with the certainty that it has the right to demand from the outer world the satisfaction of its needs.'[28]

Hegel's use of the term 'ideal' to describe a baby's cry is instructive. Ideal for Hegel refers to the irreducible unity of consciousness and action. Human action is a material counterpart to the idea it carries out, and these together construct the dialectic that makes up our social universe. Thus, a baby's cry is a call to social action. This accounts for the sudden unease inscribed on the faces of adults summoned by its aural challenge, and the rapid changes a baby can bring to the lives of those around them. In late autumn 1996, for example, a battered woman was forced to abandon her baby, which was brought into a Montreal police station. Television cameras showed case-hardened police officers taking turns rocking and nursing the four-month-old infant in the midst of their regular precinct duties.

As the child grows she attains an increasing mastery over the outside world and herself. She becomes aware of her surroundings and develops a sense of self. Soon the child wishes to unite theory with practice and 'passes to the practical inclination to test himself in this actual world'. The child proves herself against her environment by growing teeth and learning to stand, walk, and talk. Her incipient self-dependence is at first expressed in play with tangible objects. Later, play gives way to learning and curiosity, and children awake to the feeling 'that as yet they *are* not what they *ought* to be'.[29] Children succumb to the desire to be more like the grown-ups they see around them, and begin to mimic adult activities.

The children's need to grow up, to strive after knowledge, is the driving factor in all education. But children do not perceive learning as an end in itself; rather they see it as a means to achieve an ideal they connect with a particular mature and authoritative individual. School forms the transition from the family into the social world. As we have seen, this transition probably marked for Hegel the divide between infancy and childhood. At school, children learn to be accepted for what they do rather than what they are. At home a child is loved regardless of her behaviour, 'in school, on the other hand, the immediacy of the child no longer counts; here it is esteemed only according to its worth'. In the classroom the child 'is not merely loved but criticized and guided in accordance with universal principles . . . in general subjected to a universal order'.[30]

The stage of youth begins at the 'onset of puberty',[31] and although Hegel does not explicitly say so, he seems to follow Isidore of Seville's categorization of youth as the years between fourteen and twenty-seven. Hegel would probably disagree with theorists such as Erik Erikson,[32] who suggest that the turmoil of youth is confined to the teenage years.

The youth starts to see herself as separate from the surrounding universe, and opposed to it. She regards herself as representing 'the true and the good' while the world is 'something contingent, accidental'. This, says Hegel, 'is the fully developed antithesis, the strain and struggle of a universality which is still subjective (as seen in ideals, fancies, hopes, ambitions) against his immediate individuality'. The youth is caught up in subjectivity: dissatisfied with his own immature development, and disgusted with a world 'which, as it exists, fails to meet his ideal requirements'.[33] The idols of childhood – the persons who once seemed worthy of respect and imitation – are exposed as frauds and exchanged for substantive notions like the ideal of love and friendship, or the universal world order of peace and understanding. These concrete ideals are attributed by young people to themselves, while the world itself seems contingent and accidental by comparison. Not only is the youth opposed to the world, she also feels compelled to change it. The young person does not realize that the ideal she cherishes has already succeeded in unfolding itself. Not the world, but the young person is the accident; the universe will go on with or without a particular individual. And part of the world's substantial content is the ideal like love or friendship which young people take to be theirs alone.

Opposition between the ideals of youth and the nature of reality means that the young person feels unrecognized and at war with the world. In this conflict young people seem to possess a more altruistic character than the adult who has found a place in the existing order. For Hegel, however, this is a superficial way of looking at things. In contrast with the youth, who is still wrapped up in particular impulses and subjective views, the adult has plunged into the life of society and has become active on its behalf. 'The youth', Hegel observes dryly, 'necessarily arrives at this goal; but *his* immediate aim is to train and discipline himself so that he will be able to realize his ideals. In the attempt to make these actual he becomes a man.'[34]

The transition to adulthood can be a severe shock. The individual believes she must give up her ideals in order to pursue the mundane details of ordinary life. This can create, says Hegel, a state of 'hypochondria,' – or in modern terms, anxiety – which is the more serious, the later in life it strikes. 'In this diseased frame of mind the man will not give up his subjectivity, is unable to overcome his repugnance to the actual world, and by this very fact finds himself in a state of relative incapacity which easily becomes actual incapacity.'[35]

Lukàcs claims that Hegel experienced his own bout of hypochondria. While in his mid-twenties, Hegel went through a period of extreme anxiety that marked a turning point in his career that resulted in his reconciliation with the established order. However, there is no evidence for Hegel's 'Frankfurt crisis'. Hegel was lonely and depressed in Berne a few years before he went to Frankfurt, but there was no crisis. H. S. Harris insists that Hegel's reference to 'unhappy Frankfurt' (in a letter he wrote in 1810) – upon which Lukács based his whole argument – actually concerned the experience of Hegel's friend Hölderlin.[36] As we shall learn further in the next chapter, while Hegel was staying with Hölderlin in Frankfurt the young poet was involved in a tragic love affair.

In Hegel's view, hypochondria is synonymous with alienation since any disease indicates 'the isolation of a particular system of the organism from the general life, and in virtue of this *alienation* of the particular from the general life, the (individual) exhibits its finitude, its impotence and dependence on a foreign power'.[37] An alienated person is far from being a force for change; instead she is restricted and held fast by the surrounding environment. To avoid self-destruction, the young person must recognize the world as an autonomous entity 'which in its essential nature is already complete', and accept 'the conditions set for him by the world and wrest from it what he wants for himself'. Submission to the existing system appears to be arbitrary and irrational. In fact, unity of the individual with the world stems from a rational source. 'The rational, the divine,' avers Hegel, 'possesses the absolute power to actualize itself and has right from the beginning, fulfilled itself, it is not so impotent that it would have to wait for the beginning of its actualization.' Since the idea will go ahead on its own, it makes sense for the individual merely to attend to her private affairs and forget youth's illusions. 'The man behaves quite rationally in abandoning his plan for completely transforming the world and in striving to realize his personal aims, passions and interests only within the framework of the world of which he is a part.'[38]

While the mature individual is confronted with a self-dependent and objective world, this world itself is nothing but the historical result of the combined actions of individuals. At each stage of development, the social structure manifests the idea (of freedom) as it appears in the consciousness of all the persons within it. The idea is not 'something far away beyond this mortal sphere', but is found 'however confused and degenerated in every consciousness'.[39] In liberal democracies, for example, the rights of gays and lesbians are given far more respect than they were twenty or thirty years ago. The idea of freedom has grown to include people of differing sexual orientations. Of course, this does not mean that the ideas of every single person or group are faithfully reflected in social arrangements. For example, vegetarianism – the notion that eating animals is wrong – has a large following in advanced industrial societies, but is far from a standard practice. Western societies are still organized around meat-eaters. Still, there are signs that the vegetarian lifestyle is gaining ground, and is more acceptable as a way of life.

It is in this sense of society as the self-manifestation of the idea, that Hegel calls the world into which the adult enters 'complete'. The freedom or liberation of mind 'is not something never completed'. It transcends the conditions of everyday life and establishes itself within these conditions. Society leaves the individual 'scope for honourable, far-reaching, creative activity'. Although the social world is 'complete in its essential nature . . . it is not a dead, absolutely inert world but, like the life process, a world which perpetually creates itself anew, which while merely preserving itself, at the same time progresses'. The individual's work consists precisely in the conservation and advancement of the world. A person not only recreates a society that is already there, but his or her activity also pushes the world forward. 'The power of any single individual is severely limited, for the world's progress occurs only on the large scale and comes to view in a large aggregate of what has been produced.' The tempo of advance is slow, but it is there all the same and its presence is visible for the individual even if only in hindsight.

If the man after a labour of fifty years looks back on his past he will readily recognize the progress made. This knowledge, as also the insight into the rationality of the world, liberates him from mourning over the destruction of his ideals.[40]

Women and men newly emerging from the inner conflicts of youth into the reality of the outside world must ensure that what is worthwhile in their ideals is translated into practical activity: 'what the man must purge himself of is only what is untrue, the empty abstractions'.[41] For Hegel, 'empty abstractions' are notions which, when put into action, destroy themselves. Lacking continuity with the past, these ideas find no place to take root. For example, in the French Revolution – as Hegel contends in the *Phenomenology of Spirit* – freedom and equality were interpreted in an empty, abstract manner. Consequently, no distinctions of class or rank were tolerated, and government itself appeared as despotic rule by a faction. Instead of achieving their aim of liberty, the proponents of abstract freedom and equality succeeded only in annihilating successive attempts at government and order which the Revolution was meant to achieve.

Once entry into society is complete, the individual may well be unhappy and depressed with the state of the world, and may even abandon hope of ever improving it. Almost in spite of herself, however, the adult soon finds a place in the objective world and becomes accustomed to it. At first this world seems strange and new; there seems to be little pattern to what the individual does, and every event has a uniqueness and peculiarity of its own. The longer the individual works the more she comes to see that events follow certain general rules, are subject to particular laws. She begins to find herself competely at home when at work and gradually grows accustomed to what was formerly an alien world. There are now few surprises: only odd events, with little connection to the general run of things, provide diversion and interest. Without the constant opposition between expectation and reality, the individual finds herself trapped in the mechanisms of habit which eventually hurtle the person into old age.

> The very fact that his activity has become so *conformed* to this work, that his activity no longer meets with any resistance, this complete facility of execution, brings in its train the *extinction* of vitality: for with the disappearance of the opposition between subject and object there also disappears the interest of the former with the latter. Thus the habit of mental life, equally with the dulling of the functions of his physical organism, changes the man into an old man.[42]

For the old person life has lost all its meaning and interest, 'and the future seems to hold no promise of anything new at all'. The elderly individual imagines that she already knows the essence and general pattern of any event that may yet be encountered. Everything is explicable in terms of the maxims the old person has long since mastered and internalized. The mind of the elderly person is focused entirely on these substantial rules of conduct and the events in the past to which it owes knowledge of them. By living in the past, the aged person forgets the details of the present, 'names, for example, in the same measure as conversely, he firmly retains in his mind the maxims of experience and feels obliged to preach to those younger than himself'. The wisdom of the old person, 'this lifeless, complete coincidence of the subject's activity with the world', carries the elderly individual back to the days of childhood where there was also no conflict between subject and object, just 'in the same way that the reduction of his physical activities to a processless habit leads to the abstract negation of the living individuality, to death'.[43]

For Hegel, the transition from youth to maturity involves no shedding of ideals – as in Lukács – nor an abrupt Althusserian rupture. Ideals are not abandoned, they are applied in the context of an individual's life. The mature individual fights to put into place the ideals she developed as a young person. 'In my scientific development, which started from [the] more subordinate needs of man,' Hegel wrote to his friend Schelling in 1800, 'I was inevitably driven towards science, and the ideal of [my] youth had to take the form of reflection and thus at once of a system.'[44] Two decades later, Hegel commented on the active destiny of the mature individual in society. 'The absolute goal of free mind', he wrote in the *Philosophy of Right*, 'is to make freedom its object, i.e. to make freedom objective as much in the sense that freedom shall be the rational system of mind, as in the sense that this system shall be the world of immediate actuality.'[45]

The deep impact of Hegel's activist theory of human consciousness on Marx is already evident in the young Marx's *Economic and Philosophical Manuscripts of 1844*,[46] and especially in the 1845 *Theses on Feuerbach*, where Marx observes that it was left to (Hegelian) idealism to develop 'the *active* side' of '*human, sensuous activity, practice*', whereas materialism saw society 'only in the form of the *object* . . . or of *contemplation*'.[47] The ideal of Hegel's youth and its development into a system is the subject of the next chapter.

3 • Hegel's Development, 1770–1801

Introduction

This chapter will look at some of the radical themes in Hegel's development and connect them with his mature thinking. This provides an opportunity to re-evaluate not only Hegel's politics as a whole, but his intellectual career. Hegel's bitter critique of Christianity and his startling portrayal of Jesus Christ are intimately connected with the young philosopher's democratic political vision – a youthful ideal that reflects the influence of his friend, the great poet Hölderlin. The chapter begins with a brief examination of Hegel's life and education, and concludes with a discussion of his concept of the 'external state'.

Hegel's family life

Hegel was born in Stuttgart, in the Duchy of Württemberg, southern Germany, on 27 August 1770. He was the first-born child of Georg Ludwig Hegel, a successful civil servant, and Maria Magdalena Fromm. Hegel's family – which descended on his father's side from Austrian Protestants who fled to Württemberg in the sixteenth century – belonged to the duchy's comfortable upper middle class. Hegel received his first lessons in Latin from his mother before he reached the age of five. 'His mother, who was better educated than most women of her time and station, was delighted with his rapid progress and encouraged him in all his studies.'[1] By the age of fourteen, he was diligently recording, and making excerpts from, everything he read in a series of diaries – a habit he would keep for the whole of his life.

Hegel had two siblings, a sister, Christiane, who was born in 1773, and a younger brother, Ludwig, born in 1776. His family was touched by illness and tragedy, a circumstance, perhaps, that penetrated his philosophy. '[N]o one could read Hegel's texts,' writes Daniel Berthold-Bond, 'and miss the repeated language of "pain," "suffering," "sorrow," and "anguish."'[2] Hegel lost his mother, with whom he had a very close and loving relationship, when he was only twelve years old. He and his father nearly succumbed to the same disease that killed his mother, 'bilious fever'. This was Hegel's second brush with death, the boy having barely survived smallpox at the age of six. His brother Ludwig was killed in 1812 while serving as an officer in Napoleon's Russian campaign.

Hegel's sister suffered recurring mental problems in the last twenty years of her life, and Hegel consulted several physicians in the search for a cure for her. In 1814, during her first bout of the disease, she spent many months regaining her strength under the care of Hegel and his wife. 'Regard my home for the time being as a haven open to you, and ready at any time to welcome you,' wrote Hegel upon hearing of his sister's illness. 'I look forward with sincere satisfaction to being able to repay you to some extent for all you have always done for me, and to offer you peace and contentment in my home.'[3] Christiane, who 'always watched the career of her older brother with deep interest and sisterly affection',[4] committed suicide shortly after Hegel's untimely death (probably from cholera) at the age of sixty-one, on 14 November 1831. Hegel's first major work, *The Phenomenology of Spirit*, celebrates the close relationship between brother and sister – the most intimate, and equal, cross-sex relationship available in patriarchal society. *The Phenomenology* was written in 1806–7, a few years before Christiane's descent into madness.

Hegel's early love life was troubled. While writing the *Phenomenology*, he was romantically involved with his housekeeper, a married woman named Christiana Burkhardt (née Fischer), and had a child by her. They called the baby Ludwig Fischer, after Hegel's brother, who acted as godfather. Burkhardt's husband died a few weeks after the birth, but Hegel apparently reneged on a promise to marry the bereaved woman. The unhappy couple sent the child off to live with friends of Hegel's. Five years later, Hegel married a much younger woman from a wealthy merchant family, Marie von Tücher. In 1816, Hegel and his wife brought Ludwig Fischer to live with them. Ludwig's arrival at his father's house coincided with news of Christiana Burkhardt's death. 'I have just told him of his mother's death,' wrote Hegel. 'It affected him more than me. My heart had long ago finished with her. I could still only fear unpleasant contacts between her and Ludwig – and thus indirectly with my wife – and extreme unpleasantness for myself.'[5]

The boy felt rejected by his stepmother. Ludwig confessed in 1825 'that his stepmother did not treat him the same as she treated her own two sons and that he thus lived in constant fear'.[6] Hegel himself referred to the social prejudices his first son was forced to endure. 'Society always used to pose a danger for him, and the danger of leaving him among strangers without friendly supervision could only cause me concern.'[7] He attempted to place his son in business, but Ludwig resisted, choosing instead a military career. The young man succumbed to fever a day after Hegel's sixty-first birthday, on 28 August 1831, in Batavia (now called Jakarta), while in Dutch military service. Hegel died a few months later, without hearing of his first child's fate.

A few months before his brother Ludwig's demise in 1812, Hegel and his wife lost their newborn infant, Susanna Maria Louisa Wilhelmina. A grief-sticken Hegel announced the sad news to his friend, Niethammer. 'As happy, or indeed overly happy as she [Hegel's wife] was, no less was she shaken by the loss of this dear child. And I suffer doubly, from the loss I have suffered and from the pain she feels.' Eighteen years later, Hegel recollected his sorrow in a letter of condolence to his friend, Heinrich Beer, who had also just lost a child. Regretting that he had not realized Beer's tragic circumstances when they met earlier in the day, Hegel writes,

> I would have tried to talk with you right away, not to bring you words of consolation – for I would know of none that at present could have any effect on such a recent and immediate sorrow – but rather merely to offer my sympathy, share your grief, and lament with you such an irreparable loss. I could only have asked you what I asked my wife in the face of a similar though early loss of what was then our only child. I asked whether she could bring herself to prefer never having had the joy of knowing this child at all to the happiness of having had such a child at its most beautiful age and then losing it. In your heart you will likewise confess you could not have preferred the first of these two alternatives. You thus prefer the very situation in which you in fact find yourself. Your joy has now passed. Yet there remains with you the feeling of that happiness, your memory of the dear boy, his joys, his hours of happiness, his love for you and for his mother, his childlike sensibility, his good-naturedness and friendliness towards everyone. Do not be ungrateful for the satisfaction and the happiness you have had; keep its memory alive and steadily before your gaze over against your loss of his presence. In this way your son and your joy in having him will not be lost to you.[8]

Two more children were born to Hegel and his wife in rapid succession, Karl and Immanuel. The boys were only sixteen and eighteen years old respectively at the time of his death.

Hegel was called the 'Old Man' by his fellow students at university, and both Marx and Engels liked to call him 'old Hegel'. Even the editors of the English collection of his letters talk about Hegel's 'old age', and suggest that his 'concern for security in Berlin' reflected 'a philosophy of old age'.[9] Of course, the schoolboy title of 'Old Man' referred to Hegel's maturity of outlook rather than his physical and mental decrepitude. Hegel was never an old man. He died barely past sixty at the height of his mental powers. In Isidore of Seville's classification of the stages of life, mentioned in the last chapter, Hegel was less than half-way through the age of maturity, which runs from forty-nine to seventy-six.

Education

Hegel was raised in the ethic of civic activism and public service that characterized the citizens of Württemberg, a predominantly Protestant state ruled by a Catholic prince. From the beginning he was aware of conflict between the interests of the individual and those of government. To be a citizen of Württemberg meant being profoundly suspicious of the duchy's Catholic political leadership.[10] Hegel's experience would make him sensitive to the plight of peoples ruled by an alien government. He would be equally wary of rule by a wealthy elite, or by an administration representing a foreign crown.

Significantly, Hegel's first published work was his 1798 translation of J. J. Cart's 1793 *Lettres confidentielles*, a protest against tyrannical aristocratic oppression by the Berne nobility of part of the Pays de Vaud, a Swiss canton near Lake Geneva. 'Hegel sympathized with the revolutionary aspirations of the Pays de Vaud and with the goals of the American Revolution', writes Christopher Jamme. 'With Cart, he criticized the practice of princes, who sold their native inhabitants into military service much as livestock – a common practice as well in Württemberg.'[11] The French-speaking canton of Vaud was ruled by the German-speaking canton of Berne for more than two centuries. In 1791, two years before Hegel arrived in Berne, the people of Vaud, inspired by the French Revolution, rose up against the Berne oligarchy.

The uprising was crushed in 1792, but five years later the revolutionary armies united the territory with France. For Hegel, Vaud's liberation, like the American War of Independence, demonstrated that reactionary oppression can 'achieve nothing in the long run, in circumstances where reform is called for'.[12] His translation of *Lettres confidentielles* was published anonymously, and for years Hegel feared retribution at the hands of the authorities. Perhaps he need not have worried: 'It took over a hundred years to discover that the anonymous translator and commentator was young Hegel.'[13]

After graduating in 1788 from the Gymnasium (high school) at Stuttgart as class valedictorian, Hegel entered the Stift (Theological college) at the University of Tübingen to study for a theological degree. His presence in the seminary points to the contradictions in Hegel's life that would influence his philosophy. He never intended to fulfil the obligation of acceptance into the school, which was to to follow a career in the church or the schools of the Duchy of Württemberg. Hegel's first two years at Tübingen were devoted to a preparatory course in philosophy (the Magisterium) which he completed in 1790. A further three years in theology culminated in the consistorial exam which Hegel passed in the autumn of 1793.

At the seminary, Hegel witnessed an important debate between two of his teachers, G. C. Storr and K. I. Dietz. Storr was an orthodox Kantian who wished to defend Christian faith against the doubts of the Enlightenment, whereas Dietz wanted a complete break from religion. Dietz constructed a system of morality based on Kantian ethics that he claimed would need no religious underpinning. By contrast, Storr supported the traditional view that morality is founded on religious conscience.[14] Some interpreters, including Charles Taylor and Laurence Dickey, believe that Hegel later built a theological philosophy that drew on both camps. Hegel wrote an early essay, the 'Life of Jesus' – which I discuss below – to deal with the controversy, after he left Tübingen.

Hegel's circle of close friends at Tübingen included two men who would achieve great fame, the poet Friedrich Hölderlin and the philosopher, F. W. J. Schelling. Schelling contributed to the early formulation of Hegel's systematic philosophy, but it was Hölderlin who helped supply the unquenchable spiritual flame for Hegel's life work. The years at Tübingen coincided with the momentous events in France after 1789. Hegel and his friends were captivated by the French Revolution and counted themselves among its most enthusiastic supporters. This aroused the suspicions of Duke Karl Eugen, who placed Hegel and his friends under secret police surveillance. Although Hegel's planting of a liberty tree at Tübingen belongs to mythology, he never forgot to toast the fall of the Bastille to the end of his life.[15] He keenly followed events in France, remarking in a letter to Schelling on the execution of the revolutionary terrorist J. B. Carrier in December 1794. 'The trial is very important and has revealed the complete ignominy of Robespierre's party (*Hegel: The Letters*, p.29). Indeed Carrier's death was a harbinger of a 'year of revenge' when victorious Girondins would cut down trees of liberty and destroy the remainder of Robespierre's Jacobins.[16]

After leaving Tübingen Hegel tutored the children of an aristocratic family in Berne for three years, from 1793 until 1796. Hegel frequently remarked on his loneliness and depression in Berne. Nevertheless, his aristocratic employers possessed a library with rich holdings in philosophy and social science. He devoured Gibbon's *Decline and Fall of the Roman Empire*, Kant's *Religion Within the Limits of Reason Alone*, and the economic and sociological works of the Scots Smith, Steuart and Ferguson. While the lonely Hegel tutored children in Switzerland, his friend Schelling 'burst like a comet' on the philosophical scene in Germany. And Hölderlin was in Jena, 'where Fichte was lecturing (along with Schiller) and the whole culture of Germany had for the moment a living and visible focus'.[17]

With the assistance of Hölderlin, who already had a position there, Hegel secured a tutorship in Frankfurt, where he stayed between 1796 and 1801. Hegel's joyous anticipation for his coming reunion with Hölderlin is conveyed in the poem 'Eleusis' – 'Hegel's most substantial poetic effort'.[18] The poem, dated August 1796, is written in a style developed by Hölderlin at Tübingen, itself inspired by the great poet, Schiller. The two friends, Hegel is certain, will discover in Frankfurt,

> the bliss of certainty, of finding the loyalty of the old bond
> still more solid, more ripened
> of this bond no oath has sealed, to live but for the free truth
> never, never to make peace with the decree that regulates
> feeling and opinion.[19]

Before he left Berne, Hegel had to get permission from the Tübingen seminary in order to take the job in Frankfurt. He eventually resigned his position as a tutor in 1799, when the death of his father left him with a modest inheritance, but remained in Frankfurt for more than a year afterwards. In 1801, with Schelling's help, Hegel secured a post as professor at the University of Jena. In order to have his master's degree from Tübingen accepted as a Ph.D. at Jena, Hegel submitted two works to gain 'nostrification': an essay, 'Difference Between Fichte's System of Philosophy and Schelling's', and a dissertation, *On the Orbits of the Planets*, which he defended on his thirty-first birthday, 27 August 1801. The following sections will discuss some major developments in Hegel's writings up to his departure from Frankfurt. The themes of equality and love, which arise in Frankfurt, concern the democratic vision that would inform Hegel's work until his death. We will return to Hegel's career after 1801 in chapter 5.

Christianity and love

Hölderlin entered Tübingen at the same time as Hegel and graduated with him in 1793. Both were fascinated with Greek antiquity, and believed the ancient world could project an ideal universe of fulfilment for contemporary men and women. They held the dogmatic and authoritarian morality of Christianity 'chiefly responsible for the atrophy and ossification of German culture'.[20] Yet no society could survive without a common spiritual bond to unite its people. What was required to achieve true freedom, the two friends agreed, was a folk religion based on the politics and principles of beauty articulated by the Greeks.

A passage on the meanings surrounding death, written by Hegel shortly after leaving Tübingen, offers a striking example of what he (and Hölderlin) saw as the superiority of the Greek tradition over that of contemporary Christianity. This comparison is all the more telling, Hegel observes, since Christianity is a religion which 'makes preparation for death into a cardinal point, a cornerstone of the entire edifice'.

> How different were the pictures of death implanted in the Greek imagination from the ones our people harbor: among them it was a beautiful spirit, the brother of Sleep, immortalized in the monuments above their graves; among us it is Death, whose gruesome skull hovers over all our coffins. For them death was a reminder of the joy of living – to us it just smells like death. They euphemized death, moderating their depictions of it, but we, when in respectable society, altogether avoid speaking or writing of this natural thing, while our orators and preachers, determined to strike terror in us

and spoil our pleasure, paint death in the most hideous colours imaginable.[21]

For Hegel, Christianity resulted from Jesus Christ's failed attempt to bring the aesthetic and political truths of Greece to the people of Judaea, who were then under the twin yoke of the corrupt Jewish priests and the harsh rule of Rome. Hegel's account of Christ's mission appears in two of his earliest writings, 'The positivity of Christianity', and the 'Life of Jesus', both written in 1795. The incomplete essays written by Hegel between 1793 and 1794 (the 'Berne Fragments') also deal with the figure of Christ. Hegel is fascinated with Christ as a moral philosopher who brought spiritual truths to the people through everyday images. For Hegel, Christ was a great teacher of the idea of democracy that would burst on the European scene in 1789. But Hegel rejects many of the doctrines of the church promulgated in Christ's name.

For the young Hegel, even the Christian understanding of the meaning of the saviour's death is distorted and unreliable – a 'moral detour'.

> Even today, when the spirit, the ideas, of the time no longer reflect much need of repentance for wrongdoing, we are taught first (in order of importance, if not time) to know Christ as the propitiator sacrificed to appease an outraged God for the sake of all mankind – each of whom has need of expiation not just on occasion, but throughout his life, indeed for the very fact that he exists. And although millions have made similar sacrifice, giving their lives for lesser ends (their king, their country, their beloved) and done so gladly, with a smile instead of an anguished bloody sweat, we are supposed to have such gratitude for this one person who suffered and died for us that his death becomes the very centrepiece of our religion, the most solemn preoccupation of our imagination, and is supposed to lead us to reverence for Christ and God.[22]

Christ's purpose was to teach morality on earth, to create a new civilization, not to prepare the individual for a satisfying afterlife. 'The real end of morality has already been lost sight of when salvation replaced it as the ultimate purpose of such teachings.'[23]

The youthful Hegel returned to the discussion of Christ's life in his 1798 work, 'The spirit of Christianity and its fate'. As many commentators have noted, however, Hegel's tone changes in Part 3 of this essay. In the first two sections, Hegel concentrates on the 'positive', authoritarian aspects of Christianity. He contrasts, for example, the followers of Socrates, who knew and understood Socratic philosophy, with Jesus's disciples, who, 'drawn to him by miracles and wonders, loved him without ever comprehending either his virtue or philosophy'.[24] In Part 3 Hegel deepens his critique of Christianity by turning to the subject of love.

Love underlies Hegel's conception of the state as a 'divine unification of men', which also receives its initial formulation in the 'Spirit' essay. He contrasts the ideal state with the Christian notion of a 'Kingdom' which

> means only a union through domination, through the power of a stranger over a stranger, a union to be totally distinguished from the beauty of the divine life of a pure human fellowship, because such a life is of all things the freest possible.[25]

Love as the basis of the ideal state – and its importance for the relationships of labour and property – will remain a central theme in Hegel's philosophy for the remainder of his career.

The restricted conception of love in Christianity's 'heavenly Kingdom' is the key to its fate. Christ's disciples neglected every other link with the community except 'the relationship of the common faith and the revelations of this common possession in the appropriate religious actions'. Achievements in the world of work or in the state are deemed insignificant; even the right to the ownership of property is abandoned or ignored. Christianity, to be sure, preaches love, but this love is 'inactive and undeveloped . . . a love which, though love is the highest life, remains unliving'. Inevitably, Christianity becomes an instrument of fanaticism and terror. '[T]he contranatural expansion of love's scope [through Christian proselytizing] becomes the father of the most appalling fanaticism, whether of an active or a passive life.'[26]

What accounts for Hegel's discovery of the dialectical power of love in Part 3 of the 'Spirit' essay? Commentators have pointed to Hölderlin's influence on Hegel after their reunion in Frankfurt. As Christopher Jamme argues in a landmark article, 'Hegel and Hölderlin', the poet's leading concepts of love and unification appear to have been adopted by Hegel.[27]

In *The Spirit of Hegel*, Alan Olson further speculates that Hegel used the concept of love as reconciliation partly in order to comfort his friend. Hölderlin was caught in a tragic romance. In May 1796, a few months before Hegel joined him in Frankfurt, the poet fell in love with a married woman, Susette Gontard, the mother of the children he was tutoring. 'Hölderlin', writes Olson, 'clearly believed the love he shared with Susette to be the work of fate. Susette, the young wife of his aging employer was, for Hölderlin, not only a woman of rare beauty but also his Diotima, his intellectual companion and poetical muse.'[28] When Hölderlin fell out with Gontard's husband in September 1798, he left Frankfurt for nearby Hamburg.

Olson suggests that 'Hegel's discussion of infidelity and adultery in the context of the the Sermon on the Mount' is a disguised reference to Hölderlin's predicament.[29] In this passage, Hegel acidly criticizes the unfaithful husband who persists in demanding absolute loyalty from his wife despite his own violation of their love: '[T]he support which the husband draws from a law and a right and through which he brings justice and propriety onto his side means adding to the outrage on his wife's love a contemptible harshness.' Hegel continues that 'in the eventuality which Jesus made an exception [i.e. when the wife has bestowed her love on another] the husband may not continue a slave to her'.[30] If this is an indirect reference to Hölderlin, Hegel may be suggesting that Susette Gontard's marriage was already 'inwardly sundered' by her husband's own infidelities. According to Olson, the 'Spirit' essay's advice to Hölderlin 'is to "let go" of Susette through a renunciation that facilitates [the] higher presence [of divine love]'. For Hölderlin to do otherwise would be to risk the destruction of 'both the object of love and himself'.[31] As we shall see in chapter 5, Hölderlin's tragic fate fulfilled Hegel's worst fears.

The ideas of democracy and love that Hegel gleaned from Christ's teachings contrast not only with the Christian concept of the 'Kingdom' of God, but also with the authoritarian nature of states in Hegel's time. In the final section of this chapter, we will look at the young Hegel's discussion of contemporary political regimes.

The external state

During their time together in Frankfurt, Hölderlin and Hegel – possibly with their friends Jakob Zwilling and Isaak von Sinclair – prepared a document called 'The earliest system-programme of German idealism' of which only a two-page fragment written in Hegel's hand has survived. According to Jamme, '[o]ne can sum up Hegel's Frankfurt writings as an execution of what was already in mind in the 1797 sketch of the system'.[32] H. S. Harris, however, contends that the 'System-programme' was written by Hegel in 1796, a year before he arrived in Frankfurt.[33] Both Harris and Jamme agree, however, that this small fragment contains the germ of Hegel's mature system.

The 'System-programme' insists that the world of nature and society can be understood only from a moral point of view, from the standpoint of 'the free self-conscious essence', the human individual. Religious superstition must be combated and the priesthood prosecuted before the 'bar of Reason'. Aesthetics, the idea of beauty, is what unites the creations of human beings and nature. Thus, 'the philosopher must possess just as much aesthetic power as the poet'.[34]

Following up on the idea of a folk religion, probed by Hegel in Berne, the 'System-Programme' claims that 'a mythology of Reason' is required to unite the people into a perfect democracy. Here is the first delineation of the social ideal that would inspire all of Hegel's work after Frankfurt, an ideal that would survive also in the writings of Marx. In this 'eternal unity', argues Hegel, there will be,

> No more the look of scorn [of the enlightened philosopher looking down on the mob], no more the blind trembling of the people before its wise men and priests. Then first awaits us *equal* development of *all* powers, of what is peculiar to each and what is common to all. No power shall any longer be suppressed for universal freedom and equality of spirits will reign! – A higher spirit sent from heaven must found this new religion among us, it will be the last [and] greatest work of mankind.[35]

The 'System-programme' contains at least two puzzles. First, what is to be made of Hegel's emphasis on the 'aesthetic power of philosophy', given the perceived unreadableness of his later philosophical output? As Stephen Bungay amusingly puts it, the mature Hegel 'is a good example of one of those Germans who dives deeper into murkier waters than the rest of us, and who not unsurprisingly comes up muddier'.[36]

My own view is that Hegel's mature philosophy conforms to the aesthetic ideal he meant to achieve. Hegel never abandoned the poetic muse, and enjoyed writing conventional poems to friends throughout his life. He forged a special language in the poetic style he learned from Hölderlin to express his thought. This mode informs his work after Frankfurt, but it is not – as Allen Wood and others insist – a matter of 'pretentious style and abstract expression'.[37] The Berne 'Life of Jesus', for example, showed that Hegel could write with remarkable clarity and simplicity – as do the mature Hegel's lectures on philosophy and history. However, the ideal conveyed by Hegel's systematic philosophy, and the historical context in which it appears, requires a different, higher, and more subtle mode of expression. Surveillance by the secret police motivated Hegel to invent a subversive poetics that helped to mask the radical meaning cradled in the text. His philosophical writing is an innovative poetry that requires patience as well as insight from the reader. This mode of expression, a joint creation of the era of Romanticism and censorship, poses many understandable difficulties for readers in our period, but these difficulties are not reducible to Hegel's abandonment of the aesthetic ideal proclaimed in Frankfurt.

Hegel himself commented on the 'obscurity' of his style and offered an explanation similar to the one I have put forward. Replying to a friend who found the Preface to the *Phenomenology* unclear in places, Hegel – then a newspaper editor in Bamberg – contrasts the form required for journalism with that demanded by abstract philosophy. He wittily observes that, as lucid as newspaper articles might appear to be, they do not really throw much light on political events. Perhaps his own 'obscurity' was not so bad after all.

> As for the wish you express for greater intelligibility and clarity, I would gladly have fulfilled it, but it is just this which is most difficult to achieve and is the mark of perfection, at least when the content is of the more solid type. For there is a content which carries clarity along with it, such as the sort with which I am principally occupied every day: e.g. that Prince so and so passed through today, that His Majesty went boar hunting, and so forth. But no matter how clearly political news is reported, it is still more or less true nowadays that neither the writer nor the reader understands events any better. From this I might on the contrary . . . conclude that so much the more will be understood through my obscure style, which is what I would like to hope but do not therefore believe.[38]

The second puzzle thrown up by the 'System-programme' is Hegel's treatment of the political realm. While he clearly projects an ideal society, the young Hegel's critique of politics does not resemble the optimistic vision of government later constructed in the *Philosophy of Right* (1820) – the mature statement of his political theory. Instead, political governance is displayed as an ugly machine:

> The Idea of mankind . . . gives us no Idea of the *State*, since the State is a mechanical thing, any more than it gives us an idea called an *Idea*. So we must go even beyond the State! – for every state must treat free men as cogs in a machine; and this it ought not to do; so it must *stop*. It is self-evident that in this sphere of all the Ideas, of

perpetual peace etc., are only *subordinate* Ideas under a higher one. At the same time I shall here lay down the principles for a *history of mankind*, and strip the whole wretched human work of State, constitution, government, legal system – naked to the skin.[39]

Did the mature Hegel abandon his youthful critique in place of subservience to 'the whole wretched human work of State'? This is one of the key arguments canvassed by those – such as G. Lukács – who believe in the 'reconciliation thesis' discussed in the last chapter. A recent writer, Michael O. Hardimon, suggests that the reconciliation thesis means that even poverty is ultimately acceptable for the mature Hegel, provided the numbers of the poor are kept low.

> Hegel is not . . . committed to the doctrine that it must be possible for *everyone* to come to be at home in order for anyone to be . . . [H]is view is rather that if the modern social world is to be a home, it must be possible *in general* for people to come to be at home in it.[40]

On this interpretation, the 'System-programme' demand for the '*equal* development of *all* powers, of what is peculiar to each and what is common to all' must have been watered down by the mature Hegel, in order at least to exclude the poor.

The apparent contradiction between the views of the young and the mature Hegel follows a real contradiction in the nature of the modern state, one which he attempted to overcome in his later work. For the mature Hegel, there are two sides to the state. On one side, the state can be seen as a benevolent, representative force, a structure identical with, and devoted to, the full development of each and every individual. Hegel called this the 'social state'. Some existing states bear a resemblance, however slight, to the social state. Equally important, people instinctively bring this (Hegelian) view of the state with them whenever they fight social injustice. In his 1818 lectures in Heidelberg – given just before the Karlsbad Decrees imposed an iron regime of censorship on the German states – Hegel refers explicitly to the 'contradiction' between the ideal constitution people have in their minds and the oppressive laws of an outworn era which 'is the source not only of discontent but also of revolutions'.

> If the spirit [of the constitution] becomes of itself progressively more mature and institutions do not alter with it, there is genuine discontent, and if nothing is done to dispel this, we get disturbances

of the peace owing to the fact that the self-conscious concept contains other institutions than actually exist; there is a revolution.[41]

George Armstrong Kelly provides an illuminating discussion of Hegel's social state. He notes the paradox that the Hegelian aspect of government becomes most obvious when the state fails in some way to represent the interests of various groups in society. Protest movements in advanced democracies, for example, do not represent 'a fundamental attack on the state, but rather a vivid appeal to the state outside of the authorized system for transmitting political claims'. Those who practise 'representational violence', says Kelly, adopt a 'fundamentally Hegelian' view of the state.

> That is, it is implicitly conceded that the state is there to resolve the conflicts of civil society and to redistribute justice to the aggrieved in view of its higher purpose. It exists above the competitive strife in which the violent petitioners lie impacted. Disaffected groups then confront the government with violence not because *it* is the enemy, but because being conscious that public authority possesses (and might enact) effective measures of redress, they wish to make authority vividly aware of their claims, to alarm or punish authority into accepting a more wholesome justice.[42]

The other side of the state concerns its evil, unrepresentative nature. Most often, existing governments are simply the instrument of the ruling authorities, what Hegel called in the *Philosophy of Right*, the 'external state'.[43] The external state resembles the 'mechanical' state discussed in the 'System-programme' – the state that 'must treat free men as cogs in a machine'. Hegel offers a concrete example of an external state in his 1831 essay on contemporary politics, 'The English Reform Bill', written a few months before his death.[44]

Significantly, Hegel's analysis of the English state in this late essay reaches a conclusion similar to that drawn by the revolutionary democrat, Tom Paine in *Rights of Man* (1791, 1792), written forty years earlier. 'From the want of a constitution in England', writes Paine, 'to restrain and regulate the wild impulse of power, many of the laws are irrational and tyrannical, and the administration of them vague and problematical.'[45]

To summarize the results of this section, the two puzzles presented by the 'System-programme' are both connected to Hegel's democratic vision. His innovative philosophical poetics, which give so much trouble to modern readers, were meant to explicate this vision, and also to elude Prussian censorship. The concept of the 'machine state' remains critical in all of Hegel's later writings. But the mature Hegel contrasts this mode of government with an account of politics that would fulfil the yearning he shared with Hölderlin in the Frankfurt years for an ideal community such as that enjoyed by the ancient Greeks.

For Hegel, the dialectic between the representative and authoritarian sides of the state leads to the development, and sometimes the downfall, of governments – as we saw in chapter 1 with regard to Soviet and East European communist regimes. The next chapter considers Hegel's ideas on democracy and revolution in relation to the thought of Tom Paine. We shall find surprising parallels between these two political thinkers and also some important differences. Chapter 5 will return to the themes of love and the state, and their connection with the tragic figure of Hölderlin.

4 • Hegel and Tom Paine in the Age of Revolution

Introduction

In his astonishing new biography of the author of *Rights of Man*, John Keane suggests that Tom Paine's 'eighteenth-century vision of a decent life ... is undoubtedly more relevant' to contemporary politics 'than that of Marx, the figure most commonly identified with the nineteenth- and twentieth-century political project of bringing dignity and power to the wretched of the earth'. For Keane, the fall of communism has brought into question Marx's political legacy while revivifying Tom Paine's.

> Not only is Paine's bold rejection of tyranny and injustice as far-reaching as his nineteenth-century successor, but his practical proposals – as the collapse of communist utopia demonstrates – are actually more radical than Marx's, mainly because they managed to combine breathtaking vision, a humble respect for ordinary folk, and a sober recognition of the complexity of human affairs.[1]

Arguments comparable to these about Paine have also been made to support Hegel over Marx. Francis Fukuyama, for example, suggests that 'the monumental failure of Marxism as a basis for real-world societies – plainly evident 140 years after the *Communist Manifesto* – raises the question of whether Hegel's Universal History was not in the end the more prophetic one'.[2] Similarly, Richard Sakwa contends that in Russia and Eastern Europe 'Marx's approach to the state and politics of class have perhaps been the areas most comprehensively rejected.' The new politics eschews Marx's 'proposition that all states are class states' and has rehabilitated 'the social democratic proposition that the state can represent the interests of society at large'. This approach – characterized by Sakwa as 'the rejection of class categories in favour of general humanistic concerns' – amounts to a massive return to Hegel. 'One of the key features of the post-communist world, indeed, is the vindication of Hegel against Marx, that there can be no higher freedom than that achieved by the rule of law in the constitutional state.'[3]

What lies behind this return to two apparently very different political figures, and the preference for them over Marx? I want to show in this chapter that Hegel's allegiance to democracy and the liberal state may have been spurred by the revolutionary writings of his predecessor, Tom Paine. Paine's influence may have shaped a whole range of Hegel's concerns, including his conceptualization of state and civil society, the fate of America, and the idea of democratic revolution.

Impressed by the failure of the democratic revolutions of 1848, Marx tended to ignore the potential for democratic politics within the context of bourgeois society that fascinated Paine and Hegel. Instead, he opted for a utopian resolution – the communist society that would rise from the ashes of the free market. Yet Marx's critique of capitalism and his optimistic hopes for the future actually represent a profound commentary on one side of Hegel's political philosophy. In chapter 8 I will try to bring together both sides of Hegel's politics – the Hegelian critique of capitalism illuminated by Marx and what Perry Anderson calls 'the fundamental outline of liberties Hegel had perceived as the definitive form of modern freedom'.[4]

There were good reasons for Hegel to hide any affinity he might have had with Tom Paine. Germany during Hegel's period was virtually a police state; it was no haven for democrats. The 1819 Karlsbad Decrees erected a wall of strict censorship around the German states just as Hegel was preparing to publish his political textbook the *Philosophy of Right*. Even while lecturing at university Hegel dreaded the presence of the secret police. We have, for example, the testimony of the great poet and democrat Heinrich Heine, who attended Hegel's classes in Berlin. Heine relates dryly that Hegel often composed his thoughts 'in very obscure and abstruse signs so that not everyone could decipher them – I sometimes saw him looking anxiously over his shoulder for fear that he had been understood'.[5]

Hegel and Tom Paine

Hegel's view of government – both as a young man and as a mature thinker – may have been influenced by Tom Paine's *Rights of Man*. This book became 'an instant international best-seller' following its publication in two parts, in 1791 and 1792, while Hegel was at Tübingen. Hegel had an excellent command of English, but in any case, '[t]ranslations of both parts of *Rights of Man* [soon] appeared in

France, Holland, and the German lands'.[6] The youthful German philosopher, 'whose imagination was fired by the spectacle of Revolution in France ... [and] whose comments regularly reflect[ed] his commitment to the ideal of representative democracy',[7] could not have failed to investigate Paine's defence of the Revolution, 'the most widely read book of all time, in any language'.[8] There are many parallels between the *Rights of Man* and the key political work of Hegel's maturity, the *Philosophy of Right*, as we shall see. These ideas may have germinated during the period Hegel was in Tübingen, Berne and Frankfurt. Thus Hegel's unpublished discussion of the constitution of the German Empire – begun in Frankfurt in 1799 – contains echoes of Paineite ideas (such as the separation of civil society from state) that are worked out in more detail in the *Philosophy of Right*.

That the young philosopher was familiar with the arguments of Paine's *Rights of Man* is very probable, given Hegel's outright support for democratic revolution in Germany. Paine's strongest admirer in Germany, Georg Forster, was the leader of the Jacobin Club in Mainz. 'Forster had declared Mainz to be part of the French Republic and the left bank of the Rhine to be its natural and proper boundary.' Hegel's friends, Hölderlin and Sinclair, knew personally several of the Jacobin Club members, and Hegel (who visited Mainz in 1798) sympathized with the aims of Forster's group. Like his friends, Hegel hoped for a revolution in Southern Germany, 'and he was ready to support a minority government of "patriots" in the Republic of Württemberg established by French arms'.[9]

My claim that Hegel knew about, and likely was influenced by, his contemporary Tom Paine is controversial. Writers on politics tend to contrast Paine with Hegel, since their views are supposed to be quite different: Hegel, the German statist conservative versus Tom Paine, the proponent of radical democracy. John Keane's influential essays on this subject are only a late example of this established contrast. There is no direct textual evidence that Hegel actually read the English pamphleteer. Hegel pointedly ignores Paine's important contributions in his lecture cycles on political philosophy, which were not published until after his death. This is a surprising omission, for Paine was then perhaps the world's most prominent living theorist and historian of freedom. The clearest indication that we have of Hegel's interest in Paine is the remarkable section devoted to North and South America in the Introduction to the lectures on the philosophy of world history. Hegel may be thinking of Paine when he refers disparagingly to the proposition that the experience of the United States 'proves that republican states are [possible] on a large scale'.[10] This, of course, is a key thesis in *Rights of Man*. Hegel's objections to Paine's argument are discussed below.

In fact, Hegel's political philosophy may helpfully be seen as the product of a long and argumentative conversation with Tom Paine. It was Paine and the American revolutionaries who injected the ideal of representative democracy into political debate; and Hegel's writings on politics are an attempt to come to grips with this. Yet the fruitful encounter between Anglo-American democracy and German idealism is absent from most commentaries on both figures.

Hegel's understanding of history is remarkably similar to Paine's. Accordingly – in sharp contrast to the general evaluation of the relationship between the two thinkers – Z. A. Pelczynski points to their shared belief in 'the law of reason'.[11] Both saw freedom as the underlying motivation of human action; and both equated reason and rationality with a system of just and equitable government. Paine's hatred of despotism was matched by Hegel's contempt for aristocratic rule that would – like the Berne nobility in the Pays de Vaud – trample the rights of the people. When Hegel was translating J. J. Cart's account of the uprising in the Pays de Vaud he may have had in the back of his mind Paine's amusing story about the bear of Berne, chronicled in *Rights of Man*.

For centuries, relates Paine, the populace of Berne kept a bear at public expense whose existence was believed to ward off evil happenings. One day the town bear unexpectedly sickened and died, and the town was left without its mascot until a substitute could be arranged.

> During this interregnum the people discovered that the corn grew, and the vintage flourished, and the sun and moon continued to rise and set, and everything went on the same as before, and taking courage from these circumstances, they resolved not to keep any more bears; for, said they, 'a bear is a very voracious, expensive animal and we were obliged to pull out his claws lest he should hurt the citizens.'

Paine notes that the French newspapers picked up the story of the bear of Berne in the summer of 1791, when Louis XVI fled to Varennes, 'and the application of it to monarchy could not be mistaken in France; but it seems that the aristocracy of Berne applied it to themselves, and have since prohibited the reading of French newspapers'.[12]

Rights of Man was a fiery rejoinder to Edmund Burke's conservative tract, *Reflections on the Revolution in France*, written in 1790. Burke was repulsed by the events in France, and disgusted by their defenders, especially Paine. He considered the Revolution as 'part of a systematic plan to propagate a false philosophy and wreck the foundations of European civilization'.[13] Paine was equally stunned and outraged by Burke's unqualified support for traditionalism and aristocracy. He could not believe that Burke – an outspoken advocate of emancipation for the American colonies – would turn so savagely against the principles of reason. As with Paine's writings, there is no direct evidence that Hegel actually read Burke. But it is almost unthinkable that Hegel the political philosopher could have ignored one of the greatest political controversies of all time. On the contrary, he may have cheered Paine's riposte to Burke every step of the way. As Pelczynski says of Burke and Hegel, 'it would be difficult to find two thinkers whose basic political beliefs and preferences were more opposed or whose mutual opposition went deeper'.[14]

Christ the 'revolutionist'

There are even striking parallels between the young Hegel's and Paine's analysis of Christianity, which go beyond their mutual debt to the Enlightenment critique of religion. Paine's 1794 text, *The Age of Reason*, takes up some of the themes in Hegel's unpublished writings on religion in Berne and Frankfurt between 1793 and 1798. Hegel had a much more sophisticated grasp of theological issues than the English revolutionary, and he would have baulked at the *The Age of Reason*'s uncritical Deism. Yet Hegel would certainly have enjoyed Paine's ruthless attack on the Christian church. At the time, Paine was personally immersed in the swirling events of the French Revolution, and under threat of death by the guillotine. Paine's notoriety meant that *The Age of Reason* was published and discussed across Europe, and especially in the German states, where 'the translated work was quickly published in three separate editions, adding to Paine's wide reputation as a courageous "outlaw" and "a most original writer" '.[15] Resident in the Swiss capital, about 100 kilometres from the French border, Hegel is likely to have been an avid reader of Paine's anti-religious tract.

Like Hegel, Paine believed that Christ was a moral philosopher and revolutionary who carried the message of the ancient Greeks to the people of Judaea, and struggled against their corrupt religious and political authorities.[16] Both writers focus on Christ's mortal life and discount what Paine called the 'fabulous' biblical pronouncements on the circumstances of Christ's birth and death. Writes Paine:

> That Jesus Christ existed, and that he was crucified, which was the mode of execution at that day, are historical relations strictly within the limits of probability. He preached most excellent morality, and the equality of man; but he preached also against the corruptions and avarice of the Jewish priests, and this brought upon him the hatred and vengeance of the whole order of priesthood. The accusation which those priests brought against him was that of sedition and conspiracy against the Roman government, to which the Jews were then subject and tributary; and it is not improbable that Jesus Christ had in contemplation the delivery of the Jewish nation from the bondage of the Romans. Between the two, however, this virtuous reformer and revolutionist lost his life.

For both Paine and the young Hegel, the doctrines of the church bear little resemblance to Christ's message of freedom and equality. Instead Christianity preaches the opposite. Thus Paine mocks the doctrine of redemption in much the same fashion as Hegel did while in Berne. According to Paine, the Christian is

> taught to contemplate himself as an outlaw, as an outcast, as a beggar, as a mumper, as one thrown, as it were, on a dunghill at an immense distance from his Creator, and who must make his approaches by creeping and cringing to intermediate beings.[17]

Civil society and the state

Hegel would not have made reference to Paine, even if (as I believe) he admired, and was profoundly affected by, the Englishman's revolutionary writings. In Part 2 of the *Rights of Man*, for example, Paine encouraged his friend, the Marquis Lafayette, to wage war against the German princes who at the time were harbouring counter-revolutionary French émigré armies. This alone could not have endeared Paine to the German authorities. Powerful princes were likely to look with a bloody eye at any German subject who professed admiration for the seditious revolutionary. Like Paine, Hegel celebrated the 1792 victories of the French over Prussia and Austria, and looked forward to the establishment of liberal freedoms in the autocratic German states.

Germany in Hegel's period was a perilous place for democrats. Private letters sent through the post were in danger of being opened by the secret police. Lecturers had to fear that some of their students might be working for the authorities. Published writings were vetted by right-wing university professors in the employ of the intelligence apparatus. Hegel's enthusiasm for Paine would have had to be kept under wraps, if he were to avoid loss of gainful employment, or worse. As we shall see in the case of Hölderlin (discussed in chapter 5), suspicion of radical sympathies could have tragic results.

In his mature political writings, Hegel borrowed ideas connected with Paine, but he also transformed them, as we shall see. Among these borrowings are the notions that 'civil society' is separate from the state; and that government has two quite different identities. Influenced by the Scottish political economists, Steuart and Ferguson, Hegel deepened Paine's analysis of civil society. He also attempted to rectify the dangers suggested by the experience of the Great Terror – an event that took place amongst all the formal trappings of democracy. Perhaps the largest difference between the two writers concerns their attitude to the growth of capitalism. Paine was more optimistic than Hegel about the favourable impact of free markets on democracy; Hegel saw the mushrooming capitalist economy as a potentially corruptive force that required state intervention.

Referring to the English political administration, Paine suggested 'two distinct characters for government'. The first is the domestic, or internal, government – 'the government of laws, which operates at home'. The second 'character of government' is focused on the external world of trade and foreign conquest, 'and operates abroad, on the rude plan of an uncivilized life'. According to Paine, foreign dealings are financed 'with boundless extravagance', while domestic affairs are handled cheaply, with most actual governing delegated to local communities. These two aspects of government are 'so distinct', he writes,

> that if the latter were to sink, as it were by a sudden opening of the earth, and totally disappear, the former would not be deranged. It would still proceed, because it is the common interest of the nation that it should, and all the means are in practice.

The external side of government, ruled by a tiny elite ('court or cabinet government'), draws the whole nation into a 'perpetual system of war and expense, that drains the country, and defeats the general felicity of which civilization is capable'. This system, upon which ordinary individuals had little influence, was responsible for high rates of taxation that benefited a few powerful men, and created large masses of poor people. For Paine, only revolutionary France had managed to escape the depredations of this system; the rest of Europe was at its mercy.

> All the European governments (France now excepted) are constructed not on the principle of universal civilization, but on the reverse of it. So far as those governments relate to each other, they are in the same condition as we conceive of savage uncivilized life; they put themselves beyond the law as well of GOD as of man, and are, with respect to principle and reciprocal conduct, like so many individuals in a state of nature.[18]

Hegel agreed with Paine's distinction between the character of government at home and abroad (a distinction also made by Kant and Rousseau). Like Paine, he saw nations acting towards one another like 'individuals in the state of nature'. In fact, he uses exactly these words in the *Philosophy of Right*: 'since the sovereignty of nations is the principle governing their mutual relations, they exist to that extent in a state of nature in relation to one another'.[19] As we shall see below, however, Hegel dramatically altered the meaning of what he called 'the external state', and applied the term to government's domestic, as well as its foreign affairs. Contrary to Paine, he depicts a nation's strictly domestic affairs as the root cause of corruption in the state, along with the predilection for overseas adventures and war.

Hegel adopted another duality suggested by Paine, the distinction between civil society and the state. Paine's 1776 pamphlet, *Common Sense*, writes Keane, 'was the first political essay in modern times to make and defend the distinction'. As Keane documents, in the early modern tradition of political thought, civil society and the state were considered to be one and the same. Civil society 'describe[d] a type of political association that ensured good government and peaceful order by placing its members under the influence of laws'.[20] The consensus among commentators about a happy unity in this political coupling began to be questioned in the mid-eighteenth century. Thus, the Scottish Enlightenment writer, Adam Ferguson, in his *The History of Civil Society* (1767) – a work that also had a profound effect on Hegel – charted tendencies in civil society that led to corruption in the state, and the danger of despotism. According to Ferguson, the modern division of labour divides people from each other, creates huge disparities of wealth and power, and exposes society to bureaucratic manipulation, and even military rule.

Paine disregarded Ferguson's warnings about the division of labour, and directly challenged the traditional unity of state and civil society. Where Ferguson saw danger arising from civil society, Paine contended that civil society retained a separate source of identity from government, an identity that was threatened by inroads from the monarchical state.

Paine saw limited republican government, and free commercial exchange within and between nations, as the solution for the evils associated with European despotism. He believed the evidence for this could be found in England's lively civil society, which had no need for the state. 'It is from the enterprise and industry of the individuals, and their numerous associations, in which, strictly speaking, government is neither pillow nor bolster, that these improvements have proceeeded'.[21] With the growth of commerce and the market (civil society), Paine predicted, despotic states would crumble and perish. Restrictions on government would reduce the potential for international conflict, and universal peace would eventually prevail.

Government could never be about a contract between the individual and the state (as Rousseau believed) since individuals in society long preceded the advent of government. Government, Paine thought, should be responsible to citizens, but instead autocratic states have ensnared the individual in a choking nest of fealties and prohibitions. Paine's emphasis on the priority of the individual, and the importance of civil liberties reappears in Hegel's *Philosophy of Right* (1820), where the self-conscious individual – not the state – is the opening character, and the defence of 'classic human rights' is a primary concern.[22]

Hegel agreed with Adam Ferguson that civil society and the state are identical, but (dialectically) he also accepted Paine's argument that the two are separate entities. Let me try to unravel this conundrum. Like Ferguson, Hegel accepted that civil society is a corrupting force that endangers rational government. He saw this as early as 1799 when he described, in *The German Constitution* (p.190), the growing '*bourgeois* sense, which cares only for an individual and not self-subsistent end and has no regard for the whole'. For Hegel, this '*bourgeois spirit*' is part and parcel with 'the dominance of trade and commercial wealth' in civil society.[23] Its negative consequences are laid out in the *Philosophy of Right*. '[C]ivil society', writes Hegel, 'affords a spectacle of extravagance and want as well as the physical and ethical degeneration common to them both.'[24] Inevitably, government becomes subject to the same wealthy powers that rule civil society. The mature Hegel called this potentially corrupt form of government, 'the external state'. Significantly for our argument, Hegel defines the state in civil society much the same way as Paine does in *Rights of Man*. Here is Paine's definition:

> Government is nothing more than a national association, and the object of this association is the good of all, as well individually as collectively. Every man wishes to pursue his occupation, and to enjoy the fruits of his labours, and the produce of his property in peace and safety, and with the least possible expense. When these things are accomplished, all the objects for which government ought to be established are answered.[25]

Compare this with the definition of the external state in the *Philosophy of Right*.

> In the course of the actual attainment of selfish ends – an attainment conditioned in this way by universality – there is formed a system of complete interdependence, wherein the livelihood, happiness, and legal status of one man is interwoven with the livelihood, happiness, and rights of all. On this system, individual happiness, &c., depend, and only in this connected system are they actualized and secured. This system may be prima facie regarded as the external state, the state based on need, the state as the Understanding envisages it.[26]

Hegel sees the basis of the external state as the understanding consciousness, not reason. As we saw in chapter 2, the understanding tends toward capriciousness and unpredictability because it depends on objects that remain external to it. The external state is primarily concerned with private property, finance, and industrial production – in other words, the production and circulation of commodities. A state founded on this limited form of rationality is constantly in jeopardy of succumbing to irrational forces.

Like Paine, Hegel believed that government has two different 'characters,' to use Paine's words. Again, though, Hegel departs from Paine in a very significant way. The evil character of government is a direct result of its overly intimate connection with civil society; the benevolent aspect of the state depends on the degree of government autonomy from corruptive market forces. Paine, of course, would have been shocked by this deduction, since, for him, civil society was the fount of democracy and human rights, not the cause of political debauchery. Accordingly, Paine's hatred of taxes left Hegel cold. For Hegel, England's high taxes were intimately connected with its lively civil society. Low taxes were an indicator of political failure, of the public's distance from government due to absence of representative institutions.[27]

A strong advocate of Paine's vision of a democratic civil society, John Keane contends that, compared to *Rights of Man*, Hegel's vision of the state 'contains a weakened sensitivity to political power and its authoritarian potential'.[28] Yet Hegel's project aims at guaranteeing the autonomy of civil society from government. Although Keane (like Paine) fails fully to realize it, this separation goes both ways. Civil society must find a space autonomous from the state but, equally, the state must distance itself from civil society. Part of the problem is that Keane, like the vast majority of commentators, overlooks the distinction Hegel makes between the external state and the social state. For Hegel, the problem with the external state is that it is too close to civil society, and therefore prone to the arbitrary exercise of political power. Hence, in *The German Constitution* (1799–1802), he criticizes 'recent theories' of the 'machine state' – already 'carried partly into effect' – which see the state as 'a machine with a single spring which imparts movement to all the rest of the infinite wheelwork, and that all institutions implicit in the nature of a society should proceed from the supreme public authority and be regulated, commanded, overseen, and conducted by it'. He singles out the contemporary French regime and the Prussian state as examples of 'this pitch of pedantry in domination', and calls for maximum freedom of movement in civil society. The best thing, Hegel says, is for the 'public authority' to be able to

> count ... on the free devotion, the self-respect, and the individual effort of the people – on an all-powerful invincible spirit which the hierarchical system [of the machine state] has renounced and which has its life only where the public authority leaves as much as possible to the personal charge of the citizens.[29]

Hegel's concept of the autonomous state – which he called the 'rational' or 'social' state – was borrowed from the work of the great German poet Schiller and the philosopher Fichte. In *Letters on the Aesthetic Education of Man*, Schiller contrasts the 'natural state' which is based on 'force and not laws' with the 'state of reason' or 'state of freedom' founded on a 'moral unity'. For Schiller, '[t]he task of humanity is to exchange the state of necessity with the state of freedom ... Like Schiller, Fichte identifies the "state of necessity" with the existing state, and looks for a gradual progress from it toward the "social state"'.[30] Unlike Schiller and Fichte, however, Hegel contended that the project for the rational state was already under-way, that the existing state contains the germ of the social state of the future. Just as the French Revolution unearthed the rational elements slumbering below the surface of society, the task of the philosopher is to illuminate the elements of the rational state concealed in the present. And this was the enterprise toward which Hegel devoted his mature political work.

For Hegel, the revolutionary governments of the United States and France achieved an important advance toward the rational state. As Paine detailed in *Rights of Man*, these administrations had for the first time in history constructed democratic constitutions consciously designed to guide and restrict the actions of government. 'A constitution', wrote Paine, 'is a thing *antecedent* to a government, and a government is only the creature of its constitution. The constitution of a country is not the act of its government, but of the people constituting a government.' The last third of the *Philosophy of Right* amounts to a discussion of the democratic constitution – of what Paine sums up as 'everything that relates to the complete organization for a civil government, and the principles on which it shall act, and by which it should be bound'.[31] But Hegel disagrees with Paine on several critical points. Constitutions are required not only to restrain the power of government, but also to regulate the ebb and flow of civil society. Moreover, true democracy involves more than the right to vote. The representative structure is only one part of the state, and it must find a place in an organic social order. As Francis Fukuyama writes,

> It is true that Hegel was opposed to direct elections and favored the organization of society into estates. But this did not arise from opposition to the principle of popular sovereignty *per se*. Hegel's corporatism can be understood as comparable to Tocqueville's 'art of association': in a large modern state political participation must be mediated through a series of smaller organizations and associations to be effective and meaningful. Membership in an estate is based not on birth but occupation, and is open to all.[32]

Paine's ideas on civil society and minimal government were drawn from the experience of the American Revolution, and the defeat of British despotism in the lower half of British-occupied North America.

His defence of the French Revolution in *Rights of Man* assumed that this democratic experiment would proceed along the same lines as the revolutionary occurrences in America. Paine himself learned to his great cost of the falsity of equating the two revolutions. Under Robespierre and the Jacobins in 1793–4, democracy and revolution spun out of control and resulted in the death of thousands under the guillotine (almost including Paine himself). Hegel's political works may be read (in part) as a dialogue with Paine about the fate of these two revolutions, and their ultimate meaning. Hegel's enigmatic comments on the USA in his lectures on politics and history cannot be read, I suggest, except as the other side of a running debate with the author of *Rights of Man*.

Two revolutions

Paine was a central figure in the American Revolution. His 1776 pamphlet, *Common Sense*, had a dramatic impact on events in North America. Never a person to mince words, Paine himself averred that *Common Sense* 'met with [success] . . . beyond anything since the invention of printing'.[33] The pamphlet's converts to the idea of independence from Britain included Benjamin Franklin and George Washington.[34] *Common Sense* carried the debate around the relationship of the colonies with England, and helped steel the colonists' resolve to break with the distant monarchy. Among what Paine's most recent biographer calls 'the profoundly original' ideas in *Common Sense* was the notion that the people are ultimately the judge of any political regime, and that no despotism can hold against the combined power of an aroused populace.[35] As we have seen, this was the lesson Hegel applied in his translation to J. J. Cart's account of revolution in the Pays de Vaud. It is also the obvious subtext of his sketch of the decline and fall of states in the *History of Philosophy*, as discussed in chapter 2.

Paine favoured republican government, and was bitterly opposed to unrepresentative European monarchical regimes, such as those of Britain, Holland and Prussia. He realized, however, that republican government without an adequate system of representation could be as despotic as any monarchy. Furthermore, when Paine wrote *Rights of Man* and hailed France, along with the USA, as the world's leaders in the achievement of freedom, Louis XVI was still on the throne. Paine admired the French monarch for his support of the American Revolution, and did not believe that constitutional monarchy on the model of 1789 was at odds with freedom. Later, when the people turned against the king following exposure of his plans to betray revolutionary France to its foreign enemies, Paine agreed that the monarch would have to be removed. However, he helped lead the (almost successful) fight to spare Louis XVI from the guillotine.

In the *Philosophy of Right*, Hegel outlines a system of constitutional monarchy in which the prerogatives of royalty are strictly controlled. This is not unlike the monarchical set-up in the first years of the French Revolution. According to Douglas Moggach, early versions of the *Philosophy of Right*, written before the Karlsbad Decrees, even 'admitted the possibility of popular sovereignty' but Hegel withdrew this alternative from the published text.[36] Yet for Hegel, it was immaterial from the point of view of democracy whether a nation is led by a crowned head or a democratically elected president (this is discussed in more detail in chapter 8). The key point is for a nation to have a strong central government, with a visible leader. Accordingly, in Hegel's unpublished work, *The German Constitution*, he writes, 'it does not matter . . . whether this centre has a strictly monarchical or a modern republican form, since the latter also falls under the principle of a limited monarchy, i.e. one bound by law'.[37] In our own time, for example, both Canada and the USA are democracies, though one is led by a royal (Queen Elizabeth II) and the other by an elected president (William Clinton).

Despite deep resonances with Paine, Hegel turned sharply against the English revolutionary's proposals for representative democracy. Hegel could not accept that the political solutions adopted in the infant North American republic were directly applicable to Europe. He felt the Terror in France resulted from the naïve application of abstract republican principles to a complex social whole that bore little resemblance to the comparative simplicity of the American colonies. The following sections look at these two sides of Hegel's debate with Paine.

The US example

Hegel shared Paine's belief that the American Revolution of 1776 ignited the spark of freedom that eventually crossed the Atlantic into

France and the rest of Europe. But he found the New World experience deeply troubling, as is indicated in his lectures on the philosophy of history delivered at the University of Berlin between 1822 and 1830.[38] Although Paine is not mentioned, Hegel's remarks are clearly aimed at the author of *Rights of Man*. More than a century and a half later, Hegel's insightful discussion of the strengths and foibles of the US republic retains much of its interest.

In his lectures on world history, Hegel refers to the geographical basis of history. He cautions that too much can be made of mere geography. Nevertheless, certain principles are inscribed in the internal nature and external relationships of the continents. These, in turn, shape the relations and consciousness of the nations formed within them. His observations have been criticized by some as Eurocentric, even racist, and his knowledge of geography was necessarily limited by what was known about the globe in the first third of the nineteenth century. A great deal of what Hegel discussed under the heading of geography we now call geopolitics. In a manner reminiscent of the Hegelian approach, the American sociologist Randall Collins has pointed to the geopolitical relationships connected with the internal development of nations. From this point of view, military relations rather than economic ones are 'the key external dynamics of states'.[39] We will look at these dynamics from a Hegelian perspective later in this section.

The globe in Hegel's time was divided into the Old and New Worlds. He observed that the New World exhibited an 'astonishing contrast' between North and South America – a contrast which has not diminished to this day. This striking dissimilarity is extremely important to understanding the character of the USA and its revolution, upon which Paine hung so many hopes. North America was characterized by mass colonization which 'destroyed and suppressed' the aboriginal population. '[N]early seven million have been wiped out.'[40] Although the European invaders of South America were even more ruthless and violent than northern settlers, the indigenous peoples were not altogether extirpated. Completely erased in southern cone countries of the continent like Chile and Argentina, aboriginals in Mexico and Central America were conquered and governed by the Spanish.

Founded on the knowledge and skills of immigrants – which were the product of thousands of years of development in the Old World – the North American colonies ruthlessly destroyed the indigent culture.

'[T]he citizens of the independent states of North American are all of European descent, and the original inhabitants were unable to amalgamate with them.' While highly critical of the 'violence' and 'degradation' meted out upon the original Americans by Europeans, Hegel rehearses contemporary assumptions about the cultural inferiority of the aboriginal peoples. 'The Americans . . . are like unenlightened children, living from one day to the next, and untouched by higher thoughts or aspirations.'[41]

Hegel, however, is no racist. The viciousness of the European settlers appals him. He observes that racial segregation laws imposed by the British in India were designed to prevent the 'urge for autonomy and independence' nurtured by the mixture of native and European cultures exemplified by the Creoles in South America and Mexico. He notes the development of independent aboriginal governments, and attributes the general weakness of the native peoples in North America not to genetics, but to geography, culture and the experience of genocide – to the 'lack [of] a focus of communal existence without which no state can exist'. Like Paine, Hegel opposed the enslavement of Africans in the Americas, noting that the relatively humane rule of the Portuguese (compared to the Dutch, Spanish and English) 'made it easier on the coast of Brazil than elsewhere for slaves to gain their freedom'. Hegel reports that among the freed slaves 'was the black physician Dr. *Kingera*, who first acquainted Europeans with quinine'. This medical discovery, as Hegel knew, was of world-historical importance.[42] Quinine was the first effective drug against malaria, and perhaps the first drug to tackle the cause of any disease.[43]

Hegel compares the success of the American colonies with the growth of towns around the imperial German cities at the close of the Middle Ages. The great cities attracted immigrants who settled nearby to take advantage of the commercial privileges they enjoyed. 'In this way, Altona grew up near Hamburg, Offenbach near Frankfurt, Fürth near Nürnberg and Carouge near Geneva.' Bankrupt citizens expelled from the imperial cities 'would settle in the adjoining territory; they would have there all the advantages which such a town can offer – exemption from the dues which the older cities extracted from them, and from all obligation to belong to a guild'. Similarly, American settlers fled from the 'burdens and levies which are imposed on trade and commerce in Europe [and which] no longer apply in America'. Any European emigrant 'willing to work hard' will find an 'ample scope' of opportunity in the New World.[44]

For Hegel, the USA offers the paradigm case for civil society and limited government celebrated by Paine. The American colonies enjoyed thriving industries on the English model, a Protestant faith characterized by numerous sects, a rapidly growing population, 'civil order, and firmly established freedom'. Thanks to the exclusion of natives and blacks from citizenship, the country was ethnically homogeneous. 'These were industrious Europeans', writes Hegel,

> who applied themselves to agriculture, tobacco and cotton planting, etc. Soon, their whole concern was with their work; and the substance which held the whole together lay in the needs of the populace, the desire for peace, the establishment of civil justice, security and freedom, and a commonwealth framed in the interests of the individuals as discrete entities, so that the state was merely an external device for the protection of property.[45]

Civil society on the classic American pattern did not yet exist in South America; and the republican card on which Paine placed so much faith was a non-starter. The new republics of South America – which appeared in the years after Paine's death in 1809 – were marked by continuous 'military revolutions', the singular dominance of the Catholic church, and a harsh ethnic hierarchy based on a subject native populace. The peoples of South America, Hegel opined, 'still have to extricate themselves from the spirit of the hollow interests before they can attain the spirit of rationality and freedom'.[46]

Anticipating Max Weber's famous Protestant-ethic thesis, Hegel suggests that, for the Protestant church, all of life's work is divine in the eyes of God. So people in the USA throw themselves into their labours, secure in the 'mutual confidence and goodwill of their fellows'. Among the Catholics of South America, however, 'there can be no grounds for any such confidence. For in worldly affairs, force and voluntary subservience rule supreme, and the forms which go under the name of constitutions are in this case merely a necessary expedient, offering no protection against mistrust.' The secular independence of the citizens of the USA rests on devotion to industry, to industrial production and agriculture. Accordingly, the understanding mode of thought is supreme. 'The industrial principle was imported from England, and industry itself contains the principle of individuality: for in industry, the individual understanding is developed and becomes the dominant power.'[47]

Hegel grants to Paine that all the trappings of democracy and constitutional law exist in the USA. Yet the American settlers do not yet have a state. The state can only arise from a fully developed civil society; and despite surface appearances, civil society in the United States remains incomplete. The 'absence of taxes' in the former colonies – a cause for joy according to Paine – is a symptom of a disease that wastes the American consciousness. Opines Hegel,

> Universal protection of property and the almost complete absence of taxes are facts which are constantly held up for praise. This indeed sums up the basic character of the community: the private citizen is concerned above all with industry and profit, and particular interests, which look to the universal only in order to obtain private satisfaction, are dominant.

The lack of an actual political centre; the habit of referring everything to the will of the individual; the subordination of everything else to the rights of private property: these are signs of corruption, a basic disregard for law, at the root of the American experiment. Certainly, the USA possesses a justice system and a formal code of law, 'but this formal justice is devoid of genuine integrity, and the American traders have the bad reputation of practicing deceit under the protection of the law'.[48] Interestingly, another distinguished commentator on the United States, Alexis de Tocqueville, also comments on the American penchant to use the formalities of law to achieve evil ends. In *Democracy in America* (1835), written four years after Hegel's death, de Tocqueville shows how the greedy policies of the states, combined with the show of benevolence of the federal government, managed to vanquish the Indians and deprive them of their human rights.

> The Americans ... have accomplished this two-fold purpose with singular felicity, tranquilly, legally, philanthropically, without shedding blood, and without violating a single great principle of morality in the eyes of the world. It is impossible to destroy men with more respect for the laws of humanity.[49]

Hegel never mentions the most unsettling contradiction at the heart of the American Republic – one recognized both by Paine and de Tocqueville – the institution of black slavery. This omission is mysterious since it would have greatly strengthened Hegel's argument against employing the USA as a model for Europe, where most countries had outlawed slavery. However, this strange lapse may, perhaps, be explained by the political conditions in Hegel's Germany. The international battle against the slave trade was connected with the fight against 'wage slavery' and child labour in Europe, both of which were extremely controversial issues in the 1820s and 1830s. Hegel's criticism of the 'formal' character of American law, and the 'deceit' of American 'traders' may be a veiled reference to the slave trade, and the position of slavery as a protected practice in the US Constitution. In his 1817–19 *Lectures on Natural Right and Political Science*, given at Heidelberg before the Karlsbad Decrees extinguished free debate in Germany, Hegel submits that 'to make and keep a human being as a slave is the absolute crime, since the personality of the slave is negated in all its expressions'. Slavery, he argues, is worst than murder, for the latter merely negates 'only the possibility of all expressions of my personality, not, as by slavery, their actuality'.[50] Clearly, on this basis, the pro-slavery US Constitution formally justified the most heinous crimes against humanity.

Introducing a twist to the Protestant-ethic thesis, Hegel notes that Protestantism, by making the individual conscience supreme in matters of religion, bolsters self-confidence but also surrenders mind to feeling. If everything depends on how you – as an individual – feel about principles of faith, then almost anything goes. 'This explains why their religion has split up into so many sects, culminating in the extremes of insanity; many of them practice forms of worship characterized by transports of enthusiasm, and sometimes by the most sensual forms of self-abandonment.' Without an external structure and hierarchy, the various churches dissolve into anarchy, where ministers are hired and fired as the congregations see fit and 'religious affairs are simply regulated according to the desires of the moment.' This ethical giddiness gains astonishing momentum under the private-property system nourished and sanctioned by Protestantism. 'In North America, the most unbridled licence prevails in all matters of the imagination, and there is no religious unity of the kind which has survived in the European states, where deviations are limited to a few confessions.'[51]

Hegel rules as 'inadmissable' the argument most closely connected with Paine: that the USA provides an example of republican government that could be emulated by large European nations. 'North America cannot yet be regarded as a fully developed and mature state, but one merely in the process of becoming; it has not progressed far enough to feel the need for a monarchy.'[52] Hegel does not necessarily mean that the USA would eventually regress to the feudal rule of kings and queens. Rather, he means, I think, that the former colony would someday require a strong chief executive with a powerful state apparatus like those of the European states. Unlike most European nations, the USA has no fierce rivals at its borders, and requires no standing army. 'Canada and Mexico present no serious threat, and England has found over the last fifty years that a free America is more useful to it than a dependent one.' Trade is mostly composed of raw materials, 'not yet factory goods or industrial products'. Most productive activity centres around agriculture. The vast open frontier provides ample outlet for social tensions and the country feels little need for a powerful central authority. As Hegel puts it in a celebrated passage, 'if the ancient forests of Germany still existed, the French Revolution would never have occurred'.[53]

For Hegel, civil society creates conflict and tensions that undermine its own independence and produce the need for a state. Devoid of these inner stresses, the USA has neither a true civil society nor a true state.

> [A] real state and a real government only arise when class distinctions are already present, when wealth and poverty are far advanced, and when a situation has arisen in which a large number of people can no longer satisfy their needs in the way to which they have been accustomed.[54]

America, says Hegel, in a famous phrase, 'is the country of the future, and its world-historical importance has yet to be revealed in the ages that lie ahead.' He saw war between North and South America as a possibility, because of the great cultural and political disparities between them. Indeed, the USA has been involved in a series of conflicts with Latin American states throughout the nineteenth and twentieth centuries. The current hostile policies directed at Fidel Castro's Cuba have a long history. Economic integration of the hemisphere through trade agreements on the pattern of the North American Free Trade Agreement is a substitute for the war Hegel predicted, and may accomplish the same end. Although he claims not to be concerned with the future, Hegel offers a pretty detailed forecast. The country will eventually fill up with immigrants; the old forests will disappear; large cities and extensive communications networks will develop, 'and the whole will turn in upon itself and become consolidated'.[55] Once this takes place, class divisions will erupt and become severe, and with these, an independent government apparatus will evolve. At the end of the twentieth century, the agenda Hegel lays out for the USA has mostly been achieved. Arguably, everything is in place except the powerful and autonomous state he predicted would eventually make its appearance. So far the USA has only an external state, in Hegel's terminology. Admittedly, it has a vast and powerful military-industrial organization, but the goal of government remains largely the defence of private property and personal interests. As was the case with the despotic regimes Paine loathed, the federal government's impact on domestic affairs is dwarfed by its overpowering presence in the international arena. These characteristics have been exaggerated by the neoconservative ascendancy in the nation since 1980. 'It is the success of the nation's elites', write Petras and Morley, 'in converting the domestic economy into a trampoline for global leadership that has seriously undermined the domestic foundations of global power and eroded domestic society.'[56] Compared to Europe, and even its next-door neighbour, Canada, the USA lags far behind in social and cultural provision for its populace. Where Tom Paine was able to lay the blame for poverty and social decay at the feet of despotism, his wondrous republic is now characterized by dramatic disparities of wealth and the most pathetic scenes of want. A few years before the second millennium, the USA finds itself in the very dilemma Hegel prophesied. A situation has indeed 'arisen in which a large number of people can no longer satisfy their needs in the way to which they have been accustomed'. US economist Thomas Palley observes that in the past quarter-century the country has experienced an unprecedented shift in economic fortune.

> The period between 1950 and 1970 is often referred to as the Golden Age of American capitalism. Real per capita income grew in those years at 2.25 percent a year, and prosperity was democratized as huge numbers of Americans entered the middle class ... Since 1970 this expansion and diffusion of prosperity has stopped, and the Golden Age has been replaced by a Leaden Age, in which economic growth has been accompanied by falling wages and rising unemployment.[57]

Because it has no long history, notes Hegel, the North American republic's future place in world affairs can only be divined by its geopolitical position. The USA is a coastal country. External relations most important to it are with countries and regions beyond the oceans. In contrast with the continents of Asia, Africa and Europe, the New World lacks a unique principle inscribed by its physical composition.

According to Hegel's unabashedly Eurocentric perspective, Africa is the undeveloped land of natural unity, Asia the brooding, inward-looking crux of conflict and division, Europe the vigorous centrepoint of spirit. 'The only principle left over for America', Hegel muses, 'would be that of incompleteness or non-fulfilment.'[58]

The country of non-fulfilment is as apt a title as any for the USA in the era after the fall of communism.[59] As Hegel expected, the presidency has accumulated great power, especially in foreign relations. But the sense of longing, of incompleteness, that inspired the western movement in the USA has turned outwards. A military analyst suggested that without the Soviet Union as a check for its ambitions, the United States 'could wield its power in a way not possible since World War II'. Hence, constant non-fulfilment applies to the geopolitical imperial ambitions of the USA – 'the only surviving great power'. Unrivalled world dominance marks the fate of the USA which in geopolitical terms is – like Great Britain – an island. The difference from the Soviet Union, its vanquished challenger, is remarkable. '[A]s a continental power,' suggests Colonel Harry G. Summers, Jr., 'the Soviet Union didn't need all that air and sea lift. They could march to the Middle East if they chose to do so. And they could march to Western Europe, South Asia and East Asia as well.'[60]

Tom Paine's conviction that republican constitutions would bring peace to the world has not wholly been borne out. Hegel's scepticism about the virtues of this form of political organization has proven a better guide, especially in the case of Paine's America. The coincidence between the beginning of Operation Desert Storm against Saddam Hussein's Iraq (the most recent war fought by the USA) and the razing of Baghdad by Mongol hordes on 17 January 1259 has been mentioned by several writers. On the impact of the Mongolian raids, Hegel writes: 'they . . . rush as a devastating inundation over civilized lands, and the revolution which ensues has no other result than destruction and devastation'.[61] As Canadian philosopher John McMurtry points out, the American empire has distinguished itself from previous imperialisms by wild episodes of destruction, including those in Vietnam, Laos, Cambodia, Chile, Nicaragua, El Salvador, Panama and Iraq.

> Since the Roman empire, the technologically powered engines of Western civilization have invaded other countries with the traditional effect of building modern infrastructures of roads, communication,

water supplies, scientific method and the application of codified law. US military interventions, since the Second World War, have increasingly had the opposite effect.[62]

Still, Hegel shared Paine's hopes for the future of the new republic. Like all Europeans, he looked across the ocean with profound expectations. Perhaps even now, on the cusp of the second millennium, Hegel would think it too early to divine the principle America will carry into world history. He might still see the USA as 'the country of the future', and repeat his wistful reflections of 150 years ago:

> [America] is a land of desire for all those who are weary of the historical arsenal of old Europe. Napoleon is said to have remarked: *Cette vieille Europe m'ennuie.* It is up to America to abandon the ground on which world history has hitherto been enacted.[63]

Whatever the future of America might be, the initial importation of its republican constitution into Europe had tragic consequences that Tom Paine never anticipated. This is the subject of the next section.

The Terror

When Robespierre's Jacobins ascended to unquestioned power in June 1793, Paine wondered at his own folly of equating unrestricted democracy with freedom. The American experience, in which the founders of the revolution were celebrated and rarely reproached, could offer Paine little guidance. The maelstrom of the French Revolution devoured its heroes. Ideals Paine espoused in *Rights of Man*, says his biographer John Keane, were

> clearly being used by a minority government acting in the name of the sovereign people to justify a new species of dictatorship. This minority government was rash and precipitate, and inconstant. These cold-blooded schemers were committing atrocious crimes *against* the people. [Paine's] head rang with thoughts about the age-old prejudice of conservatives that democratic government is despotic by nature because, acting in the name of the people, it supposes itself to be the only fountain of power, against which there can be no appeal.[64]

Fourteen years later, Hegel, in *The Phenomenology of Spirit* (1807), diagnosed the horrifying events in France. The 'absolute freedom' of the Revolution, he wrote, detached everyone from the organic links of vocation and social class.[65] The subjective ideal expressed in the philosophy of Rousseau, in which – according to Hegel – the individual will was indistinguishable from the general will, took on real, social form.[66] Here Hegel echoes Paine in *Rights of Man*: the French Revolution, wrote Paine, 'is no more than the consequence of a mental revolution priorily existing in France. The mind of the nation had changed beforehand, and the new order of things has naturally followed the new order of thoughts.'[67]

The Revolution had explosive consequences no one could have predicted. As Hegel observes, the line between each individual's will and the universal will of the state disappeared, so that one individual (Robespierre) could represent himself as the government. The self-enclosed world of revolution could not embrace anything outside of itself, and therefore was incapable of creating anything positive. '[T]he Jacobins', writes Robert Wokler in his instructive commentary on Hegel's treatment of the Terror, 'were obliged to cleanse the nation of its internal differences, closing the Catholic Churches, for instance, and forcing the Commune of Paris, from which they had drawn so much of their own strength, to surrender its powers.' The Jacobin 'idea of the sublime unity of the nation . . . required a lofty purity of public spirit that made the vulgar purity of democracy seem an uncouth substitute for virtue'.[68]

With nothing to interfere with its absolute sway, declares Hegel, 'there is left for it only *negative* action; it is merely the *fury* of destruction'. Driven mad by abstraction, the revolutionary divides the world in two, 'into a simple, inflexible cold universality, and into the discrete, absolute hard rigidity and self-willed atomism of actual self-consciousness'. There is nothing to connect, or mediate, these two extremes, with terrible results.

> The sole work and deed of universal freedom is . . . *death*, a death too which has no inner significance or filling, for what is negated is the empty point of the absolutely free self. It is thus the coldest and meanest of all deaths, with no more significance than cutting off the head of a cabbage or swallowing a mouthful of water.[69]

Established as the government, the individual will of the revolutionary at once becomes opposed to the universal will of the people. Anything the government does can be construed as an insult to the individual will of those outside. '[C]onsequently, it is absolutely impossible for [the government] to exhibit itself as anything but a *faction*.' Unmasked as a faction opposed to the universal, the government falls, only to be replaced by another faction. Because opposition to the regime has no real basis – no democratic groundwork in actually existing institutions, like a free press, political parties, churches, and other autonomous organizations – government can respond only to the suspicion of opposition, to perceived 'intention'.

Being suspected, therefore, takes the place, or has the significance and effect, of *being guilty*; and the external reaction against this reality that lies in the simple inwardness of intention, consists in the cold, matter-of-fact annihilation of the existent self, from which nothing else can be taken away but its mere being.[70]

Poor Tom Paine could vouch for the wisdom of Hegel's diagnosis. Hailed as a hero when he first entered revolutionary France in 1791, and made an honorary citizen and elected a member of the Convention, he was later vilified, hounded by the authorities, and finally, on Christmas Eve 1793, thrown into a death cell from which he obtained release after ten harrowing months only as a result of Robespierre's fall, and the belated intervention of the American authorities. Paine's philosophy of revolution could offer nothing to prevent the bloody events of the Terror, though he did extend a chill warning in *Rights of Man*. 'The danger to which the success of revolutions is most exposed, is that of attempting them before the principles on which they proceed, and the advantages to result from them, are sufficiently seen and understood.'[71]

The poet Schiller understood the perils involved in departing too hastily from 'a State of compulsion [to] a State of Freedom'. If this transition is attempted prematurely – before human beings are educated to freedom, and before they can cast aside their 'selfish and violent' natural character – the outcome would be 'the destruction of society rather than its preservation'. People cannot exist without a state, and transforming government without injury to the vital infrastructure that is necessary for human life, is the same as trying to repair a clock without letting 'its wheels run down. The living clockwork of the State must be repaired while it is still striking, and it is a question of changing the revolving wheel while it still revolves.'[72]

Hegel wondered how to replace 'the revolving wheel while it still revolves'. With his friend Hölderlin, the young Hegel advocated a new civic religion, a living spirit of reason that could provide the sure foundation for dramatic social and political change. Opposition to this ideal eventually crushed Hölderlin, as we shall see, and it forced Hegel to turn from active politics to a philosophical vision of the future based firmly on the realities of the present. This vision would include a solution to the greatest problem thrown up by civil society – poverty. 'When, in countries that are called civilized', writes Paine, 'we see age going to the workhouse and youth to the gallows, something must be wrong in the system of government.'[73] Ironically, his words describe the condition of the USA more than 200 years after *Rights of Man*, where young men (40 per cent of them black) fill up death row, and forced labour is required from millions of Americans on welfare. The next chapter examines Hegel's solution for the most intractable problem faced by civil society.

5 • Revolution, Despotism and Censorship, 1801–1831

Introduction

This chapter examines the oppressive political context in which Hegel responded to Schiller's challenge to create a 'State of Freedom'. The environment in which Hegel composed his ideas was much closer to the totalitarian atmosphere of communism during the Stalin period than it was to the free conditions experienced today by intellectuals in the West. Grasping Hegel's thought requires sympathetic acknowledgement of the difficulties that intolerance placed upon writers in his time. The radical disjuncture often noted between Hegel's early, unpublished writings and the published works of his maturity was, in part, a result of the prison-like climate in which the later Hegel lived and breathed. The philosophy of freedom that he sought to communicate in all his writings did not change. But despotism forced Hegel to express his thought in novel and enigmatic terms.

Hegel first began his project for a revolution in civil society and the democratization of the state following his Berne and Frankfurt acquaintance with Ferguson and the other Scottish Enlightenment thinkers – and Tom Paine. But these ideas came to fruition after Hegel began his academic career with a position at the University of Jena in 1801. By 1820 they were part of the structure of the *Philosophy of Right*. The following sections examine Hegel's university years, and the politics surrounding them; the tragedy of Friedrich Hölderlin and its meaning for Hegel's life in academia and for his philosophy; Hegel's secret political career in an age of despotism and censorship; and Hegel's relationship with Eduard Gans, and their theory of poverty. The chapter concludes with an examination of Hegel's alleged reconciliation with absolutism, as evidenced by his adverse reaction to France's July Revolution of 1830. Hegel's own version of Schiller's 'State of Freedom' – and its contrasts and similarities with Marx's communism – forms the subject of the concluding chapters of this book.

Hegel's career

When Hegel left Frankfurt to take up a teaching post at the University of Jena in 1801 the age of revolution epitomized by the life of Tom Paine was coming to a close. The French Revolution ended in 1802 with re-establishment of the Catholic church by Napoleon, then First Consul (Bonaparte became Emperor of the French in 1804). Fichte had been hounded from the University of Jena in 1799 by accusations of atheism in the famous *Atheismusstriat*, which augured the approaching era of reaction. Nevertheless, Hegel's first years in Jena were happy and productive. He lived close by his friend Schelling, and enjoyed an eventful social life in the so-called 'Jena Circle'. Together with Schelling he edited a short-lived *Critical Journal of Philosophy*, and worked on the first elements of what would become his system. At this time, Hegel was widely known as a disciple of the much younger Schelling. Soon Schelling's troubled love affair with Caroline Schlegel, the wife of August Schlegel, intruded on the harmonious Jena social scene. Amidst intense censure from family and friends – though with the approval of her husband – Caroline divorced Schlegel and married Schelling, in 1803. The couple, along with August, fled the gossip and hostility of Jena in the summer of the same year. By 1805 Hegel had plunged into the massive labour of his most famous work, the *Phenomenology of Spirit*. The book was completed in October 1806, literally on the eve of the Battle of Jena, where the French trashed the Prussian Army. Hegel wrote to a friend describing his encounter with the victorious Napoleon on the streets of Jena on 13 October, the day after the battle. 'I saw the Emperor – this world-soul – riding out of the city on reconnaissance. It is indeed a wonderful sensation to see such an individual, who, concentrated here at a single point, astride a horse, reaches out over the world and masters it.'[1]

The French Emperor later entered Berlin, and in the wake of the French invasion Hegel's job at the University of Jena disappeared. Cash-strapped, Hegel went to Bamberg in the state of Bavaria to become a newspaper editor in March 1807. By then his friendship with Schelling was over. Schelling saw the *Phenomenology of Spirit* as a personal rebuff, and after a stiff round of letters he and Hegel rarely communicated. Their final meeting in 1829 happened by accident. They were both taking a cure at the Karlsbad health spa. 'We are both pleased about meeting again', Hegel wrote to his wife, 'and find ourselves together as cordial friends of old.'[2]

Politics hastened Hegel's move to Bavaria. Jena was solidly pro-Prussian; Bavaria was allied with France. Even so, Hegel was not entirely content in Bamberg, where the cultural level was low compared to North Germany; he jokingly referred to Bavaria as 'Barbaria'. The former professor of philosophy quickly became disillusioned with his new position. The newspaper was under strict censorship and, in a letter to his friend Niethammer, Hegel complained that:

> [e]ven praise in our [German] states can appear *disrespectful*. We are still perhaps much accustomed to this traditional German habit of gawking admiration, this heaping up of praise like the good Catholic singing the praises of his Creator, instead of the sort of intelligent discernment and recognition that shows insight.

Hegel admired Napoleon's attempt to bring constitutional monarchy to the German states, but in the same letter he noted that '[t]he German princes have neither grasped the concept of free monarchy yet nor sought to make it real. Napoleon will have to organize all this.'[3]

Hegel's support for Napoleon's initiatives in Germany reflects the ideal of representative democracy he shared with Tom Paine. Under the French Constitution of 1804 universal suffrage was still the letter of the law, but the German princes grasped, writes Hegel, 'only half the example' offered by the French, 'The other half, the noblest part, is left aside: liberty of the people, popular participation in elections; governmental decisions taken in full view of the people'. Powers inherent in constitutional monarchy were abused by the German royals and transformed 'into arbitrariness, rudeness, barbarity, above all dumbness, hatred of publicity . . . exploitation, and wastefulness'. Instead of vibrant democracy the people got 'torpor, ill-humor, indifference to every public interest, servility, and baseness'.[4] There was no free civil society, the 'essence of liberty'; instead the state bore down on every detail of social life. As a newspaper editor Hegel personally experienced the arbitrary arm of German authority. Thanks to an overly candid report on troop movements the newspaper was almost shut down, and Hegel was subjected to yet 'another inquisition' by the press police.[5]

Leaving Bamberg in the autumn of 1808, Hegel become rector of a secondary school (Gymnasium) in Nuremberg. This move, too, had a political inspiration. Hegel's position was part of his friend Friedrich Immanuel Niethammer's plan to implement neohumanist reform in secondary education.[6] Like Hegel, Niethammer was pro-French, and both men hoped to establish idealist philosophy in the schools as a firm basis against the rising tide of reaction in Germany. Hegel was excited at the prospect of being involved in an educational revolution. The great idea was to provide universal free-tuition education at the primary level, and to extend this to the secondary level as well. The experiment in Bavaria would spread across the Western world, though it would take almost a century for universal education of any kind to reach Great Britain.

Although many scholars contend the opposite, Hegel helped bring this revolution to women's education as well. In his commentary on Hegel's letters, Clark Butler suggests that Hegel opposed building a secondary school for women in Nuremberg because he held 'a disparaging attitude toward the education of women [that] reflects less concern for human rights in this area than was shown by contemporaries such as Fichte, Schleiermacher, or Kant'.[7] In fact, however, Hegel pushed for the establishment of a secondary school for females. After a young woman was pressured to withdraw from a teacher's college in the city, he enthusiastically responded to a petition from three teachers demanding a new school for women. Terry Pinkard observes that, 'Hegel wrote a reference for the project, pushed it through the Bavarian bureaucracy and got the school opened within a year . . . Had Hegel been opposed to women's education, he would hardly have taken any of these steps.'[8] Despite the demands of teaching and administration amidst this huge change in education, Hegel's years at Nuremberg culminated in the publication in three volumes (1812, 1814 and 1816) of his greatest work, *Science of Logic*.

Hegel's reputation – though not his financial situation, which was always perilous – blossomed following publication of the *Phenomenology of Spirit,* and the initial volumes of the *Logic*. He began to put out feelers for a university post, but remained rector at Nuremberg until 1816 when he finally received the call from the University of Heidelberg. Hegel's concluding years in Nuremberg saw the German wars of liberation against the French; Napoleon's ill-fated invasion of Russia (and the death of Hegel's brother, Ludwig, who fought under Napoleon); and Napoleon's fall in 1814. Bonaparte's Hundred Days ended with Waterloo in 1815 and exile to the lonely rock of St Helena. These events shook Hegel to the core. 'It is a frightful spectacle to see a great genius [Napoleon] destroy himself,' he wrote to Niethammer in 1814.

There is nothing more *tragic*. The entire mass of mediocrity, with its irresistible leaden weight of gravity, presses on like lead, without rest or reconciliation, until it has succeeded in bringing down what is high to the same level as itself or even below. The turning point of the whole, the reason why this mass has power and – like the [Greek] chorus – survives and remains on top, is that the great individual must himself give that mass the right to do what it does, thus precipitating his own fall.[9]

An enthusiastic advocate of Napoleon's social and economic reforms, Hegel never believed that the French could equal the Germans in philosophy and education. The revolution in France would create a deeper, more sustained revolution in Germany, he thought, because of German's spiritual depth. Thirty years later, the young Marx would reach the same conclusion. But Hegel's hopes (like those of Marx a generation later) were dashed by events. Now German reaction was at the helm; and the forces of liberalism and democracy were in retreat. Divisions within Germany reappeared in families. These splits created a charged atmosphere of suspicion, censorship and spying in Germany that would mark the last fifteen years of Hegel's life.

Heidelberg was the centre of German Romanticism, in politics and the academy. This was the birthplace of the German radical student movement, the *Burschenschaften*, which wanted the constitutional gains of the Napoleonic years to be extended and deepened – a cause which Hegel warmly embraced, though he was suspicious of its nationalistic and anti-Semitic edge. He spent two years in Heidelberg, where his fame increased and the first disciples of his philosophy appeared. The Heidelberg period produced *The Encyclopaedia of the Philosophical Sciences* – the three-volume version of Hegel's system, comprising the *Logic*, the *Philosophy of Nature* and the *Philosophy of Mind*. Hegel also prepared the first version of the *Philosophy of Right*, the *Lectures on Natural Right and Political Science* (1817–18), which were lost until the 1980s. This lecture series is extremely important since it was the final relatively unencumbered statement by its author on politics before the curtain of absolute censorship fell over the German states. A year later, in 1819, the assassination of the German nationalist poet Kotzebue by the student Karl Sand led to the declaration of the Karlsbad Decrees, which imposed draconian prohibitions on the expression of opinion in Germany.

When Hegel at last took the chair in philosophy (vacated by the death of Fichte) at the recently founded University of Berlin in autumn of 1818 his fame was guaranteed. His lectures drew large enrolments, and he enjoyed the attention of students who came from across Western Europe. His celebrity reached its height in 1829–30 when Hegel became rector of the university, about a year before his death. He published the *Philosophy of Right* in 1820, a compendium meant to be used along with his lectures on politics, and lectured widely on history, aesthetics, religion and logic. His fifty-fifth birthday festivities were so lavish that the jealous king of Prussia decreed that birthday celebrations for private individuals henceforth would be strictly limited. For his fifty-sixth birthday Hegel discreetly left Germany on a holiday tour. Even this got him into trouble, however. 'He was suspected of having undertaken the trip to bring to a successful conclusion some projects of political opposition.'[10]

Hegel's appointment at Berlin has been taken by many critics as evidence of his conservative Restoration sympathies. Nothing could be further from the truth. Under State Chancellor von Hardenberg, Prussia was in the throes of an ambitious revolution from above. Von Hardenberg intended to match the liberal successes of the French Revolution without bloodshed, though he met powerful resistance from the feudal hierarchy in Prussia, and was forced to make significant compromises.

> Because the bureaucratic reformers could not justify their activity or maintain their power on the basis of a popular mandate, they were forced to compromise with existing political and social powers – the arbitrary authority of the monarch, the social and political privileges of the aristocracy – in order to survive.[11]

Hegel's move to Berlin was initiated by von Hardenberg's ally, the Education Minister Baron von Altenstein. At that time, Altenstein was involved in a controversy with factory and mine owners who objected to his request that Prussian children under the age of eight be excluded from the workplace.[12] (The plight of labouring children would soon become a huge social issue in England, as Marx documented in *Capital* fifty years after Altenstein's initiatives; I deal with this in *Hegel, Marx, and the English State*, University of Toronto Press, 1996.) The conflicted politics of Prussia meant that Hegel could take no direct role in affairs of state. He was barred from the Royal Academy of Sciences and found himself unable to assist distinguished friends like Niethammer in obtaining posts in the government. The Prussian secret police had a special interest in Hegel, as we shall see.

Hölderlin's fate

When Hölderlin left his 'beloved Diotima', Susette Gontard, and travelled to Homberg in 1798, he and Hegel remained close. During these two years, Hölderlin secretly met and corresponded with Susette Gontard. He also wrote his epic verse tragedy *Empedokles*, and contributed some of the most beautiful and mysterious translations from the ancient Greek ever written. Hölderlin and Sinclair were now familiar figures among radical political groups in Homberg. The young poet met Susette Gontard for the last time in May 1800. In the same year, he and Hegel apparently parted ways. From then on, Hegel never refers to Hölderlin, except very briefly in response to letters from Schelling and Sinclair. He is not mentioned in Hegel's lectures and published works. As a result of Hegel's silence, scholars remained unaware of Hölderlin's importance for Hegel's thought until the twentieth century. Wilhelm Dilthey, who initiated the study of Hegel's intellectual development in 1907, noticed parallels between Hölderlin's *Empedokles* poem fragments and the early Hegel's *Spirit of Christianity*. In following decades, scholars saw intriguing connections between the two, but the relationship remained enigmatic. 'Only in the mid 1960s – in the work of Otto Pöggeler and Dieter Henrich – was firm proof attained of a connection between Hölderlin's philosophical fragments and the genesis of Hegelian philosophy.'[13]

In December 1801, profoundly disappointed by the cold reception of his art in Germany, Hölderlin accepted a comfortable position in Bordeaux as a private tutor. He resigned suddenly the following March, after only three months in the post. He finally returned to Stuttgart in June 1802, a changed man. A friend wrote that Hölderlin appeared 'as pale as a corpse, emaciated with hollow wild eyes, long hair and beard, and dressed like a beggar'. Shortly after his return to Germany, Sinclair informed Hölderlin that Susette Gontard was dead.

Writing to Hegel from Stuttgart in 1803, just before his marriage to Caroline Schlegel, Schelling mentions Hölderlin's condition and pleads that Hegel become his guardian.

> The saddest spectacle I have seen during my stay here was that of Hölderlin. Ever since his trip to France ... his mind has been completely disturbed. And though he is still to some extent capable of doing some work – for example – translations from the Greek – he otherwise finds himself in a state of total mental absence. The sight of him quite shook me: he neglects his exterior to the point of

disgust; and though his speech does not greatly indicate a state of insanity, yet he has completely adopted the outer manner of those in such a state. There is no hope of curing him in this land. I have thought of asking you if you wished to take charge of him if he perhaps came to Jena, which he wanted to do. He needs quiet surroundings and probably could be put back in shape by sustained treatment. Anyone who wanted to take charge of him would absolutely have to function as his governor and rebuild him from the ground up. If only one had first triumphed over his exterior he would no longer be such a burden, since he is quiet and withdrawn.[14]

Replying to Schelling, Hegel echoes his friend's concern but does not volunteer to help Hölderlin.

You are certainly right that he will not be able to recuperate [in Swabia]. Yet, what is more, he is beyond the point where Jena can have a positive effect on a person. And the question now is whether, given his condition, rest will suffice for him to recuperate on his own. I hope that he still places a certain confidence in me as he used to do, and perhaps this will be capable of having some effect on him if he comes here.[15]

In the years between 1802 and 1806 Hölderlin produced 'the hymns and fragments upon which his reputation as the first great modern of European poetry rests. In late 1806, at the age of thirty-six, he [was] committed to the Tübingen clinic for the insane.'[16]

A debate rages as to the ultimate cause of Hölderlin's madness, and whether his poetry was the product of an insane genius. As early as 1804, Schelling speculated that Hölderlin's versions of Sophocles' *Oedipus* and *Antigone* were further proof of his friend's 'obvious derangement', and at least one reviewer sarcastically dismissed them as poor satires upon the contemporary German public.[17] Hölderlin's magnificent translations of Sophocles and Pindar had to wait for the twentieth century to find an appreciative audience. The sparkling achievement of his hymns and fragments went unrecognized during his lifetime.

Hölderlin spent almost a year in the Tübingen clinic. Ernst Zimmer, a local carpenter and admirer of Hölderlin's epistolary novel, *Hyperion*, agreed to look after the distressed writer, who was given only three years to live by his doctors. But Hölderlin survived for thirty-six years – long after Hegel, who died twelve years earlier – living in the now famous *Turm* (tower) built by Zimmer and located on the River Neckar only a few yards away from the Tübingen theological college, where he and Hegel and other friends first heard the astounding news about the French Revolution. Hölderlin became something of a tourist attraction as visitors gathered to hear him mumble his poems as he wandered about the tower.

What accounts for 'one of the most famous silences in the history of philosophy'?[18] Why did Hegel abandon his old friend? Alan Olson suggests that Hölderlin's illness must have devastated Hegel and caused him to repress his feelings of friendship and love. There was a similar silence in Hegel's life: he never again mentioned his mother, Maria Magdalena Hegel (née Fromm), after her early death. Yet he returns again and again in his writings to his mother's namesakes, the various Marias present at Christ's resurrection, including the prostitute Maria Magdalen, who washes Christ's feet in a loving gesture of faith. Similarly, Olson claims that Hegel's discussion of madness, in the third part of the *Encyclopaedia*, is actually a veiled reference to Hölderlin.

There may be, however, a more compelling reason for Hegel's silence. Since the late 1980s, scholars in Germany have argued that Hölderlin was not insane. Textual evidence indicates that the poet was feigning madness to avoid prosecution for high treason, and an inevitable death sentence. His friends, including Hegel, conspired in the hoax. If the secret police had managed to penetrate this deception, Hölderlin would have been executed, and his friends imprisoned for conspiracy.

Like Hegel, Hölderlin remained true to his revolutionary ideals; but while Hegel's last recorded connection with pro-French radicals was his visit to Mainz in 1798, Hölderlin along with Isaak von Sinclair did not stray from this increasingly dangerous path. Their dream of establishing a revolutionary Swabian republic exploded in 1805 when Sinclair and Hölderlin were denounced to the authorities by a turncoat for a claimed plot to assassinate the reactionary elector of Württemberg. This was most likely a trumped up charge meant to silence critics of the Swabian regime. In a similar case a year earlier, the English poet William Blake was arrested and falsely charged with sedition. '[I]n a sense the fate of both poets is emblematic of the plight of radical political and/or imaginative vision during the era of reaction following the French Revolution.' Sinclair was arrested for high treason but released four months later due to lack of evidence. When Hölderlin learned he too was implicated in the plot his mental condition deteriorated markedly. 'I refuse to be a Jacobin. Down with all Jacobins,' he cried. Hölderlin was certified insane and therefore unfit for trial. A year later, Hölderlin was transported by force from Homberg, where he lived under Sinclair's protection, to the Tübingen psychiatric facility. An eyewitness described how Hölderlin fought the officials who came to collect him. 'Screaming that he was being abducted by military guards ... and redoubling his efforts to escape, Holterling scratched the attendant with his enormously long fingernails until the man was completely bloodied.'[19]

It is certain that the German secret police entertained deep suspicions about Hegel. His long association with both accused conspirators would have been enough to qualify him for a special place in police files. If he did visit or correspond with Hölderlin, he would have had to do so under cover. This was only another black mark in Hegel's record that would grow much larger once he became a professor in Berlin.

In the twentieth century Hölderlin was first claimed as the poet of reactionary nationalism by Hitler's brown shirts. By the 1960s, however, he came to be seen as a lover of the French Revolution, a member of the secret Jacobin societies in Swabia, and a bitter critic of reaction and German provincialism. The playwright Peter Weiss sealed this new image with his 1971 *Hölderlin*.

> Explicitly underscoring Hölderlin's radical legacy, Weiss closed his play with an apocryphal scene in which the young Karl Marx comes to pay homage to the mad prophet in his Tübingen Tower and in allegorical rite of passage, apostolically receives from him the revolutionary flame.[20]

Later in this chapter we shall see how Marx received 'the revolutionary flame' from Hegel (and from Hölderlin too). Hegel had to give up the immediate dream of revolution for the exigencies of the present. 'I was driven towards science', he wrote to Schelling in 1801, 'and the ideal of [my] youth had to take the form of reflection and thus at once a system.'[21] Hölderlin, too, had to refashion the ideal, but it retained its lustre of hope in his mind as in Hegel's. The following fragment illustrates the modernist tone of Hölderlin's late poetry – its 'perfect economy' of meaning and silence[22] – and the philosophical ideal which inspired it.

> I want to build
>
> And raise new
> the temples of Theseus and the stadiums
> and where Perikles lived
>
> But there's no money, too much spent
> today. I had a guest
> over   and we sat together.[23]

The secret Hegel

After Hölderlin's confinement to the Tübingen tower, Hegel and Isaak von Sinclair remained friends and corresponded episodically between 1806 and 1813. Hegel never shunned the former 'traitor', and both he and Sinclair reflected upon their devotion to the revolutionary cause of their youth. In 1812, Sinclair – a lawyer and civil servant who served the liberal Count Ludwig V of Homberg – responded critically and affectionately to Hegel regarding the latter's *Phenomenology of Spirit*, and recalled the revolutionary pact he, Hegel, Schelling and Hölderlin had made during their life together at the University of Tübingen. This was the bond Hegel had referred to fifteen years before in his poem to Hölderlin, 'Eleusis': 'to live but for the free truth,/never, never to make peace with the decree that regulates feeling and opinion'. Now Schelling had drifted away from the ideal, and Hölderlin was confined in his tower. Only the two old friends remained. 'In the style and exposition [of the *Phenomenology*]', wrote Sinclair, 'I recognized well you and your zeal . . . and thought of the times when our spirits had concluded that pact from which fate has torn away the other members.'[24] Sinclair died of a stroke in 1815, at the age of 40.

Sinclair once described the flow of the young Hegel's political oratory as 'a flaming sword'.[25] When he resumed his professorial duties at Heidelberg in 1816 Hegel became renowned for the halting character of his speech, and the extreme care with which he expressed his ideas. Hegel, too, was imprisoned in a tower like Hölderlin, though his was ivory instead of wood. 'I am not an independent man like yourself', Hegel wrote to the French philosopher, Victor Cousin, 'but am subject to regulations from on high and from below, and thus have to adapt my plans to them.'[26] More than once he asserted that the times had cruelly thrust him out of active affairs into the pure realm of the absolute. Even in this weightless atmosphere Hegel had to move with extreme caution. His private letters (usually personally delivered by travelling friends rather than entrusted to the official mail) and his lectures sometimes betray the old fire, as in his ironic missive to Niethammer, describing the monarchs at the 1814 Congress of Vienna, gathering like vultures on the corpse of the Napoleonic age.

> It is a new, unforgettable experience for the peoples to see what their Princes are capable of when they convene to devote themselves in mind and heart to discussion of both their own peoples and the world – all to be sure, according to the most noble declared principles

of universal justice and welfare for all. For centuries we have only seen action taken by cabinets or individual men for themselves against others. The present phenomenon, however, is unique and calls for a brilliant result . . . (*Hegel: The Letters*, p. 314)

But Hegel's published works are always written in code. As I suggested was the case with Tom Paine, Hegel often 'does not name his sources lest he be tarred as dangerous himself'.[27] The French Hegel scholar Jacques D'Hondt observed that because Hegel could not publish everything he wanted to say about politics, he actually had three philosophies of right. The first is the published version 'which had difficulty in penetrating the barricades of censorship'. The second is the *Philosophy of Right* as it was read between the lines by his friends and followers, fleshed out with Hegel's spoken words, and interpreted in the context of the events that constrained it. 'Finally there is the philosophy of right whose maxims Hegel actually followed in his daily life.' Like all trinities, says D'Hondt, this one, too, becomes a unity over time. 'They move in the same direction, but to a greater or lesser extent. It is in his actions that Hegel shows himself to be the most intrepid and . . . the most dynamic.'[28]

The celebrated professor of philosophy had more than enough opportunities to demonstrate courage under fire. During the most fully documented period of his life – the time he spent in Berlin between 1818 and 1831 – reaction reached its apex and chose its young victims from among those who aspired to the revolutionary ideals Hegel cherished. The doomed Jena student Karl Sand (beheaded in 1820) hoped to overthrow the Restoration by murdering the Russophile poet Kotzebue. His act achieved the opposite effect. Prince von Metternich, the Austrian diplomat, used the assassination to promulgate the 1819 Karlsbad Decrees in co-ordination with the German Confederation of states. Universities were placed under government control; the *Burschenschaften* was banned; the screws of censorship were tightened; and a special secret police unit, the Central Office of Investigation, was established 'to enquire more deeply into the revolutionary intrigues uncovered in several German states'.[29] Emboldened by this turn of events, Frederick William III imported the Decrees to Prussia in their full severity. He cancelled or postponed the reforms of von Hardenberg, reversed self-government in the countryside, and re-established the Prussian union of church and state.

Hegel was quickly caught in the spiderweb spun by Metternich. Acknowledging to Niethammer that any philosopher 'is in and for himself a born *expositus* [vulnerably exposed individual]', Hegel nevertheless thought himself fairly safe. Unfortunately, this was not true of his students. His first teaching assistant in Berlin, Friedrich Carové, faced prosecution for a pamphlet he wrote on the Kotzebue assassination. It is likely that he wrote the pamphlet with Hegel's advice and approval. Hegel's own estimation of Kotzebue was not high, as is shown by the colourful language he used to discuss the poet in an 1803 letter to Schelling. Expletives were a rare occurrence in Hegel's correspondence.

> I have not caught sight of any literary news other than a pile of shit by Kotzebue, *Explorations*, a diarrhoea he emitted while still in Germany. It is the old song about Goethe and the Schlegels ... Goethe swore at a dinner that these people [i.e. Kotzebue and company] should never gain a foothold in Jena.[30]

Thanks to the pamphlet on Kotzebue, Carové was thrown out of the University of Berlin and spied on by the police, his career effectively ruined. Though it compromised him in the eyes of the police, Hegel remained close friends with his former student long after these incidents. Hegel describes the fate of his second teaching assistant, Leopold von Henning:

> For one year now a teaching assistant ... has been made available to me for my lectures. His job is to attend my *lectures* and then go over them with the students four hours a week ... He ... was under arrest for ten weeks on suspicion of demagogy, with a gendarme guarding him day and night in prison.[31]

Interestingly, Henning was arrested on the strength of a private letter from his mother-in-law! Besides Hegel's students, the Prussian police took a special interest in Hegel's friends and relatives. 'The sons of close friends such as Karl Friedrich Frommann, Niethammer, and the Jena lawyer Ludwig Christoph Asverus were members of the *Burschenschaften*' (*Hegel: The Letters*, p. 445) and were spied on by the police. Hegel's son Ludwig Fischer befriended Robert Wesselhöft, a leading student dissident, who had to flee to Switzerland. Gottlieb von Tucher, Hegel's brother-in-law, was also a member of the *Burschenschaften*.[32] Hegel posted a 500 thaler bond (about three months' salary) for Asverus's son Ludwig, who was arrested on Bastille Day (14 July) 1819, and languished in prison for almost a year. 'His trial ... lasted seven years with numerous periods of detention and all sorts of incidents, until, in 1826, the king in an act of clemency ordered an end to the affair.'[33] In 1821 Hegel's confidence in his own safety was eroded by the Prussian monarch's edict that prohibited the teaching of any philosophy that might lead to atheism. Hegel's outlook was at risk since it held that religious thinking was inferior to philosophy's infinite vision. He urged his followers to avoid loose talk about religion because of the horrendous consequences. '[O]nce one has been branded in a given place – no matter where and no matter what label such as "demagogy" or, ultimately, "atheism" – one is a marked man everywhere in the German Empire . . . and regions of the Holy Alliance.'[34]

Hegel hurried to the assistance of Victor Cousin, the French philosopher and a personal friend, when Cousin was arrested in 1824 by the Prussian police while attending a relative's wedding in Dresden. Prussian authorities were acting on behalf of their French counterparts, who secretly accused Cousin of having 'dangerous opinions'.[35] Cousin was whisked to Berlin, imprisoned for three months, and kept under house arrest for most of a year. Later Cousin dedicated his 1826 translation of Plato's *Gorgias* to Hegel. He worried that Hegel might be upset by a reference to the Prussian police which accompanied the dedication:

> When, as I recently travelled again in Germany, an extravagant police, directed unbeknownst to it by an odious political line, dared attack my liberty, making the most atrocious accusations, declaring me proven guilty and convicted in advance, you [Hegel] spontaneously rushed forward to tell my judges that I was your friend.

Hegel reassured Cousin that he did not have to bother about the secret police, 'for whose omniscience Plato . . . is probably an obscure corner into which it has not likely penetrated'.[36]

Both men were perfectly aware that the secret police had indeed 'likely penetrated' the 'obscure corner' that Plato scholarship inhabited. Cousin was a marked man; his works would have been read in detail by scholars acting on behalf of the intelligence authorities. The French police had a direct line to the Prussian secret service, as Cousin's arrest in Dresden indicated. Jacques D'Hondt argues that Hegel had to tread carefully throughout his career, a skill he learned in his seminary days at Tübingen when he and his friends organized a secret political club and read prohibited French newspapers. Hegel's early essays on the life of Jesus (discussed in chapter 3) were unpublishable in the cold German climate, and remained unknown until 1907. Most of his early political essays were destined to a similar fate, or – as with his translation of J. J. Cart – published anonymously. Hegel's private letters were either 'closed' or 'openable'. The 'closed' letters were delivered through alternatives to the regular post; the 'openable' ones were delicately phrased to mislead the censors. Directly incriminating correspondence was destroyed by Hegel upon receipt. We know of his communication with the exiled radical Karl Ulrich only because of a single missive from Ulrich to Hegel which survives. In it Ulrich instructs Hegel to address his reply to a false name, and promises to 'shred [Hegel's reply] as usual after having read it closely'.[37] Letters between the two would doubtless not have been sent through the regular post. 'Hegel knew that he was condemned to live in a dangerous environment,' concludes D'Hondt. 'The equilibrium constantly threatened to shatter. Hegel walked a tightrope.'[38]

Reciting verse, playing the piano, entertaining guests with elaborate formality, Hölderlin inhabited his wooden tower and followed the covert maxims of an imprisoned revolutionary poet in an age of despair. Hegel stumbled through a tower of mirrors – the revolutionary *manqué*, the tongue-tied university professor and subversive theorist.

Eduard Gans and poverty

Hegel's friend and protégé, Eduard Gans, provided a direct link between Hegel's philosophy and the revolutionary politics of Karl Marx. It was through Gans, I believe, that the 'revolutionary flame' was passed from Hegel to Marx. Between 1836 and 1838, the young Marx attended, and must have been influenced by, Gans's enormously popular lectures on law, which he delivered at the University of Berlin up to his untimely death in 1839.[39]

Neglected by scholars in Germany until the past two decades, Gans's work is slowly gaining prominence after a 150-year eclipse. Only a tiny sample of his voluminous writings has so far been translated into English. Born in 1797, Gans was the offspring of a wealthy Berlin Jewish family. As a university student, Gans had to put up with anti-Semitic taunts from fellow members of the *Burschenschaften*, and was a founder of the Union for the Culture and Science of Jews. In 1825 he converted to Protestantism to be eligible for an academic post at the University of Berlin. He was appointed to the law faculty the following year, and became full professor in 1828. There he attained fame as a top expert on legal philosophy and world systems of law. 'Gans had been an associate of Hegel's before his formal conversion. In the years that followed he became Hegel's closest companion.' A supporter of representative democracy in a dark period of reaction, Gans devoted his academic life to 'a progressive and social interpretation of Hegel's doctrine'.[40]

Following Hegel's death, Gans was the leader of the critical Hegelian school that gave birth in the 1840s to the left-Hegelian movement whose adherents would include Karl Marx and Friedrich Engels. Although Gans, like Hegel, had to contend with censorship, this was nowhere near as rigorous as the blackout imposed by the Karlsbad Decrees. After 1830 – when the Bourbon king of France Charles X was overthrown in the July Revolution – popular protest and agitation in Germany revived, and the regime of censorship eased. Gans was able to say openly what Hegel could only hint at. 'In Gans's lectures and writings', observes John Toews, 'the interpretation of the present as a Moment in the progressive actualization of Reason in history found earliest and most forceful expression.' Gans taught the eager students who jammed his lecture hall that the philosophical comprehension of the present and the past could throw light on the future 'and thus provide an orientation for progressive political opinion'. He sympathized with the 'post-1830 liberal movements in France, England, Belgium and Switzerland' that would kindle the revolutions of 1848, and encouraged 'his Prussian contemporaries to take up the cause of liberal reform in their own country'. Like Hegel, Gans embraced the cause of radical democracy first propounded a half-century before by Tom Paine. 'The task for the future was to end the minority of the "subjects" of administration and extend the actualized ethical community to the whole society.'[41]

Throughout the 1820s, Hegel and Gans communicated regularly with radical circles in Paris inspired by the figure of Henri de Saint-Simon. Saint-Simon, who died in 1825, was a precursor of Marxism. Engels, in his famous essay, 'Socialism: utopian or scientific', called Saint-Simon – along with Charles Fourier and Robert Owen – a 'utopian socialist' because of his far-reaching critique of industrial society. In the last few years of his life Saint-Simon became an impassioned advocate of the working class. As Toews relates, Gans maintained his connection with the Saint-Simonians and agreed with their critique of liberalism. There could be no doubt, Gans assented, that the unrestricted competitive market 'produced political anarchy and unconscionable exploitation of the propertyless working class by bourgeois property owners'. But Gans rejected Saint-Simonian solutions such as abolishing market relations, ending the right to inheritance and restricting occupational choice. He feared that these strategies, which anticipated some put forward by Marx and Engels after 1848, 'would destroy the very foundation of ethical life in the modern world'. Politics is the essence of life in the community, and the way to ensure freedom is not to retrict the individual, but rather to raise him or her to the universal through 'political integration and cultural education'. While Gans's greatest concern was for the impoverished working class, he felt that a socialist revolution, with its attendant dangers of terror and dictatorship, was unnecessary to achieve liberation.

The working class could be elevated to full membership in the political community through legal protection of their individual rights, social legislation that alleviated their competitive disadvantage in the marketplace, and the creation of 'free corporations' that would form a bridge from the particular to the universal will.[42]

Gans shared Hegel's view that poverty had subjective as well as objective causes. Individuals could become destitute through accident and misfortune, or by neglect of finances and health. The dependents of such persons would also be dragged into poverty. But the major (the 'objective') cause of poverty in civil society is wealth. 'Poverty is the shadow of wealth', wrote Gans. 'Extreme wealth will create extreme poverty.' To use a contemporary example, the richest man in the world – William (Bill) Henry Gates III, the Microsoft lord – has amassed a fortune estimated at $18 billion, 'enough to purchase half a dozen poor countries'.[43] Capitalism creates an abundance of goods, but the bourgeois property system restricts the income and purchasing power of workers so that they cannot buy all the commodities they produce. Meanwhile, profits for the rich pile up and some of these earnings are directed back toward additional production. Ultimately, economic crises throw masses of people out of work. Keynes would later call this fateful mechanism lack of 'effective demand'.

According to Hegel and Gans, the conventional solutions for poverty are singularly ineffective. Charity undermines the confidence and independence of the person on the receiving end, while puffing up the ridiculous self-regard of the giver. The public dole, though much to be preferred to charity, means that the individual is excluded from meaningful relationships in the world of work, and made dependent on the state. Makework projects to create employment add to the problem by competing with existing businesses and injecting more goods into the system. Emigration of the working population to foreign lands opens up new markets and relieves the pressure on the home country, but also strips the nation of some of its best workers. Moreover, countries like the USA which absorb waves of migrants will ultimately also become crowded, and will face identical problems of overproduction and unemployment.

What is today called 'globalization' is another alternative considered by Hegel and Gans: firms and investors can aggressively exploit foreign markets to dispose of excess goods and capital. But this solution too is self-limiting, as world economic crises develop. Besides, globalization means that firms escape the oversight of states, and are prone to violate the welfare of citizens in the home country and of people in foreign nations. In today's terms, this leads to a 'global race to the bottom' as each country outbids the other by lowering wages and government social provisions to attract investment, hence worsening the crisis.

I noted in chapter 2 that Hegel – in his supposed drift toward reconciliation with the established order – is considered by most commentators not to have found a solution for poverty. Having outlined the conditions that would haunt capitalism right up to the twenty-first century, Hegel fell silent. Gans, however, saw poverty as a social problem capable of eradication. 'This hope to find a better solution to the problem of poverty', writes Norbert Waszek, 'has a programmatic edge to it which must have been a trumpet call to Gans's students, among whom a young law student by the name of Marx was to be found.'[44] According to Waszek, Gans visited England in 1830 and 1831, while Hegel was still alive, having a first-hand look at the miserable conditions of the factory workers. During the same period, he achieved a greater understanding of the Saint-Simonian system. Under the twin impact of these experiences, Gans constructed a view of class struggle – 'the fight of the proletariat against the middling classes of society' – that, according to Waszek and many other authorities, was foreign to Hegel's original system. In this view, Hegel utterly ignored the claims of the proletariat and excluded workers from the basic institutions of civil society – the corporations – and barred them from the state.

Gans enthusiastically adopted the Saint-Simonian idea of association. Workers, he contended, should create their own corporations (unions) to offset the power of business owners. By organizing their own centres of power, workers could avoid the mass poverty sanctioned and encouraged by the capitalist free market. He modified Hegel's corporation so that the educational function Hegel allotted to it was preserved. 'The purpose of Gans's *Vergesellschaftung* or free corporation', says Waszek, 'is not restricted to material living conditions but, like Hegel's, it attempts to to extend . . . "ethical life" to the insulted and the injured.' However, Gans stopped short of accepting the Saint-Simonian ideal of communal ownership. The expert on Hegel's concept of property and world systems of law could not accept abolition of private property. As Waszek emphasizes, this is 'an aspect which marks the line between Gans and his more radical successors, Ruge, Marx, *et al*'.[45] Hegel's concept of private property and the corporation is discussed more fully in the concluding chapters of this book.

Hegel's reconciliation?

As we saw in earlier chapters, many commentators suggest that Hegel's politics turned in a conservative direction during his career. This has often been described as Hegel's 'reconciliation' with the existing order. However, there is no consensus on when this crisis in Hegel's development occurred. Some, like Charles Taylor, point to the year 1800 as the decisive date. Others, such as Georg Lukács, put the event forward to the period after publication of the *Phenomenology* in 1807. Herbert Marcuse, in *Reason and Revolution*, avers that Hegel's transformation took place in 1818 when he took up his professorship at the University of Berlin. A final date for Hegel's supposed transformation into a conservative is the July Revolution of 1830, which toppled the French monarch. This political about-face also involved Hegel's relationship with his friend, Gans.

On 30 July 1830, an attempt by Charles X to suspend parliament and restrict freedom of the press caused a revolt in Paris. The Bourbon monarch was replaced by the constitutional monarchy of the Orleanist Louis Philippe. Gans was visiting Paris when the revolution occurred and wrote Hegel a glowing account of the proceedings. Hegel, however, was not as sanguine about the possibilities in France, referring derisively to the event as a 'great carnival',[46] and recording his own anxiety about its impact. Hegel's death a little more than a year after the revolution prevented him from fully analysing its consequences. The July Monarchy quickly disappointed radical hopes, and he and Gans no doubt came to a meeting of minds about prospects in France. Within a few months, radicals like Charles Fourier would agree with Hegel that the revolution was little more than a 'great carnival', a surface incident that changed little.[47] For a few years France enjoyed a climate of freedom of expression unknown since the first hopeful days of the revolution of 1789. But the old controls and restrictions were soon back in place. Real change had to await the revolution of 1848.

Hegel's doubts about the revolution were more likely aroused by its probable reactionary result than by any radical threat it posed. Earlier Hegel had gently broken with Victor Cousin, who would take a leading role in the July Monarchy, because of Cousin's arrogant treatment of German idealism in his *Introduction à la histoire de la philosophie* (1828). Cousin declared that Hegel's philosophy would be superseded by a new position that consisted of a mixture of contradictory standpoints. As Minister of Public Instruction in the Orleanist administration, Cousin opposed Hegel's 'pantheism' in favour of the later Schelling, 'as if to suggest that Hegel's own philosophical position ought to have made him politically apprehensive'.[48] Cousin's opportunistic trajectory from bourgeois radical to defender of God and throne must have worried Hegel, and added to his ambivalence about the July Monarchy.

The lectures on the philosophy of right given by Hegel at Heidelberg in 1818 provide some support for my explanation of Hegel's antipathy towards the July Revolution. He warns that revolutions which result from parliament's 'hostile attitude toward the executive power' often bring no substantial improvement in the condition of the people, but only a change in the ranks of 'those who hold the executive power in their hands'. It makes no difference whether the new leadership is genuinely interested in what is best for the community. Real progress in the state depends on enlisting the desire and will of the whole people.

> Only so is right present for itself, even if it may previously have been present in itself. For it is a matter of contingency if the government's actions bring about the universal, and the sole reason why there must be an organized state is that what is fitting may occur necessarily.[49]

The best evidence for Hegel's alleged late conservative turn is his final publication, 'The English Reform Bill' (1831), interpreted by many as a 'somewhat ill tempered essay' opposing liberal reform of English electoral law.[50] In fact, as I have shown in *Hegel, Marx and the English State*,[51] Hegel's essay is actually a radical critique of the illusory measures proposed by the Whig government. In any event, the essay got Hegel into trouble with the Prussian monarch. Fearing that its criticism of England was too strong for an official journal, the king banned publication of its concluding sections in the *Prussian State Gazette*. This was merely one more in a series of political harassments spanning Hegel's initial appointment in Berlin and his final years of teaching.

In 1831, the Prussian Crown Prince asked Hegel to take over Gans's lectures on the philosophy of law, supposedly because of Gans's advocacy of the July Revolution. The Crown Prince's request was in line with criticism directed at both Hegel and Gans for 'anti-Prussian and revolutionary' sympathies. According to the testimony of Arnold Ruge, Hegel apologized to the Prince for Gans's conduct and stated (untruthfully) that he was not aware of what his colleague was teaching. Hegel resumed lecturing on the philosophy of law in autumn 1831, but he did not require Gans to give up his own lectures. Instead, Gans publicly announced that he would suspend his class in deference to Hegel. This action apparently infuriated Hegel, who on 12 November wrote a bitter note to his colleague accusing Gans of 'placing me in a foolish light with colleagues and students'. Hegel had only a brief time to live. He fell suddenly ill with cholera hours after sending the note to Gans. The friends reunited two days later 'as Hegel lay on his deathbed'.[52]

We know that since entering the University of Berlin Hegel had endured censorship, political baiting, accusations of atheism and arbitrary arrest of his best students. In the light of this history, Hegel's words of apology to the Prussian Crown Prince, and his show of an emotional exchange with Gans, may have been part of the tightrope strategy that he had learned since his undergraduate days at Tübingen seminary. As Michael Hoffheimer submits, Hegel's so-called breach with Gans is known mostly through the (biased) testimony of Arnold Ruge 'whose criticism of Hegel's conservatism provided a motivation to exaggerate Hegel's differences with Gans'. Ruge was a founder of the left-Hegelian organ, the *Hallische Jahrbücher*. In the early 1840s his journal featured the writings of Bruno Bauer and Ludwig Feuerbach which pilloried Hegel's conservatism and directly influenced the young Marx. Hegel, notes Hoffheimer, 'had announced renewed lectures on the philosophy of law the year before [his interview with the Crown Prince], in 1830, though he did not give the course at that time'.[53] In other words, it is doubtful that Hegel resumed the course purely as a result of political pressure. The short 'breach' with Gans may well have been a creation of Arnold Ruge's imagination.

As for Gans himself, he never doubted that he and Hegel were political and philosophical allies. Gans helped prepare the first edition of Hegel's collected works. He edited the students' notes on Hegel's lectures on politics which are still included in the latest English editions of the *Philosophy of Right*. Gans's preface to Hegel's *Lectures on the Philosophy of History* was included in the 1857 English translation by J. Sibree. Although Sibree's translation remains in print, Gans's preface was dropped in 1899. In the preface Gans remarks on the liveliness and excitement of Hegel's lectures. He relates how Hegel, contrary to his received image as an uninspired speaker, designed the lectures to appeal directly to his young audience. In the edited version of the lectures, notes Gans, 'the naiveté, the *abandon*, the enthusiastic absorption in the immediate subject which makes the speaker indifferent as to when or how he shall finish, had to be left intact'. Gans's description of Hegel's lecture style recalls Isaak von Sinclair's observation that the early Hegel's oratory was like 'a flaming sword'. For proof of Hegel's 'didactic gift' Gans recommended – with good reason, given their continued popularity and influence today – the lecture manuscripts themselves.[54]

Gans also supplied a preface to the second edition of the *Philosophy of Right* (1833). He decried interpretations of the book which caused 'every freedom loving man [to] keep his distance from its doctrines and basic principles'. Gans argued that Hegel's text, far from slavishly justifying the present order, was actually a democratic critique of absolutism. Gans observed that '[i]n a difficult time', Hegel called for 'open judicial proceedings, open assembly meetings, and trials by jury as the only institutions appropriate to rationality'. Nor did Hegel deify monarchy. To be sure, 'monarchs [are] the necessary and intellectually suitable summit of the state'; but they are also, for Hegel, 'merely the product of contingent historical circumstance'.[55]

For Jacques D'Hondt, Hegel was a radical liberal who constructed a political project that was superseded only a quarter-century later by Karl Marx: 'Although [the *Philosophy of Right*] continued to be in advance with respect to the institutions of 1820, it no longer retained first place in the range of doctrines.' The birth of the German proletariat sealed the fate of Hegel's text. Hegel 'did not contribute to the socialist movement that had just been born. Even less did [he] anticipate the economic, social and political theory that Marx was beginning to articulate.' Hegel, says D'Hondt, concealed the real contradictions of the bourgeois state by transposing them into his own doctrine. Marx's greatest advance was to show that, instead of civil society being 'dependent on the state, as Hegel proposed . . . the state rested on civil society'.[56]

Did Hegel labour for years to produce a political mouse? Were his struggles with censorship and the secret police aimed at concealing a critique of a feudal social order that was already in its death throes? I want to suggest another alternative. When the young Marx entered Gans's lecture hall in 1836–7, and again in 1838, he was exposed to a radical Hegelianism that he later converted into his own devastating analysis of capitalism. Marx captured the spirit of Hegel's demolition of the bourgeois order, but he ignored the elements that make Hegel's system so pertinent to the challenge offered by the fall of communism. Some of these elements, as we saw in chapter 4, bring Hegel close to the democratic theories of Tom Paine, especially the notion of a free civil society untrammelled by the arbitrary dictates of an authoritarian state. In addition, Hegel offered a radical theory of private property, and an outline of politics that would protect minorities and bring government closer to its citizens. We turn to an outline of Hegel's democratic vision in the final chapters of this book.

6 • Property and the Corporation

Introduction

What did the eighteen-year-old Marx learn when he stepped into Gans's crowded lecture hall in Berlin? What arcane elements of Prussian and Roman law did Gans unfold before the teenage intellectual from the ancient Roman town in the Rhineland? Perhaps Marx sensed behind Gans's expert theatrical lecture style the ghosts of Hegel and Sinclair and the unfulfilled revolutionary desires of Hölderlin, soon to die in his forlorn tower. Did he seize the revolutionary flame from Hegel's gifted follower? This chapter – and the next two concluding ones – offer a glimpse of Hegel's vision, its reception by Marx, and its promising future in the era after the fall of communism.

These final chapters bring into focus the lectures on politics Hegel gave in Heidelberg between 1817 and 1819. The Heidelberg lectures – which remained in obscurity until 1982 and were not available in English until 1995 – make up the earliest version of the *Philosophy of Right*. They were given shortly before a mantle of censorship settled over the German lands. The lectures offer a frank and devastating analysis of poverty. They are also more critical of monarchy and friendlier to democratic institutions than the published version of the *Philosophy of Right*, which appeared in 1821.

The next section of this chapter introduces the central difference between Hegel's system and Marx's: the concept of private property. This concept involves a key dilemma of the post-communist era. With the collapse of state power in the Soviet Union, and the trend toward privatization of government services in many countries, the threat of unrestrained capitalism has replaced the old fear of communism.[1] This underscores the importance of the differences between Hegel and Marx, for private property defines the disputed borderline between civil society and the state.

The following section examines the democratic corporation – Hegel's solution for the dilemma of poverty – and considers its connection with the doctrine of property rights as understood by Hegel and Marx. The struggle for recognition that characterizes Hegel's rational state (and Marx's vision of communism) is the subject of the final two chapters.

Communism and private property

Even if Gans's lectures are examined closely, there is no telling what the adolescent Marx might have recovered from them. We have some clues, however. In November 1837, a year after Marx first enrolled in Gans's law courses, he wrote to his father that he had been converted to Hegelianism. 'It becomes clear from this letter', writes Shlomo Avineri, 'that even at this early stage Marx was drawn to Hegel's philosophy because he saw in it a powerful instrument for changing reality'.[2]

Hegel's philosophy taught Marx the dynamics of social change, but it also demonstrated to him the dangers inherent in revolutions. Although the Terror was as remote from the youthful Marx as the Second World War is from today's university students, his first published writings echo Hegel's analysis of the French events. As we saw in chapter 4, Hegel in the *Phenomenology of Spirit* connected the Terror to the breakdown of class and property relations in France, and dissolution of the separation between individual will in civil society, and the state. Throughout his life Marx warned against imposing a political revolution on a society where economic and social conditions are not yet ripe. For Marx, an insurrection of this type, comments Avineri, would 'collapse immediately or ... lead to political terrorism'.[3]

For many of Marx's followers, the origin and development of the Soviet system provided a striking example of the situation he warned against. Lenin led the revolution in backward Russia under the impression that the new socialist state would soon be joined, and aided, by revolutionary governments in the West. The mature conditions Marx prescribed for a successful revolution were never present in Russia. Following the end of the First World War, socialist revolution failed in Germany and elsewhere in Europe. In place of assistance from a sympathetic communist leadership installed in advanced industrial countries, the new Soviet Republic met grim hostility from the capitalist powers. Similarly, the socialist regimes of Eastern Europe emerged not from autonomous revolutions growing out of mature social and political soil, but were imposed on war-ravaged countries by the Red Army (with Western connivance) after the defeat of Hitler. From this perspective, the circumstances of its birth made the authoritarian nature of Soviet socialism inevitable, and compromised any chance it had to reflect the ideals of equality and freedom that Marx associated with communism. 'The revolution in a precapitalist society, which nevertheless aspired to achieve socialism', declared Isaac Deutscher, 'produced a hybrid which in many respects looked like a parody of socialism.'[4]

As R. N. Berki avers, Marx's vision of communism involved something like Hegel's concept of the state as a source of unity and 'concrete moral identity'. Marx rejected the organizing principles of Hegel's constitutional theory, but he never abandoned its underlying moral quality, which he absorbed as a student at the University of Berlin. 'Marx's emerging vision and understanding of Communism as the unity of the individual and the species actually build on, and merely verbally define, his own original Hegelian view of the state as "true moral association".'[5]

Despite his admiration for Hegel, Marx turned away from a key premiss of the Hegelian system. For Hegel (and for his friend and associate, Gans), the structures of the state and private property are expressions of universal human interests. These institutions are grounded in human reason, though their actual appearance on earth is everywhere entwined with compromise and evil. As an instrument of the universal, the state rises above the clash of social forces that constitute civil society – the field of individualism and private property. By asserting the state's ability to transcend civil society, Hegel also affirms the relative independence of these two realms. 'Hegel's description reflects the fundamental dualism of the modern age: social on the level of the state, individualist on the real level of civil society. One is the spiritual realm of history; the other the physical world of necessity.'[6]

Against Hegel, Marx contended that the independence of politics from civil society is an illusion. There is even, in Marx, a sense that politics and government are modes of human *self-estrangement*. 'The atomized individuals ostensibly "represented" in modern state institutions', writes R. N. Berki, 'are in truth people estranged from their proper human selves.'[7] Even the differences between a republic and monarchy are merely semantic. Political power grows out of the economic relations of civil society, and is ultimately reducible to them. Instead of being an instrument of reason, as Hegel thought, the state is actually a tool of the ruling capitalist class. To get rid of this state civil society, together with its determining relationships of social class, must be overthrown. Bourgeois property relations are rotten, Marx would show in *Capital*. Tear them apart and start anew. There was nothing to be gained from Hegel's (and Gans's) interminable dissection of a doomed order. 'The knell of capitalist private property sounds,' wrote Marx of the advent of communism. 'The expropriators are expropriated.'[8]

Capitalist private property would not be the only victim in a communist revolution. The classless society Marx envisioned would lack professional distinctions. 'In a communist society,' he declared in *The German Ideology*, 'there are no painters but only people who engage in painting among other activities.'[9] How would Hölderlin, who devoted his life to the poetics of revolution, feel about that communist anodyne? Proletarian revolution, claimed Marx, would erase the division between government and civil society. Bureaucrats — those self-interested servants of a parasitic state — would become an endangered species. For Marx, 'bureaucracy is the image of prevailing social power distorted by its claim to universality'.[10]

As Jürgen Habermas suggests, Marx's vision of communism is founded on a 'Janus-faced' perspective that 'looks back to an idealized past as much as it looks forward to a future dominated by industrial labour'.

> The idea of a free association of producers has always been loaded with nostalgic images of the types of community — the family, the neighbourhood and the guild — to be found in the world of peasants and craftsmen that, with the violent onset of competitive society, was just beginning to break down, and whose disappearance was experienced as a loss.[11]

In contrast to Marx's communism, Hegel's 'state of freedom' (as we shall learn in chapter 8) is founded on the concept of professionalism. Hegel's state respects the distinction between civil society and government. The civil service, far from being a pariah class, is a catalytic agent of change in the good society. Marx implicitly retained a Hegelian concept of bureaucracy in his account of the English factory inspectorate in *Capital*, but he did not openly incorporate it into his vision of communism.[12]

Marx rarely addressed the long-term probable result of the communist revolution. If, as he recommended in *Capital* and elsewhere, the organic links of class and property were destroyed, what would prevent a new episode of terror? The Paris Commune of 1871 – which in some ways Marx's *Civil War in France* presented as the living model of communist society – provided him with an opportunity to assess the effects of revolution. As Berki points out,[13] however, Marx turned his eyes from the implications of the terror and repression that the short-lived Commune inflicted on Paris.

The Soviet revolution was certainly immature from Marx's viewpoint, but it took seriously his strictures against private property and class. Stalin's ascent to the Kremlin's throne of blood, after arch rival Trotsky's banishment in 1928, depended on the same factors that thrust Robespierre's Jacobins into power. 'What Jacobinism and Bolshevism had in common', notes Isaac Deutscher, 'was – substitutism. Each of the two parties had placed itself at the head of society but could not rely for the realization of its programme on the willing support of society.' In both Russia and France, the revolutionary class disintegrated, 'the social basis of the revolution narrowed and power was exercised by ever fewer people'.[14] The organized centres of dissent were gone; one individual could represent himself as the government. In the Soviet Union, as in Robespierre's France, the result of this process was horrific. 'Already before the defeat of Nazism', notes Perry Anderson, 'Stalin's regime had made war on its peasantry and unleashed the purges, in two great waves of mass terror that can only be compared in toll of lives to the First World War, and may have exceeded it.'[15]

Prior to Lenin's death in 1923, while Stalin was one of six members of the powerful Politburo, the future dictator took bi-weekly tutorials on Marx's *Capital* and Hegel's *Phenomenology of Spirit*. His teacher, the leading Marxist philosopher, Jan Sten, related that Stalin had difficulty in absorbing Hegel's dialectic. Perhaps Stalin understood the dialectic of terror only too well. A friend of Stalin's tutor remarked that,

> Jan often dropped in to see me after a lesson with Stalin in a depressed and gloomy condition. The meetings with Stalin, the conversations with him on matters philosophical ... opened his eyes more and more to Stalin's true nature, his striving for one-man rule, his crafty schemes and methods for putting them into effect.[16]

The concept of private property forms the controversial nub of the relationship between Hegel and Marx. It also once constituted the key difference in social and political relations between the Soviet bloc and the West. Today as governments across the world privatize – or sell off – their operations, the issue of private property, and the dividing line between civil society and the state, becomes critical. Management theorist Henry Mintzberg points out that the collapse of communism occurred because Soviet bloc states 'were totally out of balance. In those countries, the state controlled an enormous proportion of economic activity. There was little or no countervailing force.' Victory over communism has dangerously shifted the scales. 'The belief that capitalism has triumphed is now throwing the societies of the West out of balance, especially in the United Kingdom and the United States. That the imbalance will favor private rather than state ownership will not help society.'[17]

Shrinking government also involves a related difference between Marx and Hegel. In a strange dialectical reversal, the political right has taken up Marx's battle cry against the parasitic state.[18] Under Marx's ideal of communism, political power would flow into the hands of the associated producers as the state withered away. Today's neo-liberal right intends to make state power the private property of capitalist elites. 'Neo-liberal thinkers see the modern state as an increasingly domineering and malign influence, imposing itself upon society ... They argue that the modern state has grown to become a "New Leviathan".'[19] Government bureaucrats and red tape are prime targets of this new *Zeitgeist*, which seeks to dissolve the separation between civil society and the state. Whether in the West, the Third World, or the former communist republics, the cry is to 'make government more like business'. Reformers advocate 'the perfomance model' that would break up government departments into separate 'businesses' serving various 'client groups'.

> Carry the performance model to its natural limit and you end up with a model that can be called virtual government. Popular in places like the United Kingdom, the United States, and New Zealand, virtual government contains an assumption that the best government is no government. Shed it all, we are told, or at least all that it is remotely possible to shed.[20]

Hegel sought to preserve the institution of private property while Marx urged its overthrow. Avineri writes that 'property was to Hegel human freedom realizing itself in the world of phenomena, and the lack of property prevents man [sic] from participating in this universality'. Instead of confirming the human personality, as Hegel supposed,

Marx argued that property denies individuality and alienates the individual from others.

> For Marx property is not the realization of personality but its negation: not only are the property-less alienated, but so are those who have property. The possession of property by one person necessarily entails its non-possession by another – a dialectical relation totally absent from Hegel. Consequently the problem is not the assurance of property to all – to Marx an inherent impossibility and immanent contradiction – but the abolition of all property relations as such.[21]

Despite Avineri's claim, Hegel was acutely aware that under the capitalist system, 'the possession of property by one person necessarily entails its non-possession by another'. As argued below and in chapter 7, Hegel had little love for capitalist private property. This form of property, as Hegel wrote in *The German Constitution* (1799–1802), was built on 'the *bourgeois* sense, which cares only for an individual and not self-subsistent end and has no regard for the whole'. It was responsible for the 'inequality of resources' that underlies the class system in civil society. 'In these times', Hegel said, referring to poverty, 'the most fearful evil rages unchecked.'[22]

I contend that Hegel would have agreed with Marx's critique of capitalist private property. Yet, unlike Hegel, Marx failed to probe the positive side of private rights; instead, he recommended abolition of property in favour of common ownership of the means of production. Joseph McCarney, an advocate of Marx's view of communism, notes that his

> community of freedom ... is a transformed social world in which people are treated not as rights-bearing citizen consumers but as 'freely associated producers'. The producers retain a public power and public authority for certain collective purposes. But these are not, as in Hegel, the uniquely appropriate focus of emancipated social life.

In contrast with Marx, Hegel's 'community of freedom is the rational state, a political and juridical order whose members encounter one another primarily as citizens and bearers of rights'. Hegel's ideal social order, McCarney adds, 'coexists with the familiar arrangements of civil society: that is, of market capitalism, curbing their excesses and reconciling their contradictions'.[23]

The history of communist regimes implies Hegel's triumph over Marx in one respect, admits McCarney. 'This has to do with [Hegel's] basic insight that freedom has to be embodied as justice, and, hence, as a constitutional system incorporating explicit and effective guarantees of rights.' At the same time, says McCarney, Hegel's social theory violates these fundamental rights through its support of capitalist private property and wage labour. Wage labour amounts to alienation of the worker's bodily powers under the merciless compulsion of market forces. Alienation occurs every moment the worker is employed by the capitalist. 'The self must be active in its own forced alienation – a paradigm case, one might suppose, of Hegelian unfreedom.'[24]

I will discuss Hegel's view of wage labour and its connection with private property in the next chapter. In the mean time, however, it is significant that, in his critique of Hegel, McCarney avoids the question of what would safeguard constitutional rights in the absence of private property. The former Soviet Union had a fine constitution but it was unenforceable in the absence of a source of private power that could compete with the awesome might of the state. For this reason, as Richard Sakwa points out, movements for democracy that developed in the 1980s within the former USSR, and in other communist republics, demanded 'the rebirth of civil society, a sphere independent of and legally guaranteed by the state'. While Marx condemned civil society 'as the site of capitalist exploitation', proponents of democracy argued that 'civil society entails the autonomy of social organisations and the role of individual choice and political pluralism, based on private property'.[25]

Actually, Marx's antagonism toward property rights was equivocal. In his 1875 *Critique of the Gotha Program*, where he outlined two stages of communism, wage labour remains in the first stage. This primary form of communism, recently liberated from the 'womb' of capitalism, resembles the old society because it retains the principle of inequality of possessions among individuals. Workers receive back from society what they contribute in their labour; but their contribution, and hence their income, varies. Some contribute more, and are rich; others contribute less, and are comparatively poor. Property right in the first phase of communism, says Marx, 'is a right of inequality'. While individuals may have personal possessions, ownership of the means of production is limited to the state. As Marx eloquently reveals in a famous passage in the *Critique*, total abolition of private property comes only with the second stage of communism.

> In a higher phase of communist society, after the enslaving subordination of the individual to the division of labor, and therewith

also the antithesis of mental and physical labor has vanished; after labor has become not only a means of life but life's prime want; after the productive forces have also increased with the all-round development of the individual, and all the springs of cooperative wealth flow more abundantly – only then can the narrow horizon of bourgeois right be crossed in its entirety and society inscribe on its banners: 'From each according to his ability, to each according to his need.'[26]

Both modes of communism assume, as R. N. Berki suggests, 'a more highly bureaucratized system than capitalism'. Although Marx rejects Hegel's universal class, there can be no doubt that such a class must be a part of Marx's ideal society. 'Communism means planning and planning involves an increase in the volume of tertiary functions.' Marx's dualistic conception of communism leaves the property question unanswered. The first stage of communism deposits most property in the hands of the state, which resembles a 'universal capitalist', to use Marx's own words from *The Economic and Philosophical Manuscripts of 1844*. Berki asks how such a society could be much of an improvement over capitalism.

> In the *Critique* [*of the Gotha Program*] the lower phase has society, separated from and confronting the producers and consumers, dispensing burdens and benefits according to the 'value' of labour. 'Society' here has its own mind, own will, own rationality, own interest: it is a *buyer* of labour-power and the *seller* of goods for consumption. If this is not 'capitalism' in the most pertinent, profoundest and classical Marxist sense, then I don't know what is .[27]

Ironically, Marx may have developed his idea of the first stage of communism from some passages in Hegel's *Philosophy of Right*. There Hegel speaks of the 'system of needs', or the modern economic system, 'which appears to each individual in the form of *universal and permanent resources* . . . in which through his education and skill, he has an opportunity to share'. In this system, the individual 'is assured of his livelihood, just as the universal resources are maintained and augmented by the income which he earns through his work'. As in Marx's initial stage of communism, inequality is inevitable in Hegel's system of needs.

> The *possibility of sharing* in the universal resources – i.e. of holding *particular* resources – is, however, *conditional* upon one's own immediate basic assets (i.e. capital) on the one hand, and upon one's skill on the other; the latter in turn is conditioned by the former, but

also by contingent circumstances whose variety gives rise to *differences* in the *development* of natural physical and mental ... aptitudes which are already unequal in themselves ... In this sphere of particularity, these differences manifest themselves in every direction and at every level, and, in conjunction with other contingent and arbitrary circumstances, necessarily result in *inequalities in the resources and skills of individuals.*

If Marx's preliminary stage of communism was partially borrowed from Hegel, he ignored the outcome Hegel claimed was its logical result. Inequality in the system of needs, Hegel argued, leads to profound class divisions, even in the presence of a government or 'public authority' which attempts to guarantee each individual a 'share in the universal resources'.[28]

Marx's first phase of communism resembles in some ways the economic and political system of the former Soviet Union and its satellites. In these societies the government attempted to control production and consumption. Far from being all-powerful, these regimes were weak. Bureaucratic rules and regulations were resisted at all levels; inefficiency ruled, and a widespread black market developed. Katherine Verdery, an expert on post-socialist societies, resists labelling the former Soviet countries 'state capitalist'. They were not interested in making a profit, but rather in 'accumulating resources for distribution'. She compares the Soviet state to a lemonade stand. Capitalist lemonade stand owners attempt to make a profit by catering to thirsty customers and outperforming competitors. The Communist Party ran the lemonade stand in order to assert 'paternalistic superiority over its citizens – that is, its capacity to decide who got more lemonade and who got less'.[29]

> In socialism, the point was not profit but the relationship between thirsty persons and the one with the lemonade – the Party center, which appropriated from the producers the various ingredients (lemons, sugar, water) and then mixed the lemonade to reward them with, as it saw fit.[30]

Marx's dramatic account of the second stage of communism in the *Critique of the Gotha Program* begs the question of the nature of property and class relations in the future society. There is no mechanism of transition from the lower to the higher form of communism. 'The lower phase ...', Berki declares, 'is no more than a rationalized capitalism, and the promised *big change*, Marx's vision, is shifted further and further away, into the unconnected historical distance.'[31] We do not know why the lower phase of communism would necessarily give rise to the higher one; it would seem just as likely for it to revert back to the capitalist form – as Hegel might have predicted. Some would say this latter alternative describes exactly the fate of the former Socialist bloc. 'What is socialism?' the joke goes. 'The longest and most painful route from capitalism to capitalism.'[32]

For Hegel, ownership-in-common, as in Marx's highest phase of communism, was a false ideal. Nor is this because Hegel was against equality, as many interpreters suggest. Hegel makes this plain in his 1817-19 *Lectures on Natural Right and Political Science*, given at Heidelberg. These lectures have vital importance for our knowledge of Hegel, since they are the last he gave before declaration of the Karlsbad Decrees in 1819. As discussed in chapter 5, the Decrees established a regime of censorship and terror across the German states, and made it impossible for anyone to speak freely. The existence of Hegel's lectures was unknown until the early 1980s, when they were published in Germany. The Heidelberg lectures offer a damaging analysis of capitalism that is muted in the published version of the *Philosophy of Right*. They are likely very close, however, to the account of law and private property offered in the lectures by Gans that Marx attended in Berlin about twenty years later, when the fear of censorship had lifted somewhat. I will refer to these lectures often in the sections which follow. Regarding equality of property rights, Hegel avers that: 'Each of us has, so we are told, equality of right, properly speaking in regard to the whole earth; such a distribution is immensely difficult, and with each newborn child the division should really be undertaken again.' The problem is that in modern economies property is about exclusion of others from ownership, so that property rights necessarily involve inequality. 'All have equal rights since each has equal abstract right in regard to the world; but abstract right must be realized, and in the process of realization right enters the sphere of contingency, e.g. of whim and need, and thus the sphere of inequality.'[33]

Hegel observes that access to wealth – the 'universal resource' – depends on education, 'on one's capability to satisfy one's needs by aptitude'. Human beings must 'train themselves and give themselves aptitude'. Because of this universal requirement for education, Hegel argues that education should be freely available to everyone 'and [should] not [be] confined to individual classes or conferred by birth' – a condition, of course, hardly met in most advanced industrial countries today. '[T]he possibility of educating oneself . . . calls for a capital resource; and the possession of this is again something contingent, a contingency that must, however, be sublated by the state.'[34]

In an important, though neglected, essay, C. B. Macpherson pointed out that property is narrowly understood as the right to exclude others from a thing. Yet property also involves the universal right not to be excluded.[35] Hegel analysed this dialectical truth in the *Phenomenology of Spirit*. The value of a thing, he wrote, 'lies in being *mine*, which all others acknowledge and keep themselves away from. But just in being acknowledged lies rather my equality, my identity with everyone – the opposite of exclusion'.[36] In other words, a true system of property rights involves equality and mutual recognition among all members.

The implications of this radical conception of property rights are slowly unfolding in modern jurisprudence. For example, anti-smoking laws which prevent smokers from damaging the health of others by polluting the air – the universal element which we all breathe – are actually property laws, in Hegel's sense. As Hegel himself points out (though he doubtless was unaware of the health issues involved) smoking is a 'habit and a self-imposed need'; breathing is a universal requirement. By preventing access to clean air, second-hand smoke endangers our bodies, which are, for Hegel, the primary sites of the right to property. Similarly, anti-pollution laws aimed at transnational corporations are also based on the right of private property. Any type of environmental regulation which attempts to preserve the universal, whether it is an endangered species or a vital part of the ecosystem, is a property law.

> I can never take possession of something universal; it is mine only so long as I have it. So [it] is with breathing the air. The sea is a universal possession and is for the use of all because no one else is excluded by my using it.[37]

The issue raised by environmental laws is that inappropriate use of a universal resource may result in the exclusion of others from that resource. As Macpherson argues, such use is a fundamental violation of the right to property. An oil tanker break-up can ruin a nation's coastline and destroy uncounted wildlife, thus preventing access by citizens to the natural beauty of the sea, and its resources. States certainly make ownership claims on bodies of water, and set fishing limits and other restrictions. These, however, are not property laws, since property should concern only individual rights. 'The basic factor here is the power relationship. All nations lay claim to right over the sea to the furthest limits at which their guns can protect them.'[38]

Since the nineteenth century in the USA and other countries, corporations have been treated as persons under the law. This effectively transforms property rights from something enjoyed by individuals into rights enjoyed by an artificial entity, one with access to far more resources, including an unlimited lifespan, than are enjoyed by individuals. A key precedent for this was the early Christian church, which was recognized by the Roman state as a legitimate corporate body in the Edict of Milan of 313. 'Under the protection of the state the Church thus emerged as a group-entity, a legal *persona*, capable of holding rights independent of its individual members.'[39] Corporate power now rivals that attained by the medieval church. Global trade agreements have granted corporations enhanced powers to overstep national boundaries; these are unavailable to ordinary citizens. Extension of unlimited property rights to corporations, warns social critic William Greider, may reduce citizens 'to a political position resembling that of serfs or small landholders who followed church or nobility in the feudal system. They will be utterly dependent on the fortunes of the corporate regimes, the dukes and barons flying their national flag.'[40] Wide corporate rights, which render national laws impotent, constitute a clear violation of Hegel's concept of property. Hegel agreed that collectives, such as limited liability corporations or the church, may hold property.[41] But the ability to hold and enjoy property necessarily places the corporation directly under the power of the rational state.[42] The position of the corporation in Hegel's system is discussed further below.

According to Hegel, police and bureaucrats have to determine the limits within which the rights of private property can be exercised without injuring the rights of others. The powers of the state in this area must be carefully monitored and controlled, 'for otherwise the police can interfere ad infinitum in the use made of private property. Apart from this, no limit can be set with which this supervision must be confined.'[43]

On one hand, a system of strictly imposed equality in property would stultify and oppress the creative forces of civil society. On the other, unlimited property rights lead to toxic extremes of wealth and poverty. The contradiction between equal property rights and the evils of capitalist private property will be sublated (*aufgehoben*), Hegel proposed, through a dialectical process that abolishes the irrational elements of both, and retains their rational core. This process takes place within Hegel's corporation, a chief vehicle in his proposed solution to poverty.

In contrast with the modern transnational business enterprise, Hegel's corporation operates within democratic constraints imposed by the state. Management in the typical modern corporation is answerable only to the stockholders. The managers of Hegel's corporation must keep in mind the interests of the workers, and those of the communities within which they operate.

The democratic corporation

Hegel saw poverty as an ethical as well as an economic dilemma endemic to bourgeois society. Poverty strips the individual of the chance to enjoy the rights and freedoms of civil society, and demeans him or her in the eyes of others. 'Poverty', Hegel writes, 'is a condition in civil society which is unhappy and forsaken on all sides.'[44] The worst examples of this 'cancer', as Hegel called it, existed in industrial England, where the poor were left on the streets and little children laboured in factory towns across the land. '[A]s factory workers, who always have a single abstract type of work, have great difficulty in switching to another kind of work, and factories are easily ruined by [changing] fashions and . . . [other] contingent factors . . . poverty easily arises.'[45] According to Hegel, both rich and poor are afflicted with a 'rabble' mentality by this social sickness. The poor lose their respect for society and become resentful, filled with 'an inner indignation'. The wealthy think everything can be purchased with money – from commodities to human flesh and morality.

Money, says Hegel, becomes capital when it is placed in the service of making more money. Capital may take the form of factors of production, such as labour and machinery; or it may appear as finance capital, devoted to the exchange of the surplus of one industry for the surplus of another.[46] The nature of capital remains the same today as when Hegel described it. 'Capital', writes Greider, referring to the global economy of the 1990s,

> is basically the money accumulated from past enterprise, savings from profits or wages, the stored wealth that is available to finance new enterprise. Physical capital exists as factories and machines;

finance capital exists as wealth invested in enterprise through loans or stock shares or other financial instruments. This exchange – the past lending to the future, old money invested in new ventures – is the energy core of capitalism, the transaction across time that enables the creation of multiplying new wealth.[47]

Hegel observes that the capitalist economic system, based on avarice, has as its outcome the impoverishment of a large part of the population and the corruption of society. As Marx famously observed in *Capital*, '"If money . . . comes into the world with a congenital bloodstain on one cheek", capital comes dripping from head to toe, from every pore, with blood and dirt.'[48] The spread of the victorious capitalist system across the previously protected former communist states, and its growing presence in every sector of the world economy, has had results Hegel might have expected. Huge contrasts of wealth and poverty have erupted worldwide. Corruption in business and politics has become commonplace.

> Something like five thousand Italian businessmen and politicians have been formally accused in the past few years. American politics has experienced so many money scandals that they now seem routine. Businessmen sometimes grumble, in a low voice, about the bribery extracted by political leaders in the poorest nations – the *guanxi* in China, the military partnerships required to do business in Indonesia – but this is not peculiar to the poor. Every major capital is regularly scandalized by more sophisticated versions of the same thing.[49]

Hegel's instrument for taming the rabble mentality of the wealthy and restoring the dignity of the worker is the democratic corporation – an instrument, I shall argue, that retains its relevance in our own era of globalization.

My interpretation of Hegel's corporation is controversial. For some commentators, Hegel's corporation is a throwback to the feudal guild, a wishful, anachronistic recapitulation of a vanished way of life.[50] For many others, the corporation is part of Hegel's attempt to create an organic order in which the individual is subsumed by the whole, instead of the whole emanating from all individuals. Hegel feared the spread of democracy would ultimately leave the individual isolated and defenceless. According to proponents of this view, such as Peter Singer, Hegel did not envision a free democratic process within the corporation. Instead, he constructed a model in which corporations send appointed officials to the estates or parliament. Universal suffrage was unnecessary since only essential, large-scale interests rather than individual citizens 'are suitable for representation'. Democratic processes that might work in a small community break down in large nation states. An ordinary citizen's vote has so little influence, comments Singer, 'that there is widespread apathy, and power falls into the hands of a small caucus of particular interests'.[51] For Singer, and many other commentators, Hegel's corporation offers a form of 'virtual representation'. This was Edmund Burke's proposal that the majority of people in society are best represented by those who are superior in wisdom, expertise and wealth.[52] As Steven Smith puts it, 'Hegel is less concerned that the members of the estates be selected by universal suffrage than that they be tied to their constituents by common needs, interests, and experience.'[53]

Although my view of Hegel's corporation differs from most interpreters, I will show that there is plenty of textual support for it, especially in the Heidelberg *Lectures on Natural Right and Political Science*. Moreover, recent commentators have provided an account of Hegel's corporation that, in certain respects, is not dissimilar from my own. In addition, we saw in chapter 5 that Eduard Gans, Hegel's intimate colleague and follower, offered a theory of class struggle and the corporation in his 1832–3 lectures at the University of Berlin. This theory is close to the one I suggest Hegel puts forward. Norbert Waszek speculates that Gans's theory must have had an impact on Marx, who took his courses on law in the late 1830s. According to Waszek, Gans perceived the Saint-Simonian idea of workers' associations 'in analogy with a stock corporation of which the workers were supposed to be the stockholders. Although the workers were said to *possess* the stocks, they were not granted full discretionary powers of disposition.' Gans was dissatisfied, says Waszek, with the Saint-Simonians' casual treatment of private property, but he found their idea of workers' corporations very compelling as a solution for poverty in civil society. Waszek concludes that Gans's

> aim is twofold: a) he hopes to improve the material conditions of the poor by means of an institution strong enough to replace previous domination by effective participation; b) he intends to raise an atomized 'rabble' to be an organic part of the ethical life of the state.[54]

Hegel's corporation, I suggest, is an independent centre of organized power and enjoys influence within the state through electoral representation. (The machinery of representation in Hegel's state is discussed further below, and in the concluding chapter.) A 'legally recognized, state sanctioned organization', the corporation is 'derived from the usual trade and vocational groupings within the community'.[55] It brings together individuals from particular segments of the 'business class' – professionals, industrial workers, manufacturers and traders – in an effort to improve prospects and working conditions for its members. 'After the family,' writes Stephen Houlgate, 'the corporations represent the second form of genuinely ethical life in which individuals find freedom in a willing union with others.'[56] The business class belongs to the system of classes in civil society, which includes the agricultural class (farmers, peasants, nobles) and the universal class (government bureaucrats). Over time, the agricultural class grows very close in nature to the business class and loses its autonomy.

> With us, the agricultural class has also joined the business class, and the main thing is no longer to preserve the farmer's [means of] satisfaction. Instead the farmer has an eye to what is most profitable in order to exchange it for other people's products – [an eye] in other words, [to] the kinds of produce for which human labor is least needed since he no longer regards the people in his service as belonging to his family.[57]

In contrast with Marx, who foretold the destruction of classes under communism, Hegel felt that classes would have a role in the ideal state. His political community would not consist, as does Marx's, of a nebulous jumble of individuals with identical (non)occupations. Communism, averred Marx in the *Critique of the Gotha Program*,[58] 'recognizes no class differences because everyone is only a worker like everyone else'. For Hegel, social class is the pathway to meaningful connection with the universal. Accordingly, Smith writes that it 'introduces a sense of esprit de corps into the "playground" of civil society by means of the sentiments of professional pride and integrity'.[59] Class is the social bulwark against dictatorship and terror. Writes Hegel:

> Human beings must resolve to be something particular in the class relationship, they must assign themselves to a class status. In maintaining themselves within the restricting confines of class status, they confer on themselves the essential moment of actuality, a moment that is necessary in order for them to attain their freedom.

Hegel's concept excludes hierarchy between classes, with its dangers of snobbery and social superiority. Each class has a functional position in the state that makes it equal to others in power and influence. Social class allows the individual to become part of society through her own 'activity, industry, skill, and conformity to right; and through this process of mediating with the universal, to *be* something and to be *recognized* both in one's own eyes and the eyes of others'. Hegel remarks that even casual chatter between strangers rests ultimately on the foundation of class: '[P]eople ask what someone is, i.e., what status a person has, and someone with no status is nothing'.[60] Here Hegel means to remind us of the Terror when, as he wrote in the *Phenomenology*, classless 'universal freedom' signified 'death':

> a death too which has no inner significance or filling, for what is negated is the empty point of the absolutely free self. It is thus the coldest and meanest of all deaths, with no more significance than cutting off the head of a cabbage or swallowing a mouthful of water.[61]

The classless society Marx delineated held dangers of which he seemed unaware, despite his profound knowledge of Hegel's account of the Terror. He would have been repelled by the idea of creating communism in a country as backward as Russia was in 1917. Verdery observes that 'the entire Bolshevik experiment' resulted from the application of 'a theory created for conditions that did not obtain [which] broke down existing structures and produced more chaos than order'.[62] In Hegel's analysis, liquidation of social class leads to terror, regardless of the maturity of the society in which this occurs.

Thus, the cold and mean death suffered by victims of the Terror was also experienced by those cut down by Stalin – the waves of old Bolshevik 'enemies of the state' who went to the gallows or were shot in the back of the head; ill-fated engineers and technicians who forgot that thousands more could be trained to replace the ones executed; ten-year-old children of condemned NKVD men who meekly admitted their 'fascist' past; five million liquidated 'rich peasants' in the countryside; almost half the officer corps of the Soviet armed forces. Stalin achieved Marx's dream of eliminating professionals and bureaucracy, only they had to be destroyed over and over again. During the long years of Soviet terror, writes Alex de Jonge,

> [a] sense of the transitory quality of life within the danger zone was to be found everywhere. Soviet banknotes ceased to bear the signature of bank officials since their signatories disappeared too quickly. Offices in the *Izvestiya* building no longer had the names of

senior staff members painted on their doors. Streets were constantly having their names changed since streets had to be called something – unlike the public parks, which tended to remain nameless after the disgrace of the leader they were originally named after.[63]

Among the dominant myths about Hegel's political theory is the notion that he is not concerned with what ought to be; his philosophy is believed to deal only with what already exists. As Steven Smith observes, the 'end of history' thesis leads to the interpretation of Hegel as a conservative defender of the established order. Thus, for Karl Popper, 'Hegel's identification of the rational with the actual results in a doctrine of pure power politics where "might is right".' Hegel's dictum was 'an apology not just for Prussianism but for modern totalitarianism with its irrational forms of "state worship" and its "renaissance of tribalism"'.[64]

Another of Hegel's most influential critics, Friedrich Nietzsche, contended that Hegel's equation of the present with 'the perfection of world history'

> would have the effect of turning modern men into mere epigones, with nothing great or noble left to do. What Hegel ought to have said, then, is that everything after him was merely to be regarded as a musical coda of the great historical rondo – or rather, as simply superfluous.[65]

Contrary to these critics, Hegel was aware that his corporation was not yet a reality. In the external bourgeois state – the state based on need – there is plenty of scope for improving things. The evil represented by poverty provides strong reasons for revolutionary change, and the democratic corporation is precisely an instrument for getting rid of poverty. 'Evil should not happen, and there should be an authority that prevents it. Here we are talking about what *should* be, and this is the standpoint pertaining to the organization of the state based on need.'[66]

According to another widespread misreading, Hegel was against democracy. Even a fairly knowledgeable commentator such as Perry Anderson can contend that Hegel's 'liberalism was not democratic, of course, since it feared popular rule and rejected universal suffrage'.[67] As we saw in chapter 4, Hegel supported the radical democratic project initiated by Tom Paine and other leaders of the American Revolution. He is clear about this in the Heidelberg lectures. 'Political freedom', notes Hegel, 'is very important, and where it is lacking, where it is suppressed, the state declines.'[68] Like the authors of the *Federalist Papers*, Alexander Hamilton and James Madison, however, Hegel recognized that direct democracy was unworkable outside a very small community. A 'thorough going, complete democracy', he declares, where 'each individual shares in all rights of government and administration ... is not viable in a relatively large and civilized state'.[69] States governed by pure democratic rule were subject to the influence of organized factions, and to the tyranny of the majority.

Hegel's corporation is a completely democratic mini-state which mediates the will of the individual with the universal concerns of government. 'Corporations', notes Hegel, 'provide everyone with a state in which they can be active according to their own concrete being.'[70] In fact, Tom Paine could not have managed things better. As Hegel puts it, 'this is the democratic principle, that the individual should share in the government of local communities, corporations and guilds, which have within themselves the form of the universal'.[71] Harry Brod contends that Hegel rejects Burkean 'virtual representation', where broad interests and not individuals are represented in government. The task of corporate representation in the state

> is to ensure identification of the citizens with the political process, to be the institutionalization of the citizen's active role in politics. Hegel sides with the liberal concept of representation in insisting that what is being represented is not 'unattached interests', but 'people who have interests'.[72]

Directors and managers of corporations are selected, Hegel recommends, 'generally [by] a mixture of popular elections by the commonality . . . (or class or those having the same class status) and a separate system of appointment by higher authority'. Hegel cautioned that the problem with the old guilds was that the leadership 'chose their own successors', which gave 'rise to an aristocracy'. Every member of the corporation must be involved in elections. At the same time, the corporation must be responsible to the larger community. Accordingly, managers are 'confirmed in their office by senior officials', and some corporate appointments are made directly by the state. 'The point of view here is that the executive power brings these spheres back within the universal and must take action against their infringements on one another and on the universal.'[73] Newspapers, journals and other elements of the mass media themselves make up self-governed corporations and should 'enjoy . . . indeterminate freedom'.[74]

Despite the dominance of non-democratic, privately owned multinational corporations in advanced industrial societies, there already exist corporate models which in some respects resemble Hegel's. Co-operatively owned enterprises are common, 'whether controlled formally by their suppliers (as in agricultural co-operatives), by their customers (as in mutual insurance companies or co-operative retail chains), or by their employees (as in some commercial enterprises, such as Avis)'. What Mintzberg calls non-owned organizations are also plentiful. They are

> controlled by self-selecting and often very diverse boards of directors. These not-for-profit organizations are often referred to as nongovernmental organizations . . . but they are also non-business and noncooperative organizations . . . Indeed, we are surrounded by non-owned organizations. Among them are many of our universities . . . hospitals, charity organizations, and volunteer and activist organizations (the Red Cross and Greenpeace, for example).

Some of the world's great newspapers are run more or less according to the Hegelian model, and thus escape limitations on press freedom – whether imposed by governments or business – that Hegel worried about.

> Can any democratic society afford to have all newspapers in the private sector, especially when they are concentrated in a few hands that can exercise great political influence should they choose? Other models of ownership can be found, indeed in some of the most prestigious newspapers in the world – for example, nonownership of *The Guardian* in England and multiple cooperative ownership (journalists and readers, alongside some institutions) of *Le Monde* in France.[75]

For Hegel, the democratic corporation – which also includes churches, municipal and regional governments, and other independent institutions in civil society – mediates between the citizen and the nation state. Hegel was not against universal suffrage; rather, he was against the atomism implied in a single vote. As Howard Kainz notes in a recent study, 'Hegel was in harmony with liberal democratic theory in his emphasis on participation by citizens in government; but he was sharply at odds with democratic theorists regarding the mode of such participation.'[76] The best way to ensure that the individual's interests are represented is to apply leverage to government decision-making through organized corporate voting blocs. Voting as a mass of disconnected individuals makes it easy for élites to subvert democracy and act against the interests of the people.

> [D]eputies are chosen not by an [agglomeration] dispersed into atomic units, but in the articulated system made up of their different associations ... and thus by the vote of a commonality ... from which no actual citizen ... is excluded, regardless of means. The right to choose deputies and the political action this represents is not, in consequence, a single, recurrent action for the electors, nor is it handed over to single individuals as such but is essentially entrusted to local communities ... and other duly constituted associations.... Furthermore, there is such a close connection between the estates and the constitution of the whole that a free attitude on the part of electors and also a free and constitutionally minded attitude on the part of the deputies is only possible if the *rights of individuals* are safeguarded ... and if the *rights of the particular local communities and interests* are safeguarded by the free establishment of civic authorities and self-administering bodies.[77]

In Hegel's ideal state, citizens would elect members of parliament from among colleagues in their corporations[78] rather than – as with all modern democracies – from among candidates selected by political parties on the basis of electoral constituencies. Of course, spatial representation did make sense when all members of a particular trade or profession worked in the same place, but now it has lost any semblance of rationality. 'To be sure, the citizens of a city can ... be divided from the point of view of the public authority according to districts, but this is an external, purely spatial relationship – the basis here is the lifeless numerical one.'[79] Under the modern US democratic system, notes Howard Kainz,[80] '"control" over the federal government by average American working people is often reduced to perilous choices, every few years, between congressional or presidential candidates neither of whom is thought satisfactory'. The atomization of democracy in the late twentieth century has corrupted politics and alienated citizens from their own political institutions, as Hegel might have predicted. 'The reflective spirit of our times, this atomistic spirit, the spirit that consists in taking pride in one's individual interests and not in what is communal is harmful ... Through this spirit Germany disintegrated into atoms and the empire went into decline.'[81]

If Hegel's democratic corporation is an institution for the future, it is also one with deep roots in the past. Hegel was impatient with the suggestion, originating with Tom Paine, that democracy was a novel invention of the modern world. 'Representation is so deeply interwoven with the essence of the feudal constitution . . . that we may call it the silliest of notions to suppose it an invention of the most recent times.'[82] Hegel's corporation resembles the feudal guild, an organization which represented the democratic ethos of 'mutuality and solidarity'.[83] Guild structure based on 'common will and consent' – i.e. the notions of exchange and contract – was a subject of early German and Roman law, as both Hegel and Gans were aware. In fact, the greatest authority on the guild was the German scholar, Johannes Althussius, who wrote his *Systematic Analysis of Politics* in the early seventeenth century.[84] His definition of politics is echoed in Hegel's conception of the democratic corporation.

> Politics is the art of associating . . . persons with a view to establishing, nourishing and preserving social life together. Hence they are called *sumbiotike* (cohabiters). The first proposition of politics, therefore, is *consociatio*; in this the cohabiters . . . by an explicit or tacit pact, undertake mutual obligation to one another to communicate to each other those things that are useful and necessary for the maintenance and sharing of social life . . . These [cohabiters] are, therefore, mutual helpers who, joined and associated together by a contractual bond, shared those of their resources which are helpful for the commodious conduct of the life of the spirit and body; they are sharers, participants in a communion.[85]

For Hegel the guild structure of the late feudal era represented 'the high tide of civil life; enjoyment lay in what was communal and people did not amuse themselves for themselves but in the community'. Today the atomization process Hegel feared has greatly accelerated, the communal spirit of the guilds grown more remote. Hegel's remarks about the dangers of individualism apply with added force to modern capitalism. 'Now this [communal] spirit is undermined, so that people are ashamed of their class, are unwilling to be seen as members of it, and take pride in themselves alone.'[86] Nevertheless, the guild structure has survived in the form of co-operatives, trade unions, business groupings, learned societies, professional associations and not-for-profit organizations. The structure of the modern university – itself an invention of Hegel's Germany – with representation drawn from various corporate groupings, including students, staff and faculty, may be the clearest modern example of the democratic ideal represented by the guild. Nor is Hegel's vision of the relationship between the state and the corporation without reality today. As Steven Smith avers, the administrative set-up recommended by Hegel – where corporate organizations mediate between the individual and government – resembles 'the contemporary experience of Scandinavia, France, and Britain, with their highly structured relations between interest organizations and administrative bodies'.[87]

In his remarkable *Guilds and Civil Society in European Political Thought*, Antony Black emphasizes that Hegel's organic concept of the corporation sought 'to give guild values and aspirations a central place in political theory'. Hegel is among the very few social thinkers who 'acknowledged that solidarity and exchange – the poles around which the values of guild and civil society, respectively, rotate – are not opposites but complementary and attempted to weave these together into a texture as tough and complex as that of urban society itself'. Black laments that the work-group ethic, as propounded by Hegel, has lost out to 'the values of market exchange' in liberal democratic society. 'The problem is that today all those groups which in real life bind people together in so many ways are regarded as optional, based on taste or convenience.' In an eloquent concluding passage to which Hegel would have warmly assented, Black outlines the virtues of a community of labour.

> Working together or sharing a craft creates a specific type of relationship. It forges bonds of a unique kind, less intense and pervasive than those of personal love or friendship, but truly human bonds none the less. It is an end in itself. Its merits may be sung but not listed. This does not mean that the work group is an absolute, any more than the nation-state: it can go wrong. But as a category of social life, it has its own unique and irreplaceable place in human affairs.[88]

In the past twenty years the guild principles of mutual solidarity and communal support have come under renewed, heavy attack by politicians and ideologues of the New Right (also called neo-liberalism or neo-conservatism). New Right supporters 'are committed to the view that political life, like economic life, is (or ought to be) a matter of individual freedom and initiative ... Accordingly, a *laissez-faire* or free-market society is the key objective along with a "minimal state".'[89] Margaret Thatcher's Tories and Ronald Reagan's White House aimed their guns at union power, and transnational corporations are eager to 'privatize' the restricted range of non-market relationships still possible within the public sphere of health, transportation, communications, and education. Universities, for example, are shedding full-time instructors in favour of part-timers; regular staff are displaced by contracted-out services offered by large corporations; students are encouraged to interact with home-based computers rather than with professors and other students on campus; faculty, staff, and student participation in university governance is endangered by neo-liberal partisans on big-business-dominated boards of directors. New ordinances and statutes violate the right of the poor to free use of communal space. Public space is 'hardening', and the 'public' is being reconfigured into a private spatial dimension where people are considered only as mobile, circulating consumers.[90]

A similar drama unfolded in Hegel's time. The guilds were selectively destroyed across Europe by the rise of industrial capitalism. French revolutionaries banned corporations in 1791, and outlawed any attempt by workers to come together in order to improve working conditions and wages. The English also cruelly proscribed trade unions until the 1830s. Hegel's discussion of events in the mid-nineteenth century might have been meant for these days of world triumph for the individualistic and libertarian economic model pioneered in the USA.

> The atomistic principle – that each individual fends merely for himself and does not bother about a communal [end], the principle of leaving it to each and every one whether one wishes to join a certain class, not examining a person's suitability from a political point of view since after all (as we are told by those who favor this principle) someone whose work fails to find any favor will shift to another line of business – such a principle abandons the individual to contingency.[91]

In Hegel's approach to politics, community (in the form of social classes and corporations) comes before individual self-interest. Communal purpose must be paramount when individuals join a particular class. He criticized the appointment of nobles to important positions in the bureaucracy regardless of the individual's ability, as was done in many European countries. Equally, Hegel was against an individual obtaining leadership of a corporation simply on the strength of his or her family connections.

Hegel called for rebirth of the corporation. The human heart could not withstand the isolating principle of individualism forever. Allen W. Wood writes that,

> Hegel's conception of the corporation in civil society can be seen as quite radical. Perhaps it is even utopian, unworkable in the context

of a market economy. No doubt in actual market economies some of the functions Hegel assigns to corporations do sometimes get fulfilled for some people – by professional associations, corporate firms, or labor unions. But no institution fulfills them in the combined and systematic way a Hegelian corporation is supposed to.[92]

In Hegel's ideal work environment an *esprit de corps* will develop. Sharing 'the same vocation, [the same] concerns and interests', its members develop a communal point of view. Acting as a 'second family' the corporation provides stable resources and employment to its members. Workers in the corporation are protected from poverty and instability of work relations. The need disappears for the individual to make an impressive display for the benefit of others, since membership in a corporation guarantees social recognition. Even the capitalist will be educated. In an effort to gain social recognition and respect, Hegel suggests, 'wealth in fulfilling the duty it owes to association, loses the ability to provoke arrogance in its possessor and envy in others; rectitude also receives the true recognition and honour which are due it'.[93]

The democratic corporation, Stephen Houlgate suggests, brings Hegel close to Marx. Both are concerned with finding individual fulfilment and freedom, and both are convinced 'that an economy based entirely on self-interested pursuit of profit will end up preventing large numbers of people from enjoying such freedom and welfare'. Again, however, the contrast between Hegel and Marx remains. 'Hegel's analysis shows that bourgeois private property is a fundamental freedom,' Houlgate avers. Private ownership, wage labour and money do not necessarily lead to economic crises, and Hegel 'thus does not think that production and distribution need to be taken out of private hands altogether and into public ownership'. Hegel turns his back on 'the forcible, revolutionary restructuring of relations of production'.[94]

Most commentators agree that Hegel also differed from Marx in regard to the fate of the working class. While Marx saw the proletariat as a revolutionary force that would overthrow capitalism and establish communist society, Hegel is supposed to have excluded the working class from his ideal state. (Alan Ryan is among those few commentators who recognize that workers are included in Hegel's business class.[95]) Yet Hegel's 1818–19 Heidelberg lectures make clear that factory workers are certainly part of the business classes that form corporations, and are, therefore, also members of the ideal Hegelian state. 'The aim of civil society', Hegel observes, referring to the plight of the poor, 'is the actualization of freedom. The fact that human beings have the right to live means that they have the positive, fulfilled right: the reality of freedom should be an essential condition.' Any exclusion of one group from the state in favour of another risks creating a system of castes, 'which deprive human beings of the freedom to rise above' the class relationships into which they were born. 'No personal advantages can raise the barrier of the castes, and subjective contingency and the consciousness of freedom cannot take effect. In the Roman state too we see the abrupt distinctions between patricians and plebeians, resulting in constant inner strife.'[96]

Of course, Hegel knew that in the industrial societies of his time, in which the capitalist revolution raged unchecked, the abrupt distinctions he warned against certainly existed. The result was 'constant inner strife', or what Marx would later call class struggle. In fact, Hegel talks about many forms of class struggle. He mentions the differences between the business classes and landlords over the cost of agricultural products – an issue that shaped nineteenth-century British politics. This conflict, he writes, 'puts an end to the equilibrium between the different classes, and frequently for long periods'. Later Marx would argue that the split between landowners and capitalists over this issue provided the opening for the Factory Acts, which regulated the working day and put limits on children's labour. According to Hegel, the powerful 'commercial class' of bankers and financiers, allied with international elements of the manufacturing class, often favours trade agreements with other nations that jeopardize the interests of the domestic manufacturing class of capitalists and industrial workers. Today's debate over 'globalization', as we shall see, concerns this particular form of class struggle. Class struggle breaks out within the manufacturing class itself, as capitalist and worker are pitted against one another. Hegel (vainly as it turned out) called for state intervention to ensure that 'no interests of the one class may be exalted at the expense of those of another class'. Writes Hegel,

> If one class sells its goods in distant lands, the individual members of the class cannot clearly see how their affairs are going, and the state must see to it. [It is] the same with the introduction of new machinery, as a result of which manual workers lose their jobs. The community must facilitate the introduction of machines, but at the same time provide for those whose livelihood has disappeared.[97]

The forms of class struggle delineated by Hegel partially characterize the new globalized economy after the fall of communism. Moreover, just as the nineteenth-century state shrank from its duty to prevent the worst excesses of capital, modern governments claim impotence in the face of the global capitalist revolution. Greider describes the current global system as a 'galaxy of four broad, competing power blocs – each losing or gaining influence over events'. Labour, made up of 'organized union workers and workers in general', is losing in the struggle because it is confined to a fixed national or regional base. Capital can choose its workforce from a number of national labour markets, forcing workers to compete against each other. In a similar manner, capitalist firms in Hegel's period took advantage of workers' spatial isolation and lack of communication to turn them against one another. Governments, the second power bloc mentioned by Greider, have relinquished control to international markets, often functioning as 'mere salesmen, promoting the fortunes of their own multinationals in the hope that this will provide a core prosperity that keeps everyone afloat'. This is a losing strategy, as evidenced by falling wages and high unemployment in the advanced industrial heartland of the world system. In addition, the poor fiscal health of governments, caused by falling tax revenues, is putting pressure on the institutions of the welfare state designed 'to ameliorate the harsh inequalities of industrial capitalism'.[98]

Transnational corporations make up the third power bloc in Greider's scheme of the world economy. These firms 'are, collectively, the muscle and brains of this new system, the engineers who are designing the brilliant networks of new relationships'. They have loosened ties with their home countries, and have overtaken in importance firms with a strictly national base. In other respects, however, the multinationals resemble Hegel's domestic capitalists. They are pitted against the interests of the fourth power bloc, finance capital – what Greider calls the Robespierre of the global revolution. Despite their large size, multinationals are vulnerable to the whims of finance markets and have paid a very heavy price. 'Their stocks were hammered, their management ousted, tens of thousands of employees discarded. Behind corporate facades, the anxiety is genuine.'[99]

Finance capital, like Hegel's commercial class, specializes in trading stocks, bonds, currencies and other forms of financial paper. Its influence has exploded in the global economy. International bank loans reached $3.6 trillion in 1991.

> Foreign-exchange trading totaled more than $1.2 trillion a day by the early 1990s, compared to only $640 billion a day as recently as

1989. Since financial traders usually move in and out of different currencies in order to buy or sell a nation's stocks or bonds, this furious pace of currency exchange reflects the magnifying presence of borderless finance.

As in Hegel's day, the commercial class is relatively concentrated. Most financial trading is done by

> the world's largest thirty to fifty banks and a handful of major brokerages that do the actual trades in behalf of investor clients – wealthy individuals and the various pools of private capital, smaller banks and brokerages, pension funds, mutual funds and so on – as well as the banks' own portfolios.

Similar to Hegel's commercial class, modern finance capital is concerned only with 'maximizing the return on capital without regard to national identity or political or social consequences'. Writes Greider,

> Financial investors monitor and punish corporations or whole industrial sectors if their returns weaken. Finance disciplines governments or even entire regions of the globe if those places appear to be creating impediments to profitable enterprise or unpleasant surprises for capital . . . [T]he global financiers also adhere to their own rough version of egalitarian values: they will turn on anyone, even their own home country's industry and government, if the defense of free capital seems to require it.[100]

Hegel's democratic corporation rests on an analysis of property and the labour process very close in some respects to that contributed after him by Marx. Private property is the vital underpinning of the democratic corporation. Nevertheless, Hegel's (and Gans's) conception of property is as distant from bourgeois property relations as is Marx's 'possession in common of the land and the means of production produced by labour itself'.[101] According to Hegel, the corporation sits uneasily on a hotly contested site of contradictory property rights. The orbit of this internal struggle helps bring about the radical reform of civil society and the coming of the 'state of freedom' that Hegel, following Schiller, saw as the necessary foundation for the full flowering of the human spirit. We shall look at this dynamic process, and its relevance for our own time, in the concluding two chapters.

7 • Labour and Civil Society

Introduction

The institutional structures of Hegel's rational state are in sharp contrast to the homogeneous world of Marx's communism. Marx avoided drafting utopian blueprints for the future.[1] Perhaps Hegel was more daring. As I contend in this, and the concluding chapter, Hegel may have ventured further than Marx into the new world of struggle that was becoming visible through the smoke of nineteenth-century capitalism.

I begin by examining Francis Fukuyama's 'end of history' thesis. Fukuyama's view is defective, but it highlights a central Hegelian argument: the liberal democratic state contains the basic outlines of a future rational order. Hegel, in my view, was not saying that all human questions have been foreclosed by an overarching grand theory. Fixed grammatical language structures place no limit on what can be said by those who use them. Similarly, Hegel's rational state places no restraints upon what is possible in a new society. To borrow Habermas's formulation,[2] Hegel's project affords only the initial conditions for a way of life that participants themselves will have to agree upon.

Nor does Hegel's state resolve all forms of conflict. Instead, it institutionalizes class antagonisms in a governing structure that allows for bargaining and compromise. The democratic corporation plays a crucial role. Its fate is already being decided in our own period, I believe, by a struggle over property rights between the two sides of Hegel's business class – workers and capitalists. As outlined in the middle sections of this chapter, the battle may be illuminated by Hegel's labour theory of property, which, as I envision it, marks a radical departure from the bourgeois concept.

My interpretation of Hegel's theory of property is unusual and (I hope) interesting. It addresses key points in Hegel's concept of property that possibly have not been adequately noted by commentators. I want to stimulate the reader to think of new ways in which the relationship between Hegel and Marx may be seen. I am not suggesting that my version of Hegel's property theory contains the only possible interpretation of the connection between the two thinkers. Probably I am not likely to convince all, or even most, readers. None the less, such sceptical readers may find my account valuable and this will perhaps stimulate them to offer their own alternative interpretations.

Jürgen Habermas submits an intriguing alternative to the concept of civil society in Hegel and Marx. I explore Habermas's model of civil society below and consider its implications for Hegel's democratic project.

The end of history

In *The End of History and the Last Man*, Francis Fukuyama used Hegel's concept of recognition (which I discussed in chapter 1) to argue that the thread of history has reached its limit in the institutions of Western capitalism. Influenced by Alexander Kojève's interpretation of Hegel, Fukuyama maintained that extension of civic and human rights to the individual 'by the contemporary liberal democratic state adequately satisfies the human desire for recognition' that has heretofore driven the dialectic of history. Hegel's major premiss 'was that the principles of liberty and equality underlying the modern liberal state had been discovered and implemented in the most advanced countries'. Accordingly, 'there were no alternative principles or forms of social and political organization that were superior to liberalism'.[3]

Communism's fall, remarks Fukuyama, set the capstone on the triumph of liberal democracy heralded in Hegel's *Philosophy of Right*. The old conflict of master and slave that Hegel studied in the *Phenomenology*, and the class struggle between bourgeoisie and proletariat limned in Marx's *Communist Manifesto*, have come to an end. The best evidence for this, Fukuyama claimed, is the worldwide eclipse of utopian projects. Once it was possible for 'many reasonable people [to] foresee a radiant socialist future in which private property and capitalism had been abolished, and in which politics itself was somehow overcome'. Now that the socialist dream has been vanquished, 'we have trouble imagining a world that is radically better than our own, or a future that is not essentially democratic and capitalist'.[4]

Fukuyama admits that liberal democracy offers little in the way of community, and instead 'tend[s] to atomize and separate people'.[5]

Market-orientated authoritarian states that preserve traditional communities – such as those of South-East Asia – are economically far more efficient than the liberal democratic variety, and may yet beat out the West in global competition. 'A less triumphal message', opines Joseph McCarney in a biting essay on Fukuyama, 'would be hard to conceive.' Fukuyama winds up admitting that 'the Western way of life is doomed, just as communism was and for essentially the same reason, an inability to resolve the fundamental contradictions of desire which have driven history up to now'.[6]

Fukuyama misconstrues the Hegelian concept of recognition, 'the main pivot on which the intellectual structure of his book turns'.[7] Hegel's master–slave relationship, notes McCarney, implies that there is no human recognition available on either side. The slave is shut out of the master's consciousness; but, in the absence of recognition from the slave, the master is equally deprived. Recognition means to find the full truth about oneself in the eyes of the other. It cannot be forced from the other, but must come freely. And this implies a radical equality between the recognizers. Neither of Fukuyama's proposed winners at the end of history – advanced liberal democracy or free-market authoritarianism – achieves the degree of social equality required by Hegel's concept of recognition.

Acknowledging the egalitarian strain in Hegel's *Phenomenology*, McCarney wheels out the familiar argument of reconciliation to explain why this idea plays no role in the *Philosophy of Right*. Egalitarianism is a principle 'from which Hegel himself increasingly shrank as his thought fell into its well-known pattern of deepening conservatism'.[8] Marx's vision of a classless society alone can satisfy the human desire for recognition. Despite McCarney's trenchant critique, I think that Fukuyama grasps an essential truth about Hegel's project: institutions of liberal democracy constitute the ground for all future struggle.

The fall of communism revealed, according to Habermas, that 'Marxian theories of society were too focused merely on crisis theories, with the consequence that there are today no constructive models.'[9] I want to suggest that Hegel offered a positive model of social life along lines that Habermas recommends (as we shall see, Habermas does not share my interpretation of Hegel's social theory). Socialism, writes Habermas, cannot be about 'the design – and violent implementation – of a concrete form of life'. Instead, it should be conceived 'as the set of necessary conditions for emancipated forms of life about which the participants *themselves* must first reach an understanding'.[10]

As shown in chapter 6, Hegel's rational state retains private property, money and markets, as under capitalism. These, however, are subject to strict democratic controls, outlined below. The rational state also contains classes, though they are different in nature from those under capitalism. Each of Hegel's classes acts as a check and balance on the power of the others. None is superior in access to influence and resources, but each brings different strengths to society. Whereas Marx finds two main contending classes under capitalism, Hegel's state contains three major class groupings: the agricultural class of peasants and nobles; the business class, inwardly divided between workers and capitalists; and the universal class of state bureaucrats, mainly recruited from society's educated middle stratum. The agricultural grouping apes the manners of the business class, and eventually becomes culturally indistinguishable from it.

Marx saw unions and working-class political parties as vehicles for the proletariat's struggle against capital. Similarly, Hegel's democratic corporation forms the instrument within which individuals develop their sense of self and pursue the claims of class in the rational state. But Hegel's corporation is much broader than what Habermas calls the 'over-concrete'[11] proletarian agency Marx envisioned, and better comprehends the complexity of social and economic life in advanced societies.

For Hegel, the democratic constitutional system forms the core of the rational state. This is in strong contrast to the 'restricted and functionalist analysis of constitutional democracy', which Habermas considers Marx's greatest weakness. Because Marx saw 'democratic republics as the final form of the state in bourgeois society – on whose ground the final, conclusive battle of the class struggle was to be fought – he retained a purely instrumental attitude to its institutions'. Marx said little about the manner in which freedom would be institutionalized under communism.[12] He appeared to envision no need for a democratic forum to resolve conflicts in the new society. '[T]he spontaneous self-organization of the people, as described by Rousseau, appears to be sufficient', remarks Habermas.[13]

Alex Callinicos submits a dissenting view. 'It is . . . no part of classical Marxism', he writes, 'to equate communism with the absence of conflict.'[14] Still, he offers no convincing alternative mechanism to replace that of the democratic state, except the crude instrument of 'majority rule'. Moreover, Callinicos takes as unproblematic the idea of a society where the individual is disconnected from any kind of class organization. The type of disaffiliated individual Callinicos has in mind resembles what Hegel referred to – in his discussion of the French Terror in the *Phenomenology* – as 'the empty point of the absolutely free self'.

Callinicos argues that differences in opinion under communism 'are not likely to lead to systematic social polarization such that the same set of individuals line up against each other on every issue'. Each social issue would produce its own distinct set of supporters. The result would be 'a kaleidoscope of overlapping and ephemeral "parties", emerging in response to, and canvassing support around some specific question, and dissolving or declining as it was at least temporarily resolved'.[15] Unwittingly, Callinicos here recites exactly the cataclysm of terror outlined by Hegel, where, in the absence of organized, dissenting class power to protect individual rights, 'a kaleidoscope of overlapping and ephemeral "parties"' grew up, dissolved or declined – in a river of blood.

Callinicos's Marxist project is vulnerable to the liberal critique.[16] Steven Smith, for example, urges that the communist alternative projects a harmonious community, 'which in the modern world has not survived. The attempt to create such a community by force can only result in terror, as in the French Revolution, or in tyranny, as in present-day totalitarian regimes.'[17] We have seen that class conflict does not disappear in Hegel's rational state, as it does in Marx's communism. Indeed, Hegel recognized that the potential for open disagreement among powerful organized groups – and the need for democratic mechanisms of conflict resolution – is likely to be much higher in a society of equals than in one characterized by the iron rule of a privileged class.

Labour and possession

A long tradition of scholarship has established the importance of labour in Hegel's system. This constitutes one of his clearest legacies to Marx. For Hegel, labour – including mental effort and its productions, such as writing and art – functions as an important element in the process of recognition that constitutes a complete human being. We become human through the recognition we receive from others in society. Recognition, in turn, depends on acknowledgement by others of our personal possessions, including our privacy, and the right to our own bodies. These possessions make up what we are. The connection between personality and possession, between self and object, is the fundamental basis of property relations. It is a link that took ages of struggle to secure for human beings, and is always at risk.

In contrast to the liberal tradition of Hobbes and Locke, Hegel's theory of property does not assume an antagonistic relationship between the individual and the state. While Hegel admired the complex mechanisms of the market economy, writes Hinchman, 'he also invested the state with wide responsibility for protecting the individual from its vicissitudes'.[18] For Hegel, the individual may turn to the state in cases where her property rights have been violated by agents of the market economy. Such appeals have become a standard part of modern jurisprudence, though, as Hinchman confirms,[19] their Hegelian theoretical underpinnings have not been recognized until recently. For example, the apparently inconsequential requirement of some employers in the 1990s to check for workers' drug use through urine samples is a violation of Hegel's most basic property right – not to have the privacy of our bodies violated.[20] Urine samples deprive the individual of the property of her own body, and commodify the body as a product that can be subjected to expertise and knowledge. This procedure constitutes an individual's enforced testimony against herself in the context of the commission of a merely possible offence – itself dubious – against an employer.

One could argue that in a free and democratic society such individual rights may be waived for the public good (i.e. collection by police of breath samples of motorists), but in the case of urine samples, such testing could be construed as capital's project of homogenizing the workforce and further alienating the intellectual and material labour power of the individual. In Canada, attempts by employers to impose urine tests as a requirement of employment have been found in violation of the Charter of Rights and Freedoms.

Possession of an object belongs to an individual, but the legal right of possession – property – is obtained socially. Although Hegel learned much from the political economists, here – under the influence of the classic expositors of Roman property law – he departed from them. The economists knew nothing of social rights, and attributed everything to individual choice and action. For Hegel, notes Avineri, 'property always remains premised on social consensus, on consciousness, not on the mere fact of possession'.[21]

Possession depends on a trivial, even an accidental circumstance:

my grasping something or otherwise occupying it, or touching it. Possession becomes a concrete social fact when it is obtained through the conscious, willed action of human beings, i.e. through labour. The act of labour involved in property itself assumes the development of a social community among those who work together. 'Just as labour imposes a second, "humanized" form on matter to make it match human needs,' asserts Hinchman, 'so too man imposes a second moral-cultural identity upon his original nature in order to participate in a rule-governed moral community.'[22]

Labour is the way human beings separate themselves from animals. Instead of directly consuming the produce of nature, labour allows human beings to create a surplus of goods over what is immediately required. 'The contingent circumstance that one person has a surplus of one means [of satisfaction] leads itself to *exchange* . . . against means that the other has in surplus.' Our relationship to the the external world is mediated by tools that offer a leverage on the future. Writes Hegel in his Heidelberg lectures,

> the use of natural things no longer consists in immediate appropriation and enjoyment of them, but is on the one hand *prepared for in advance by labor or work (Arbeit)*, while on the other hand labour itself is mediated by the use of *tools (Werkzeuge)*, by means of which individuals make their activity specific and at the same time protect themselves against the mechanical relationship of wear and tear.[23]

Labour, or use, is a more advanced form of property than possession. As we shall see, it gives rise to significant rights for the individual worker. In the mean time, let us look at labour – and its social and economic consequences – more closely.

Civil society and inequality

Through labour, human beings transform desires, wishes and imagination into reality. It is an intentional activity which achieves a conscious result. We only know ourselves through the things we make, and our productions are evidence of our inner selves that we submit to others. Thus labour is a profoundly social activity. In modern civil society, no one can produce merely for the particular needs of some other person; instead production is for the market. In his 1818–19 Heidelberg lectures, Hegel puts it this way: 'Every product is a product of many others; every individual product that satisfies my needs presupposes [a] chain of production. All work in confidence that their work will be used.'[24] Moreover, needs are divided up and categorized, and these give rise to other 'more universal, more abstract' needs.

> The proliferation of needs comprises the character of rationality. A natural need, for instance to clothe oneself, is something concrete. Animals are cared for by nature. Humanity rises above the soil (from which it is sprung), and can live anywhere in the world. Hercules was attired in a lion's skin, and this is a simple way of satisfying the need for clothing. Reflection fragments this simple need and divides it into many parts; according to its particular nature, each individual part of the body – head, neck, feet – is given particular clothing, and so one concrete need is divided into many needs and these in turn into many others.[25]

The explosion of new needs in civil society feeds the desire for everyone to be equal with everyone else and 'in general to acquire what the other has'. The desire to be equal with the other is really only a form of imitation. Just as children imitate adults as part of the process of growing up, human beings strive to have what their neighbour enjoys. This is the underlying motive, for example, of the fashion industry: 'Fashion is one aspect of this, and to dress according to fashion is the most rational course, whereas we can leave it to others to bother about new fashions: one should not take the lead oneself, but one should also avoid idiosyncrasy.'[26]

Of course, the fashion industry hinges on making a statement, being something different from the other person. So while labour and the proliferation of needs in civil society is about equality, it is also about establishing oneself as a particular person. This accounts, says Hegel, for 'the greatest lapses in taste, for what is stupid is always something particular'.[27]

As needs become more complicated and diverse, individuals must assign themselves to a narrow specialization. A division of labour springs up 'as a result of which labor or work becomes less concrete in character, becomes abstract, homogenous and easier, so that a far greater quality of products can be prepared at the same time'. Ultimately, labour becomes so abstract and specialized that it can be done by machines, which replace 'human motion by a principle of natural motion that is harnessed to secure uniformity and promote human ends'. But at the same time that work is made easier, it is also made more onerous. Factory and manufacturing work reduce the individual to a single motion or function. 'This is why factory workers become deadened . . . and tied to their factory and dependent on it, since with this single aptitude they cannot earn a living anywhere else.'[28] The advent of each new generation of machinery brings successive waves of globalized production. 'Manufacturers have to seek a wider circle in which to sell their products.' Unlike the old artisan industries, factory production implies intense, international competition.

The manufacturer is confronted by a greater degree of contingency – the fact that other factories open, which invent better machines or have cheaper workers or an easier supply of materials; and in this way factories are ruined if other factories open in the area where they sell their products. For example most of the Dutch factories have been ruined by the English.[29]

Uncertainty in the international economy for manufacturers is matched by indeterminate conditions for workers. Closed factories create huge pools of poverty-stricken people.

The spread of industry across national boundaries vitally depends on readily accessible sources of capital. This increases, at one pole, the wealth, influence and power of the commercial class of capitalists, and, at the other, the depth of poverty in the general populace.

[T]he great man of commerce, who has to do with what is universal in the needs of nations, who has the map lying before him, has a great status. Wealth and profit become an indeterminate quest, not merely to the extent necessary to satisfy his needs, and the relation to individual need is more or less general.[30]

The perfection machines can achieve is not lasting and depends, in the end, on human supervision. Accordingly, after every burst of enthusiasm for a new generation of machinery, there is a return to more specialized human labour.

The mechanical tools people use are also machines, since they are not wholly dependent on human activity and instead human strength is largely replaced by mechanical means. But with mechanical motion the uniformity achieved is not lasting: the tension on a watch spring is always greater at the beginning than later, and it is we who introduce the uniformity of movement. Human beings are accordingly first sacrificed, after which they emerge through the more highly mechanized conditions as free once more.[31]

The economic cycle Hegel describes has repeated itself many times since he wrote these words. The revolution in manufacturing of the

1980s and 1990s inspired by the invention in 1958 of the silicon chip has caused another worldwide upheaval in production, such as Hegel discussed. So far, however, the sacrifice of human beings to technology has not halted, and disillusionment in the capacity of computers is at an early stage. The reason for this may be, as Greider comments, that 'the new information technology [amplifies] human intellect rather than muscle'. Instead of deadening labour, the new technology encourages employment of highly skilled people, and 'demands more sophistication and flexibility, even from many routine jobs'. The new systems allow decentralization of decision-making 'in reformed workplaces and production jobs can be scattered across many distant places, even at a computer terminal in one's home'. Information technology opens the lines of communication between top managers and factory floor, eliminating the need for middle-level executives.

As in Hegel's mid-nineteenth-century civil society, the current wave of technology has created a new impetus to globalized production. Industry, says Greider, migrates to 'undeveloped territories where it will be easier (and cheaper) for enterprises to build the new production systems, free of the old restraints like established laws and social commitments, including taxes and wages'. Similarly, finance capital dominates in the 1990s, as it did in Hegel's time. 'Commerce either persuades a society to relax its laws and social obligations or it exits to another society.' When commerce penetrates national boundaries, 'it must persuade the developing territories themselves to adopt new rules, laws to protect the free flow of commerce and, above all, to protect the property rights of capital'.[32]

A result of these developments in our era, as in Hegel's, has been concentration of wealth in the upper levels of the income structure, and an unprecedented explosion of poverty and need below. 'The inequalities of wealth and power that Marx decried', avers Greider, 'are marching wider almost everywhere in the world.'[33] Still, as Hegel might have predicted, jobs lost to new technology are already being regained in the most technologically advanced country, the USA. Computers are unlikely ever to abolish work for any significant portion of the world's labour force. Despite predictions by 'end of work' theorists, writes Doug Henwood, '[t]here's been no long-term structural change in the relationship between economic growth and employment growth'. Figures from the International Labour Office's *World Economic Report* for 1996/97 show that high unemployment in Western and Eastern Europe is connected with 'slow growth and economic collapse, respectively, not technological transformation'. In the developing world of Asia and Latin America, 'paid employment is growing, as peasants are daily transformed into industrial workers, for good or ill'. Working hours for paid employees in the USA have increased substantially since 1969, and the number of people working more than fifty hours a week has grown by a third.[34]

Class struggle in Hegel and Marx

We saw in the last chapter that Hegel's democratic corporation is meant to cancel the inequalities and uncertainties that arise in civil society. But it is an institution of the future, not one that already exists. The process of labour that results in class divisions is unmediated by the democratic corporation so that a person's life in civil society is very often beyond her control, especially if she is poor. A life of deadened factory labour at best, and unemployment and poverty at worst, is the lot of many. The comforts of property and possession are out of reach. The capitalist state cannot intervene effectively in this system because inequality 'is one aspect of the free choice present in the contingency and freedom of the individual'. Civil society constitutes a terrible judgement on the poor, since its most rational feature is inequality.

> The whole must articulate itself, and this articulation in regard to the manifold character of needs and work is the necessity of classes, whose higher necessity is founded in reason since each living individual must become inwardly unequal. To feel pity that one human being must suffer more because of his needs than another is an unjustified sentiment.[35]

Marx's answer to the dilemma of inequality is class struggle: the self-conscious effort by united workers to overthrow the capitalist system and replace it with communism. The democratic corporation is Hegel's solution to the conundrum of poverty. But while Marx offers a way to get to the ideal society, where is Hegel's route to the rational state?

Here we are back with the young Marx in Gans's lecture hall in Berlin at the end of the 1830s. He listens intently and deeply as Gans unfolds Hegel's theory of progressive change in civil society. As yet the young man has no comprehension of economics and Gans's discussion of 'The System of Needs: Political Economy' most likely goes over his head. Within a decade Marx steeps himself in the arcane mysteries of political economy and writes, along with his friend Engels, *The Communist Manifesto*. Whether or not Marx developed some of his ideas while listening to Gans's lectures, class struggle was a central item on the Hegelian syllabus. For Hegel, class is a necessary aspect of the rational state, and an important barrier against political terror in modern civil society. Class also provides the means for people to become conscious of oppression and exploitation in capitalist society, and to organize against them. For Hegel, as for Marx, class struggle is based on consciousness – an understanding of the world and one's place in it. Class is the key determinant of consciousness in civil society. Class divisions grow out of inequality in civil society, yet they are founded on consciousness, on a structure of mind.

In *Capital*, Marx would find the mainspring of class struggle in the concept of surplus value. Workers create value, but their wages are equal to only a small portion of the wealth they create. Capitalist accumulation, therefore, is founded on exploitation of the proletariat, and destruction of the capitalist market system is required for a free society. Elements of Marx's theory of surplus value had been worked out before him in the 1820s by the Saint-Simonians. Radical English economists like Thomas Hodgskin had developed a socialist theory out of David Ricardo's labour theory of value at about the same time. According to the socialist application of Ricardian theory, writes Engels, 'the whole social product belongs to the workers as *their* product, because they are the sole producers'. This insight 'leads directly to communism'. Marx's communism, however, is not based on a moral protest against exploitation, but – as Engels claims – 'upon the inevitable collapse of the capitalist mode of production which is daily taking place before our eyes to an ever greater degree'.[36] The economic and social contradictions of the system doom it to extinction.

Writing just after the fall of communism in Europe, Jürgen Habermas dispelled the illusions surrounding Marx's view of capitalism's inevitable collapse, and the consequent victory of socialism. Capitalism, noted Habermas, is much more complex and multi-levelled than is suggested by Marx's prognosis. In particular, the concept of a revolutionary vanguard of class-conscious industrial workers 'precludes consideration of both the ambivalences of the increasing domination of nature, and the potential for social integration within and beyond the sphere of social labour'. Marx oversimplified the nature of capital accumulation, and had unrealistic expectations for administrative planning beyond a market system, 'whose regulative devices cannot be replaced ... without potentially jeopardizing the level of differentiation achieved in modern society'.[37]

Habermas observes that Marx's two-class model of civil society cannot account for a social system 'in which there are no straightforward connections between the social, subcultural and regional surface structures on the one hand, and the abstract deep structures of a differentiated economic system (intertwined with complementary state intervention)'. Furthermore, the 'secretly normative' presuppositions of Marx's theory of history are 'naturalized in the form of evolutionary views of progress'. The result, on one side, is a deterministic system that abolishes 'any sense of risk in those who will have to bear the consequences of action [and] encourages a questionable form of vanguardism'. On the other, Marx's 'totalizing knowledge ... feels in a position to make clinical evaluations of the degree of alienation, or success, of particular forms of life in their entirety'.[38]

According to Habermas, these 'errors and defects' – combined with Marx's instrumental attitude to the institutions of bourgeois democracy – make 'it easier to understand how Marxism, as it was codified by Stalin, could degenerate into the ideology that legitimated what was in practice simply inhuman – "vivisection on a large scale using live humans" (Biermann)'.[39]

Though keenly aware of tensions and dangers nestled within the system of needs (recurrent business cycles and economic upheavals), Hegel is unconvinced – contrary to Marx – that civil society will choke on its own economic contradictions. '[W]hole classes, whole branches of industry can succumb to poverty when the means this sector of the population produces are no longer sold and their business stagnates.'[40] In the event of general economic crisis, however, the state can be called upon to relieve distress. A much greater danger is curtailment of civil and political freedoms by a corrupt government. Business depends on these freedoms, for without them 'the desire to enjoy, own, and acquire property disappears'. Thanks to oppression by the nobility in Poland, for example, the nation was ruined. 'The towns that were once so famous fell into decay, and now they are only known by name, and the whole country is partitioned.' The Italian cities, 'which used to be so famous', suffered a similar fate, and are now 'for the most part insignificant backwaters'.[41]

Ethnic separatism, magnified by the individualist bourgeois ethos, such as Hegel feared might claim the Germans, forms the greatest danger to political freedom. This danger was realized almost 150 years later during the Nazi period, despite Hegel's hopes to the contrary. 'The German people may not be able to carry separatism to such a pitch of frenzy', Hegel speculates, 'as to murder and be murdered until the state is wiped out.'[42] The threat to freedom posed by ethnic rivalry expands in the bourgeois epoch precisely because of the nature of capitalist property relations.

> Once man's social instincts are distorted and he is compelled to throw himself into interests peculiarly his own, his nature becomes so deeply perverted that it now spends its strength on variance from others, and in the course of maintaining its separation it sinks into madness, for madness is simply the complete separation of the individual from his kind.[43]

Bourgeois property versus rational property rights

I argue in this section that Hegel distinguishes universal human rights from the one-dimensional character of bourgeois property rights. This is a debatable position, not widely accepted among commentators. Combined with my claim about the critique of capitalist property relations in Hegel (discussed in the next section), the implications for an understanding of Hegel are staggering. As I mentioned at the beginning of this chapter, my discussion may not convince every reader. It is one interpretation of Hegel's theory of property within a plurality of possible positions, some of which are mentioned below.

At the level of what Hegel calls abstract right, each individual is entitled to fair treatment. Here are the core human values that belong, as Hinchman demonstrates, to Hegel's concept of recognition: 'the dignity of the individual person, respect for life, liberty and property, equal justice before the law, etc.'[44] For Hegel, however, bourgeois property rights subvert the concept of private property. The bourgeois concept, as we shall see, recalls the dynamic of madness because of its singleness of purpose – the quest for profit – and its lack of social content.

My argument that Hegel drew a distinction between bourgeois property and a rational system of property rights (the labour theory of property) is very controversial. But such a distinction, if Hegel did indeed make it, was not original to him. It was proposed in his day by

English radical economists, notably Thomas Hodgskin, with whose work Hegel was familiar.[45] Similarly, the Swiss economist Sismondi (mentioned by Marx in the *Communist Manifesto*) had by 1818 worked out a theory of economic crises that rested on a critique of the bourgeois concept of property.

Alan Ryan[46] offers an articulate version of the standard approach to Hegel's theory of property. In his view, Hegel saw no contrast between a rational system of property rights and capitalist private property. I will briefly survey Ryan's analysis of Hegel's concept before turning to my own. Ryan admits that Hegel's theory could be interpreted along the lines of a labour theory of property. 'One natural interpretation', he writes, 'is a rather romantic and individualist one, which stresses the way in which an individual's project for self-formation and self-expression are embodied in what he creates and owns.' Work and the products of human labour, in Hegel's theory, could be compared to the labour and creations of an artist, where the relationship between work and possession is obvious. 'The paradigm of a possessory relationship exists between a painter and his painting; the object he has created, though made of canvas and pigment, has no life at all except as *his* painting.' The conclusion is inescapable: 'it would be a reproach against the system of property rights if the creator who was the *real* owner of the object he made had no control over its ultimate destination'.[47]

Thinkers influenced by Hegel, such as Max Stirner and the young Marx, did register a connection between labour and property rights. But Hegel, claims Ryan, 'did not seem much moved by any such thought. Certainly he saw a weak connection between art and more humble forms of work, but he did not draw any radical conclusions from this.' For Hegel, there is no necessity for an individual to enjoy any particular form of property. She only needs to have a social station and duties that she freely chooses; any further requirements – outside of basic civil rights – are illusory. '[B]ecause Hegel moves easily from individual aspirations to the truth which lies in the whole, he only *seems* to be resting his case on the individualism of the romantics.'[48]

Ryan accepts that for Hegel labour is the most appropriate way to take a thing into one's possession: '[T]hings most fully become ours when our work transforms them. We endow a thing with a new essence by working on it, and this new nature supersedes the original nature; naturally, therefore, labour gives one solid title.' On the other hand, says Ryan, a thing can be taken into possession simply through the device of 'marking' – 'the legally valid declaration that it is "mine"'. He cites the example of two people swapping shares in a publicly held firm. Mere transfer of shares from one person to another gives the new holder entitlement to profits and proceeds of the firm. 'For Hegel this control at extreme arm's length is a triumph of mind over matter. We can switch the destiny of things in the world not by pushing or shoving but by an affirmation of will.'[49]

Ryan's example assumes that property law is already in place (i.e. a legally valid claim that something is 'mine') when Hegel's point is to justify the law in the first place. As Robert Dahl asserts in *A Preface to Economic Democracy*, 'We cannot leap from my entitlement to secure possession of the shirt on my back or the cash in my pocket to a fundamental moral right to acquire shares in IBM and therewith the standard rights of ownership that shareholdings legally convey.'[50] Besides, 'marking' is a primitive, abstract form of possession and property. 'So marking is the most imperfect way of taking possession', advises Hegel. Slaveholders, for example, 'marked' slaves as their human property. For this reason, Hegel includes a discussion of slavery and its 'alleged justification' in the section on possession in the *Philosophy of Right*.[51] Work, however, goes beyond the form of property called possession, and advances into the higher mode of 'use'. Ryan hints at this. 'The attractions of Hegel's development of the concept of property depend on our everyday feelings about our need to identify with and express ourselves in things we make, control, and use.' Nevertheless, 'there is no very direct connection' between these 'feelings' 'and any particular form of ownership'.[52] For Ryan, Hegel's concept of property ultimately reflects only 'the right of mankind to dominate and master mere nature'.[53]

In common with most other interpreters, Ryan avoids the implications of Hegel's concept of use for capitalist property rights. These implications, I will argue below, are spelled out in both the *Philosophy of Right* and the Heidelberg *Lectures on Natural Right and Political Science*. Before turning to Hegel's labour theory of property, it is worth noting that Jeremy Waldron's *The Right to Private Property*[54] develops a Hegelian line of argument and comes to conclusions similar, in some ways, to my own. Waldron suggests that Hegel's concept legitimates a claim on the resources of the community for every individual, and poses a fundamental challenge to the character of property rights in capitalist society.[55] However, Waldron rejects the view, which I put forward below, that Hegel's theory of property pertains to relations between owner and worker in an economy characterized by an advanced division of labour. '[Hegel's] account of property seems... obviously more applicable to a petit-bourgeois economy of small owner-occupiers than to an advanced capitalist society.' As a result, Hegel's theory 'of civil society fits ill, in many respects, with his account of the importance of private property'. According to Waldron, Hegel never really confronted the question of inequality, and failed to explore the radical implications of his own theory.[56]

Hegel's labour theory of property

This section contains the most controversial of my claims about the character of Hegel's theory of property. I should emphasize that my standpoint depends to a large extent on an interpretation of some crucial paragraphs in the *Philosophy of Right* (especially §62) which have received inadequate attention from Hegel scholars. At the very least, perhaps my assessment of these paragraphs will stimulate others to develop alternative arguments.

As we have seen, Hegel's theory of private property is intensely social. 'My existing determinately... in my ownership is a relationship to other persons, and from this stems reciprocal recognition: the free is for the free.'[57] However, the bourgeois concept remains stalled at the stage of property Hegel called possession. This is the private, single notion of ownership, the relationship between self and object. This stage of property applies not only to slavery, but to any relationship of domination, which Hegel calls 'the *master's status* as simple lordship in general'.[58] It is worth recalling that, in the nineteenth century, capital and labour were referred to in law as 'master and servant'.[59]

The higher stage of property, called labour or use, involves a relationship of mutual recognition between two property owners.[60] The worker's use of machines and raw materials in the process of labour – including the intellectual worker's mental efforts – constitutes 'concrete possession' and establishes the worker as a co-owner with the capitalist in the system of production. Instead of recognizing the worker's property rights, however, the bourgeois concept knows only 'the abstract ownership' of the capitalist.[61] The worker may be 'kept alive'[62] by her wages, but true freedom in civil society requires that the worker attain 'ownership' of property. In the following passage from the Heidelberg lectures Hegel offers a devastating critique of bourgeois private property.

> [P]ossession is *concrete possession*, partly in that I actually have the thing in my grasp, partly in that I may employ, use, and enjoy it. If this concrete possession is mine ... then I own it. But if it is only this concrete possession that is deemed to be mine, and ownership – as what is ideal, essential – is deemed to accrue to another, then this is an empty distinction, and the other has a merely abstract mastery, not over the things in question but over me, a mastery that can only consist in an indebtedness on my part to him as a condition of my ownership.[63]

In *Hegel's Theory of Madness*, Berthold-Bond observes that for Hegel insanity involves 'the presence of *two centers* of reality . . . the displaced, de-centered, lost, but still recollected trace of rationality, and the new center of its deranged consciousness'.[64] Berthold-Bond does not notice that for Hegel the bourgeois concept of property, like the insane personality, also contains two centres. One of these centres partly retains the correct concept of property as a relationship of mutual recognition; the other includes only the perverted individualist concept of property peculiar to the bourgeoisie. And this contradiction, this alienation at the base of the capitalist mind, accounts for the deranged quality of social relations in civil society. As I have shown in detail in two earlier works,[65] the following passage from §62 of the *Philosophy of Right* – which perhaps has been overlooked by the great majority of Hegel commentators – contrasts the 'abstract ownership' of the capitalist with ownership gained through use by the worker. The false separation between the two leads to a 'madness of personality' that pervades the bourgeois world.

> The distinction between the right to the *whole extent of the use* of a thing and *abstract ownership* is a product of the empty understanding, for which the Idea – here as the unity of ownership, or even of the personal will in general and its *reality* – is not the truth, but for which these two moments in their separation from one another count as something true. This distinction, therefore, as an actual relation, is one of an empty proprietorship which might be called a madness of personality (if the term 'madness' were used not just of a direct contradiction within a person between his merely subjective ideas . . . and his actuality) because the term 'mine', as applied to a *single*

object, would have to mean both my exclusive individual will and another exclusive individual will, with no mediation between them.[66]

As Hegel says in §62, there is nothing to mediate between these radically conflicting rights in civil society. The relationship between capitalist and worker, says Hegel, implies 'not two *lords (domini)*, but an *owner* on one hand [i.e. the worker] and a *lord* over nothing on the other [i.e. the capitalist]. But on account of the burdens [on the property] what we have are *two owners* in mutual relationship.' The 'absolute contradiction' between the property rights of the worker and those of the employer can only be mediated – according to my interpretation of Hegel's theory – by the rise of the democratic corporation in civil society, which institutionalizes the rights of both parties. Hegel notes that it took 1,500 years before the freedom of personality, which began to flourish under Christianity, could become a 'universal principal for part – if only a small part – of the human race'. He cautions against 'the impatience of opinion' which refuses to recognize 'the length of time which the spirit requires in order to progress in its self-consciousness'. Nevertheless, Hegel predicts that 'the transition to common ownership [i.e. of productive property] is very easy to make'.[67]

An alternative interpretation of part of the momentous §62 appears in Allen W. Wood's editorial notes to the Cambridge edition of the *Philosophy of Right*. Wood does not mention the relationship between capitalist and worker. Instead, he submits that Hegel's discussion of '*two owners* standing in mutual relationship' was influenced by Kant, and refers to Prussian feudal law. According to Wood, it concerns the distinction between a feudal landlord's ownership of land and the (non-existent) rights of a tenant. Wood explains that 'Hegel finds these (feudal) conceptions quite relevant to the philosophical science of right because he thinks they violate the very concept of property as full and free ownership.'[68]

I agree with Wood to a point. There is no doubt that Hegel was critical of feudal forms of property, and believed in the working tenant's right to free ownership of land. Indeed, Hegel's critique of feudal rights needs to be fully assessed in view of his theory of the agricultural class in civil society. However, overall, I find Wood's account unsatisfactory, for it ventures an interpretation of only part of the disputed §62. Moreover, I doubt that Hegel, an extremely careful writer to say the least, would slip an essentially feudal conception into his discussion of a relatively high stage of private property unless it had profound and direct implications for bourgeois society, which is based entirely on private property relations. Indeed, the feudal rights Hegel criticizes are highly analogous to those enforced by bourgeois property relations,[69] and, I maintain, that is why Hegel introduces them in §62.

Hegel's equation of the wage contract with a wider, social form of madness echoes a similar idea in Rousseau. The French philosopher criticized any contract in which an individual 'alienate[s]' or sells herself to another 'in return for at least a subsistence'. Rousseau noted that if a person were to be worth anything to a buyer, she would have to be fed and clothed anyway. To sell oneself for a mere subsistence wage amounts to selling oneself for nothing.

> To speak of a man giving himself in return for nothing is to speak of what is absurd, unthinkable; such an action would be illegitimate, void, if only because no one who did it could be in their right mind. To say the same of a whole people is to conjure up a nation of lunatics; and right cannot rest on madness.[70]

Bourgeois property amounts to the capitalist using the worker, employing her, as a factor of production, in the labour process – hence the word 'employee'. This is the 'abstract mastery' Hegel refers to above, the capitalist's mastery 'not over the things in question but over me, a mastery that can only consist in an indebtedness on my part to him as a condition of my ownership'. The capitalist property relationship contradicts Hegel's concept of use, which applies only to the employment by the worker of lifeless, inanimate objects. The labouring worker does not 'use' other human beings, in Hegel's sense, but the capitalist does. The capitalist's mastery over the worker – which is grounded in the bourgeois refusal to grant the worker recognition – depends 'on regarding the human being simply as a *natural being* . . . whose *existence* . . . is not in conformity with his concept'.[71]

Hegel's theory is a version of the labour theory of property. 'It would not be a complete overstatement', writes David Ellerman, 'to say that Hegel's vision was the labor theory of property writ large in the grand German metaphysical style.' The labour theory of property has its roots in the work of John Locke, and in the early nineteenth-century writings of the Ricardian socialists, Thomas Hodgskin, William Thompson and John Francis Bray. We have seen above that Marx's theory of surplus value was partly developed out of an encounter with the Ricardian socialists. Ellerman contends that the labour theory of property has two essential elements, one economic, the other juridical.

'Hegel seems to have been the first to bring together the two intellectual streams of the labor theory of property and the de facto inalienability theory.'[72]

The juridical principle of de facto responsibility declares that 'the legal responsiblity for a civil or criminal wrong should be assigned to the person or persons who intentionally committed the act, i.e., to the de facto responsible party'.[73] Thus, a gun or a knife cannot be hauled before a court and charged with commission of a crime. Only the responsible actor, who intentionally commits a crime, can be found guilty of violating the law. Applied to the realm of economics and property, this principle holds that only labour – not the means of production supplied by the capitalist – is responsible for the positive and negative results of the production process. The worker uses up the means of production (the negative side of the equation) and, in turn, creates the product (the positive side).

> In particular, the people working in an enterprise are factually responsible for using up the inputs and for producing the outputs. Hence, the juridical principle of imputation (i.e., the labor theory of property) implies that the workers (in the inclusive sense) should have the legal liability for the used-up inputs and the legal ownership of the produced outputs.[74]

Ellerman points out that the bourgeois inability to differentiate between the use of objects and the actions of human beings is a feature of neo-classical economics. In order to avoid recognizing labour's non-equivalency with machines or other factors of production, economists resort either 'to an *"active" poetical picture*' or 'a *passive engineering picture*'. In the poetic view, land and capital are pictured 'as "agents of production" that (who?) cooperate together with workers to produce the harvest'.[75] This weird vision was mocked by Marx. 'It is an enchanted, perverted, topsy-turvy world, in which Monsieur le Capital and Madame la Terre do their ghost-walking as social characters.'[76] The passive engineering view treats human actions 'simply as causally efficacious services alongside the services of land and capital. The engineering view switches to the passive voice: "Given input K and L, the outputs Q are produced."'[77]

For Ellerman, as for Hegel, the bourgeois system of private property is based on massive fraud – a 'madness of personality', as Hegel called it. 'Today's market economies', suggests Ellerman, 'are flawed by one basic fraudulent contract . . . The whole product is produced by one party ("Labor") but is laissez-faire misappropriated by another party, the employer.'[78]

Wages and contract

Hegel observes that wage labour differs from slavery because the worker's services, unlike those of the slave, are limited in time. Many commentators, including Ellerman,[79] have interpreted this as Hegel's justification of the capitalist wage contract, without recognizing that when he was writing there were no laws limiting hours of work. The time limitation Hegel recommended as the crucial difference between slavery and wage labour did not exist – a fact recognized by mid-nineteenth-century working-class agitation for shorter hours which compared wage labour to slavery. Still, the time limitation on labour is an external matter. More importantly, the ideal labour contract constitutes – and does not invalidate – the worker's claim to property. The bourgeois relationship, on the contrary, sucks away the worker's 'ability to produce' and divests her of 'ownership' of property (recall the 'deadened' factory workers always on the verge of absolute poverty). Writes Hegel,

> I can only hand over my services for a definite time, and I cannot assign to another rights over all my labours. This restriction in time and restriction in terms of number and degree constitute the aspect of externality. But if I were to hand over to someone the generality of my services, my ability to produce something that is universal or contains all particularizations, everything external, I would in so doing divest myself of something universal, what lies within ... Similarly I cannot hand over to anyone, along with what I own, my capability of ownership.[80]

Of course, the capitalist employment contract demands precisely that the worker 'hand over to someone the generality of [her] services, her ability to produce something that is universal or contains all particularizations'. The worker does, indeed – as Hegel well knew – 'divest [herself] of something universal, what lies within'. The poor worker, bereft of property, has necessarily 'handed over to [the capitalist] ... [her] capability of ownership'.

In Hegel's terms, the wage contract is a 'gift' from worker to capitalist. A proper contract recognizes equality between the wills of both parties. This is a co-operative, democratic undertaking, without any element of coercion: *'two owners* in a mutual relationship'. But the bourgeois wage deal is only a formal contract, a gift. In the gift contract, one party has 'the negative moment of the alienation of the thing', while the other has 'the positive moment of its acceptance'. A real contract, in contrast to a gift, demands that each party to the contract remains at its conclusion with the same value in property with which they started. 'But a contract may be called *real* in so far as *each* of the contracting wills ... thereby both becomes and remains an owner of property in concluding it.'[81]

Ellerman observes that Marx's surplus-value theory is a veiled form of the labour theory of property. But Marx missed the significance of the critique of the capital–labour relationship 'that lay buried in the work of Hegel'. He failed to see that the standard labour contract violates the juridical principle of de facto responsibility, i.e. that the worker is responsible for the positive and negative products of the labour process. 'Marx's analysis emphasized the unequal bargaining power of the propertyless proletariat ... and exploitative wage rates in his labor theory of value and exploitation. Neither is a critique of the wage relationship itself.'[82]

Despite these signal differences in approach, Hegel's discussion of the business-class mind bears close similarity to Marx's analysis of the conflicted consciousness of the bourgeoisie and the proletariat. As mentioned previously, there are three separate groups within the business class: the manufacturing class, the commercial class of bankers and investors with overseas links, and factory workers. 'With *business* or *trade* ... the reflective [i.e. formal] class, the chief aspect is the form and an abstract profit, one that does not serve directly for gratification.' The activity of form belongs to the worker; profit to the capitalist. The worker

> processes raw material, and the form he gives it is what makes the thing of value. He is therefore impelled in the direction of mediation with others in a variety of ways, in his reflection and in regard to his need to exchange the products of his work, and also in regard to his tools.[83]

Like Marx, Hegel subscribes to David Ricardo's labour theory of value. The value of a thing is linked to the amount of labour exhausted in its production, as well as to its relative scarcity. Exchange of commodities is based on a comparison of their value. Prices are the empirical manifestation of value.

Now the value depends on the labor needed to produce the thing, value being determined by the art and effort involved, the rarity of the object, etc. The comparison is made on the basis of this value, which is a quantitative determination, a measure. Price is the value in a particular case.

The means of 'universal exchange' – money – represents the abstract value of the commodity and 'by its circulation multiplies the amount of property indefinitely'. The commercial class specializes in the handling of money since its purpose 'is to act as a universal intermediary in the reciprocal exchange of manufactured articles'. This class 'accumulates wealth, which is subject to no inherent qualitative limit, so that the pursuit of wealth extends indefinitely and for its part in turn gives rise to the proliferation of needs and means'.[84]

The commercial class handles money and accumulates wealth, but the main source of wealth in civil society is the manufacturing class of capitalist and worker – 'it is here [in the manufacturing class] that wealth originates'. Unlike the agricultural group, the manufacturing class depends only on its own talents and abilities, and this is particularly true for the worker. 'In the business class the principal concern is not the raw material but the form produced by the worker's activity; he therefore has himself and his own activity to thank for everything.' Members of the business class develop an independent frame of mind, though they must depend on others to obtain raw materials and tools, and to provide a market for their products. This is an urban class that fills up large towns because business depends on exchange, which 'is possible only when people live side by side'. Unlike artisans or independent tradespeople, who can manage their affairs on a local level, the manufacturing class (as we have seen) must adopt an international outlook. Firms have to seek markets outside their native soil and are subject to fluctuations in the world market. Businesses can be ruined by more efficient foreign competitors. A dip in world trade or a faraway change in fashions can throw thousands out of work.[85]

The struggle for recognition that Hegel sees as the ultimate fact of human life takes place in civil society mainly within the two opposing sides of the manufacturing class. Workers seek confirmation of their own rights, and they find this in the class to which they belong. This confirmation is reached by battling against 'class distinction based on privilege . . . one of the most repugnant forms of distinction'.[86] Workers formerly scattered across the countryside are brought together in large groups in factories and cities. This creates a feeling of solidarity and community that takes a political and juridical form.

> Individuals *become* and *emerge* for themselves as free will . . . or subjectivity of will, a subjectivity that is, however, inwardly universal. *Formal right* makes its appearance, and, however intimately it is implicated and has its essential content in the aim of [satisfying] needs, it must also, as the subjective element underlying this aim, be embedded in something independent of it, namely the *administration of justice*.[87]

Under pressure from the working class, the apparatus of the state can be mobilized against poverty, and the tax system can begin to contend with the dangerous gap that has opened up between rich and poor. Hegel's proposals for dealing with excessive wealth are drawn from the experience of classical society.

> In republics an inordinate increase in wealth is dangerous, so legislators have sought to counteract it. For example, the richest citizen in a *demos* (populace) had to pay for the plays, in this way wealth was honored, but he was obliged to reduce his estate, or limits were placed on accumulation. The inheritance laws were also directed against excessive enrichment.[88]

In the *Communist Manifesto* Marx and Engels trace a dialectic of transformation remarkably like the one Hegel puts forward. The revolutionary language of the *Manifesto* is more direct, of course, than Hegel's – even in Heidelberg Hegel had to look over his shoulder. But the similarities appear inescapable. Where Hegel suggests using the state to reduce inequality, Marx and Engels discuss government intervention to restrict factory working hours. The union of the workers, write Marx and Engels,

> is helped on by the improved means of communication that are created by modern industry, and that place the workers of different localities in contact with one another. It was just this contact that was needed to centralize the various local struggles, all of the same character, into one national struggle between classes . . . The organization of the proletarians into a class, and consequently into a political party, is continually being upset again by competition between the workers themselves. But it ever rises up again, stronger, firmer, mightier. It compels legislative recognition of particular interests of the workers, by taking advantage of the divisions among

the bourgeoisie itself. Thus the Ten Hour Bill in England was carried.[89]

Unlike Hegel, however, Marx ignored the juridical concept of property, and the way it flows into a theory of workers' property rights. The labour theory of property was much discussed in Hegel's day, and Marx himself was aware of its main expositors, including the radical economist Thomas Hodgskin, whose *Labour Defended Against the Claims of Capital* was published in 1825.[90] Just as he avoided the topic of democratic political theory, Marx short-circuited the discussion of labour's claim to the ownership of property. Indeed, as Ellerman attests, the labour theory of property was completely overshadowed by Marx's intervention. 'At least since Marx's time, any discussion of the labor theory of property as a critique of capitalism has been dominated by Marx's labor theory of value and exploitation. The labor theory of property simply has not had an independent intellectual life.'[91] Marx identified private property with capitalism; ergo, communism would bring the abolition of private property.

We saw in chapter 6 that for Marx private property offers the opposite of what Hegel claims. Property is not an instrument for self-development of the individual, but rather a cause for his or her alienation from society. According to Marx, writes Alan Ryan, '[s]o far from affirming ourselves in working, owning and exchanging, we deny ourselves, suffer loss, behave in a thinglike and non-human way'. The central determining mechanism of capitalism, the one which links everything that goes on within it – including the so-called democratic state – is the 'creation of surplus value'.[92]

In the *Communist Manifesto*, Marx briefly alludes to a positive conception of property 'as the fruit of man's own labor'. This form of property, notes Marx, 'is alleged to be the groundwork of all personal freedom, activity and independence'. Under capitalism, however, property is ruthlessly monopolized by the bourgeoisie, and the worker is left in return 'with a bare existence'. Communist society, Marx avows, would recognize 'personal appropriation of the products of labor', so long as there were 'no surplus wherewith to command the labour of others'. 'All that we want to do away with is the miserable character of this appropriation, under which the laborer lives merely to increase capital and is allowed to live only in so far as the interest of the ruling class requires it.'[93]

Without a fully explicated positive theory of property, Marxian socialism could offer only state ownership of the means of production as an alternative to capitalism. 'It is obvious enough', intones Ryan, 'that socialism as practised has universally required some sort of public ownership in a form familiar from the context of private ownership.'[94] There was never any question in the Marxist tradition that private property was doomed come the revolution. Even the famed Yugoslavian experiment of worker self-managed firms, says Ellerman, 'ended up as a decentralized type of social ownership'. Wilde confirms that in Yugoslavia 'the domination of important decision-making in economic and political matters by the communists and other technocratic elites acted as a major obstacle to democratization'.[95] Elsewhere in the Soviet bloc, Marx's incomplete theory of property hardened into dogma. 'After Marx died', reflects Ellerman, 'the genetic code of Marxism was fixed. Any later attempt to introduce . . . notions' concerning workers' property rights 'was heresy'.[96] Still, the prevalence of public ownership in socialist societies did not rule out market mechanisms. As Chris Pierson observes, 'almost all *practical* experience of socialism . . . has entailed the use of markets. Even the most centralized command economies had recourse to (albeit grossly distorted) markets in labour and consumer goods'.[97] Indeed, the emergence of private economic alternatives to the central command economy, and the Leninist political structure it supported, led directly to what Walder calls *The Waning of the Communist State*.[98]

Ellerman confides that, historically, Marxian socialism has given capitalist ideology a free ride. It allows the patently false identification of capitalism with private property rights, and with democracy. The capitalist 'employment relation', notes Ellerman, 'inherently denies people the right to the fruits of their labor – which is widely, if not universally, acknowledged as the best foundation for the right of private ownership'. Capitalism and democracy are often linked. Yet, as Ellerman attests, the employment contract is profoundly undemocratic. It is 'essentially a scaled-down version of Hobbes' anti-democratic pact of subjection wherein people give up and alienate the right to govern themselves to a sovereign'.[99]

Hegel's concept of property provides inner motivation for the growth of the democratic corporation. Through struggles within the business class – struggles for recognition – the worker asserts her common property rights in the corporation and eventually assumes, with the capitalist, joint control over the workplace. According to Habermas, '[c]onstitutional democracy is becoming a project, at once the outcome and accelerating catalyst of a rationalization of the lifeworld reaching far beyond the political'.[100] If Hegel is correct, the conscious struggle for property rights within the corporation should bring Habermas's project of constitutional democracy to the workplace itself. I shall argue in the concluding chapter that this fight will be only part of a larger twenty-first-century contest to reassert the power of the public realm.

An alternative model of civil society

In the wake of communism's fall, Jürgen Habermas and others have developed a useful definition of civil society, quite different, in some respects, from Marx's and Hegel's. At the same time, Habermas's model retains much from Hegel. He offers an insightful perspective on the movement of liberal democratic societies. Yet, because it ignores some of Hegel's most significant contributions to an understanding of our own period, Habermas's model is flawed.

Both Marx and Hegel, Habermas avers, saw civil society 'as a sphere of commodity exchange and social labor governed by anonymous economic laws'. For Hegel, 'individuals were robbed of all real freedom' in the bourgeois economy – 'the system of needs'. Similarly: 'Marx saw in the autonomy of civil society nothing but structures in which the self-valorization of capital proceeded over the heads of alienated individuals in order to bring forth ever more drastic forms of social inequality.'[101] Habermas advises that the meaning of civil society current today 'no longer includes the economy as constituted by private law and steered through markets in labor, capital, and commodities'.[102] Instead of a realm of oppression and inequality, civil society should be understood as a centre of freedom and popular action.

Hegel's concept of civil society includes business corporations, municipal governments and trade unions; it also contains (among others) churches, universities and voluntary organizations. By contrast, Habermas's version of civil society omits economic and governmental organizations. His 'institutional core of civil society' comprises only non-economic and non-governmental institutions and voluntary associations. These 'more or less spontaneously emergent associations, organizations, and movements' help to communicate concerns generated in people's private lives 'in amplified form to the public sphere'. Such institutions 'have an egalitarian, open form of organization' that reflects 'essential features of the kind of communication around which they crystallize and to which they lend continuity and permanence'.[103] Habermas points to Greenpeace and Amnesty International as examples of organizations at the centre of his notion of civil society. As agents of big capital, the mass media are, of course, omitted.

Economic institutions and work groups that compose Hegel's civil society are absent from Habermas's model. Nevertheless, they form part of the private infrastructure that guarantees the freedoms (such as freedom of speech, freedom of assembly and freedom of association) upon which Habermas's new civil society is founded. Accordingly, this new civil society is a feature only of advanced capitalist societies. In the absence of an 'integral private sphere', notes Habermas, a free civil society was impossible in the 'totalitarian societies of bureaucratic socialism'. Similarly, without a liberal economic and political culture in many countries in the developing world, 'populist movements arise that blindly defend the frozen traditions of a lifeworld endangered by capitalist modernization'.[104]

According to Habermas, market structures are required to underwrite the freedoms of civil society. At the same time, civil society must be kept distinct from the state. Public opinion generated through the autonomous associations of civil society has to be filtered through procedures of democratic decision-making. Without mediation by parliamentary debates and legislation, public opinion can itself become tyrannical.

Habermas cautions that the power and influence of civil society is self-limiting. As in Hegel's model, civil society must remain subordinate, or at least functionally separate from, the realm of politics. '[D]emocratic movements emerging from civil society must give up holistic aspirations to a self-organizing society, aspirations that also undergirded Marxist ideas of social revolution.' By the same token, the state can have only limited influence in civil society. '[T]he administrative power deployed for the purposes of social planning and supervision is not a suitable medium for fostering emancipated forms of life.'[105] Government is capable of nurturing projects initiated within civil society, but it cannot bring these about through direct intervention.

Habermas defends his claim that civil society 'under certain circumstances' can have an important impact on political processes. He acknowledges that 'the sociology of mass communication conveys a skeptical impression of the power-ridden, mass-media-dominated public spheres of Western democracies'. According to this sociology, '[s]ocial movements, citizen initiatives and forums, political and other associations' can relay signals of public concern, but they are too weak to affect 'the political system in the short run'. However, the power of the media is not total. Open and transparent connections between people in civil society may pick up early signs of discontent, magnify them, and relay dissent throughout the entire system. There are times when control flies from the hands of elites into those of the masses. During these 'periods of mobilization, the structures that support the authority of a critically engaged public begin to vibrate. The balance of power between civil society and the political system then shifts.'[106]

Habermas offers the anti-nuclear movement, environmentalism and the struggle for women's rights as instances of crisis situations in which 'the *actors in civil society* . . . can assume a surprising and momentous role'. During these events the power politics surrounding mass communication are subverted; official channels of information go into reverse. Instead of governments and other establishment sources controlling the news, the media are forced to respond to public disaffection. 'Sometimes the support of sensational actions, mass protests, and incessant campaigning is required before an issue can make its way . . . into the core of the political system and there receive formal consideration.'[107]

A recent political upheaval in Canada – which at the time of writing still has not run its course – tenders additional support for Habermas's view. In the province of Ontario, a popular, hard-right Tory government decided to rid itself of a vexatious municipal government. In doing so, Premier Mike Harris (nicknamed 'Bomber Harris' by *The Economist* magazine) followed the example of Margaret Thatcher, who abolished the Greater London Council in the mid-1980s for similar reasons.[108] (Comparable actions in the US state legislatures, influenced by lobbyists from the tobacco industry and the National Rifleman's Association, have overruled local municipal restrictions on smoking and the carrying of firearms.[109])

From a Hegelian viewpoint, the dictatorial actions of Thatcher and Harris (and those of US state legislatures) are in naked violation of the autonomy of corporations – which include municipal and regional levels of government – from the state. '[P]articipation of the citizens in the governance of the corporation', writes Heiman, 'is an essential ingredient of Hegel's doctrine. Hence, communities must retain their corporate, semi-autonomous identities.'[110] Accordingly, Hegel declares in the Heidelberg lectures that democratic constitutions must ensure that 'the *rights of the particular local communities and interests* are safeguarded by the free establishment of civic authorities and self-administering bodies'.[111] In the absence of a constitution in Britain, and with Parliament given absolute sway, the Greater London Council had no legal recourse against Thatcher's edict. In Canada, municipal authorities may fight the Harris government under the country's constitution, but the outcome is uncertain because municipal rights are not explicitly guaranteed.

The citizens of Toronto, Canada's largest city, voted solidly against the Tories in the 1995 provincial election. Control of City Council resided on the left of the political spectrum. An outspoken mayor, Barbara Hall, was a thorn in the side of the Conservative government. In mid-December 1996, the Tories announced the forthcoming amalgamation of the City of Toronto with five surrounding cities. The six municipalities would be turned into a giant 'megacity' with a population of about 2.5 million people. Local governments would be folded, and placed under trusteeship, until a new 'streamlined' administration could be installed. All three of Toronto's daily newspapers enthusiastically hailed the plan, as did local radio and television stations. Business organizations jumped on the bandwagon. Centres of resistance in the unions and opposition political parties were caught off-guard. The six cities began a faltering campaign against amalgamation, but chances of success seemed dim. By the beginning of 1997 all six mayors agreed to a referendum on the megacity; Premier Harris vowed to ignore the results.

The resulting explosion of citizen protest could not have been anticipated by '[t]he sociology of mass communication', which – as Habermas suggests – 'depicts the public sphere as infiltrated by administrative and social power and dominated by the mass media'.[112] Opposition centred in non-governmental and non-economic associations which arose spontaneously to fight the Tory programme. The provincial government appeared to hold all the power, but was challenged by a mushrooming social movement. In late December 1996, a tiny group calling itself Citizens for Local Democracy and led by a former mayor of Toronto, John Sewell, met in a small church basement. Within a few weeks its meetings grew into giant public forums. Citizens throughout the six cities telephoned, faxed and e-mailed the anti-megacity message. On 24 February 1997 the megacity referendum registered a giant 'No' vote, with 75 per cent of the citizenry against amalgamation. More people voted than in regular city elections. On the night of the ballot a candlelight procession converged on Queen's Park, the seat of government. Marchers demanded official recognition of the giant tally, but received no reply. Widespread citizen discontent may yet have little effect on Tory plans for a megacity. Doubtless, however, the movement has damaged the prestige of a supposedly populist government. The balance of power between the political system and civil society in Ontario shifted, just as Habermas's model might have predicted.

Like Habermas's concept of civil society, Hegel's includes voluntary organizations and other non-governmental institutions. Moreover, Hegel anticipates Habermas by emphasizing the force of public opinion in democratic societies.[113] '[G]enuine public opinion', Hegel declares, 'shows itself ... where it matters, ... the cabinet cannot remain in office if true public opinion is against it.'[114] For Habermas, public opinion must submit to the mechanisms of the democratic process; it cannot be an independent decision-maker. Hegel makes an identical point. Public opinion ought not to rule on its own because of the manifest self-contradiction it contains. On one hand, says Hegel (echoing the title of Tom Paine's famous pamphlet), public opinion 'embodies not only the eternal and substantial principles of justice ... in the form of *common sense* but also the true needs and legitimate tendencies of actuality'. On the other hand, once public opinion is applied to 'felt needs and [to] events, dispensations, and circumstances within the state ... all the contingencies of opinion, with its ignorance and perverseness, its false information, and its errors of judgement, come on the scene'.[115]

Hegel's model of civil society differs from Habermas's in several crucial respects. Hegelian property theory suggests that business corporations themselves ought to be transformed into democratic constituencies within civil society. Moreover, Hegel would count guilds, trade unions and other such economic organizations among the associations of civil society. Such associations are especially vital for the poor and vulnerable.[116]

Habermas's exclusion of economic communities, which may be his reaction to overzealous Marxist estimates of the potential of proletarian revolt, misses the vast communicative role of the workplace in civil society stressed by Hegel and persuasively noted, as we saw in the last chapter, by Antony Black.[117] Finally, Habermas rejects activist government as a source of change.[118] For Hegel, as I outline in the next, concluding chapter, the public service is a key agent of progressive transformation.

8 • The State in Time

Introduction

Marx's critical analysis of capitalism, and his optimistic hopes for a better future, represent, I have proposed, a penetrating commentary on one side of Hegel's political philosophy. Marx never really detached himself from the Hegelian heritage and so, as a consequence, there is more of Marx in Hegel than is usually thought.[1] Will Hutton observes that the fall of communism brought with it 'a desire to return to capitalism red in tooth and claw, and a hardening of the view that the real world can be made to correspond to the nostrums of free market theory'. Yet, Hutton continues, '[w]ith the collapse of communism it is possible to argue that capitalism does indeed need to be managed and that wealth creation *is* a social act – without being labelled a communist subversive'.[2]

Regardless of his status as a 'communist subversive', Marx was not as interested as Hegel in the management of capitalism. Marx was far more concerned with conditions leading to capitalism's overthrow. This final chapter discusses my interpretation of Hegel's rational state in light of some exciting and innovative arguments offered recently by socialist and left-liberal critics of the capitalist order. As I have done throughout this book, I turn frequently to Hegel's Heidelberg lectures, which offer a fresh and revealing view of Hegel's politics.

I have referred in earlier chapters to the difficult distinction Hegel makes between the ethical substance of the state and the appearance of any actually existing state. 'The state', he writes, 'is ethical spirit, spirit in and for itself, and constitutes the essence of all individuals, but the state appears as a state in time.'[3] Occasionally, this distinction appears as one between what Hegel calls the external state and the rational state – roughly equivalent to Marx's contrast between the capitalist state and the state under communism. Hegel also talks, confusingly, about the state using force against the state. 'The state's right of coercion enters into play when the state departs in any respect from what is ideal.' He is trying, I believe, to convey the idea that the democratic character of the state ultimately lies in the consciousness of its people. Sometimes a nation has to organize itself against its own state, as happened in the French Revolution. 'The development of spirit unaccompanied by a corresponding development of institutions, so that a contradiction arises between the two,' declares Hegel, 'is the source not only of discontent, but also of revolutions.'[4] Hegel puts forward this seditious idea in code so as to elude the censors. Yet he is also taking advantage of the power of abstraction. The Hegelian-Marxist scholar Raya Dunayevskaya notes that 'there is one advantage to abstraction – if you meet a new epoch and a new crisis, a new transformation into opposite, if it's too concrete it doesn't hold anymore ... the abstraction makes it easier to try and see what is new in your age'.[5] By comparing Hegel's rational state with the condition of democracy in advanced Western countries in the 1990s, I am trying, as Dunayevskaya counsels, to find out what is new in our age.

Readers may resist this attempt to bring (a highly controversial version of) Hegel into the twenty-first century, but hopefully they will find my effort provocative, even if only as an index of failed arguments. 'Today, more than ever, in the midst of the scoundrel time we live in,' Žižek contends, 'the duty of the Left is to keep alive the memory of all lost causes, of all shattered and perverted dreams and hopes attached to leftist projects.'[6] From my own left-Hegelian perspective, the current anti-state onslaught in Western societies may bring about a dynamic reassertion of the public realm.[7]

The next section of this chapter compares Hegel's ideal to the vision of market socialism developed recently by theorists anxious to maintain the political freedoms they believe are connected with unrestricted circulation of commodities and capital. In attempting to preserve the free economic institutions of civil society, the market-socialist model resembles Hegel's, but in other respects it veers sharply from the Hegelian project.

Market socialism is part of a movement among left thinkers to reconsider the liberal tradition in which, as David Held observes:

> the political has often been equated with the world of government and the citizen's relationship to it. Where this equation is made, and where politics is regarded as a sphere apart from economy or culture, a vast domain of what is central to politics tends to be excluded from view.[8]

Hegel's social theory concerns not only an understanding of the separation of civil society from the state, but also a revised conception of private property and political representation. Proposals for new forms of property and democracy are considered against the background of Hegel's rational state in the following section.

Because Hegel paid close attention to the progressive unfolding of the bourgeois order, there is much in his ideal society that is reminiscent of modern capitalist political systems. The concluding five sections of the chapter disclose similarities and differences that exist between Hegel's social state and late twentieth-century democracy. I want to suggest that the ways in which liberal democracy falls short of Hegel's rational state may offer guideposts about the shape of future democratic initiatives.

Market socialism

The Hegelian social state may be a variant of market socialism, a democratic project reaching back to nineteenth-century English political economists, such as Thomas Hodgskin.[9] This tradition has been revived by thinkers searching for a way out of the impasse for socialism created by changes in the international economy and the fall of communism.[10]

In his instructive *Socialism After Communism*, Pierson points out that 'market socialism describes an economic and political system which combines the social ownership of the economy with the continuing allocation of commodities (including labour) through the mechanism of markets'. Market socialism shares neo-liberalism's suspicion of government. Its advocates want 'to rid socialism of the pejorative association with the domineering state and the failures of state planning, and to show that the economic efficiency promised by the market is fully reconcilable with socialist forms of ownership'.[11]

Market socialism is advocated by writers convinced of its economic and political feasibility in an era where the market experience is ubiquitous. 'It may well seem to make sense to foster a type of socialism which works with rather than against the logic of markets', advises Pierson.[12] Hegel's project, on the other hand, grows out of his dialectical finding that freedom demands universal and particular expression. Both an autonomous market-oriented civil society founded on the right of property, and a state that expresses and satisfies the needs of the whole, are required for maximum self-actualization of the individual. This Hegelian diagnosis conforms to one offered recently by writers concerned to unite 'social justice and economic efficiency' through new forms of private ownership. 'A society which becomes more individualized, in the sense of placing greater importance on individual autonomy and freedom,' counsel Gamble and Kelly, 'requires not less but more collective action if it is to be stable and legitimate.'[13]

David McNally, a critic of the market-socialist agenda, suggests that without democratic planning, an economy based on 'workers' control at the level of the firm' would inevitably revert to 'capitalist social relations . . . whether they expressed themselves in terms of capitalist competition between workers' cooperatives, state capitalism (control of publicly owned means of production by a bureaucratic group which "personifies" capital), or through the crystallization of capitalistic managers within the enterprise'. McNally grants Hegel's importance as a critic of market relations, but he rejects Hegel's ideal state.

> Hegel looked to an agency outside the market – the state – to impose a universality foreign to the 'blind and elemental' particularity which characterizes market economy . . . . Marx saw the blatant flaw in such a solution – the market and the state are two sides of the same system of alienation, the one cannot cure the other.

Later, however, McNally offers 'the political form of the state' to assist in the transition from capitalism to socialism.[14]

Conceding an integral role for the market, the Hegelian ideal community differs from market socialism in other respects. It modifies the institutional framework of liberal democracy, and assigns the ultimate commanding role in society to a fully democratized state, rather than the market.

Market socialists envision the collapse of class differences. But Hegelian theory suggests that, although differences within the business class will diminish as conflicting ownership rights of capitalists and workers are reconciled, there will remain a fundamental distinction between the universal class of civil servants and workers within the market economy. As we shall see, Hegel gives this distinction considerable weight in the structure of government. Pierson mentions the divide between public- and private-sector workers but, like the market socialists, he makes no attempt to theorize it. Assessing an anti-state market-socialist electoral strategy, he observes that 'no social democratic party would be willing to abandon overnight the potential support of many millions of public sector workers, nor should it abandon its defense of the interests of those whose sole protection against destitution is the support of the state'.[15]

While market socialism generally requires abolishing private sources of capital, Hegel's model embraces private property, and encourages circulation of large pools of private capital, though these are subject to close regulation by the state. Private property rights are required, as we have seen Hegel arguing, precisely to protect the individual from the overweening power of government.

Market-socialist thinkers seek to minimize the state; but socialist values of equity and fairness inevitably require state action. '[I]ndeed', declares Pierson, these 'interventions would almost certainly be *more* extensive than those we find in existing welfare states'.[16] Thus, the difference beween Hegel and market socialists regarding the size of the state may be more semantic than real. Hegel offers a theory of democracy strongly relevant to the market-socialist project because of its sensitivity to conflict among different social actors. As Pierson observes, not much has been written on the possibility of friction 'between differing levels of democratic governance *within* a market socialist polity. Yet it is clear that there may well be clashes between a democratically elected government and democratically self-managed firms', especially over 'allocation of scarce capital'.[17]

Private property and the democratic corporation

Market socialism is based on social ownership of property, rather than capitalist private property. However, market-socialist theorists have encountered great difficulty in defining what they mean by social property. As Pierson avers, Marx proffered few guidelines, except for a vague recommendation in *Capital* that capitalist private property should be replaced by 'individual property based ... on cooperation'.[18] Pierson's review of the concept of social ownership concludes that it is 'ambivalent' and 'theoretically undeveloped'. Market socialists, however, can take comfort, he says, from the 'serious doubt' cast by knowledgeable critics 'upon the many grander claims made for private property'.[19]

In their intriguing survey of 'The New Politics of Ownership', Gamble and Kelly concur. 'Even within most strands of New Right discourse, there is no convincing justification for the highly unequal distribution of property rights and the resulting concentrations of private power which are characteristic of capitalism.'[20] Socialist thinkers have started to revise their views about private property. Once they saw 'at best only a limited role for private ownership and advocated nationalization or highly restrictive regulation to counter concentrations of private financial power'. Now a 'new politics of ownership' has grown up, which 'means recognizing the continuing importance of ownership rights in two senses – a more equal distribution of such rights throughout the population, and more effective accountability of those who manage productive assets to those who own them'.[21]

Gamble and Kelly note that modern corporate practice assumes that shareholders alone should have control over the firm since they alone face the risk of financial loss from business operations. But this view leaves 'control . . . firmly in the hands of a small corporate oligarchy' and ignores the interests of workers, and the wider community. They advocate a 'wider conception of ownership' in which both capital and labour can claim to be owners of firms. Innovative forms of corporate governance 'can be advanced through more active ownership on the part of external owners, especially large institutional investors and associations representing individual shareholders, and through employee ownership, especially ESOPs' (Employee Stock Ownership Plans). This (somewhat Hegelian) vision of the corporation could be combined with 'the creation of a public domain through new forms of collective action in which questions of public interest and public purpose about the way corporations are run can be addressed'.[22]

The most thorough discussion of corporate governance organized along democratic lines, such as I claim are recommended by Hegel, appears in David Ellerman's *The Democratic Worker-Owned Firm*. Ellerman submits 'the democratic principle' as the key for deciding who ought to govern a firm: 'The direct control rights over an organization should be assigned to the people who are governed by an organization so that they will be self-governing.'[23] The 'governed' within the corporation are defined as: 'those who (within certain limits) take orders from the enterprise management, i.e. who are under the authority of managers'.[24]

According to Ellerman, the transition from a capitalist-governed corporation to a worker-governed one 'is a way to transform and perfect the private property system by restoring the labor basis of appropriation. It is not private property that needs to be abolished – but the employment contract.'[25] Thus, labour's claim to property that

I maintain (in chapter 7) Hegel advocates could be realized through gradual establishment of the democratic worker-owned firm.

The USA may seem the least likely country in which to expect such a transition, but even here there are intriguing possibilities. ESOPs in the USA – which have grown to cover more than 10 per cent of the American workforce[26] – fall far short of the democratic ideal.[27] ESOPs, admits Alcaly, tend to be 'controlled by management, which may use them to further its own interests rather than those of the workers'. Partly financed through employee sacrifice in wages and conditions, ESOPs 'were frequently used by management to frustrate hostile takeovers, since the large blocks of stock they tied up effectively kept a company out of the hands of corporate raiders'.[28] However, as Ellerman observes, ESOPs also implement an important feature of the democratic corporation: the linkage of ownership with employment in the firm, rather than simply share ownership. Moreover, because ESOPs are structured like pension plans,[29] and membership is guaranteed for each worker by federal law, they overcome the shortcomings of conventional worker co-operatives and worker-owned firms which are often tempted to sell out to private bidders, or to close off membership to new workers.

The pension-plan structure of ESOPs may allow for a gradual transition to the democratic corporation. 'The real innovation of the ESOP is allowing the workers to use the leverage of the company to take out a loan to buy stock, and then to have the company pay back the loan as a tax deductible expense.'[30] Another factor is that worker participation in management, as documented in many studies, leads to increased efficiency.[31] But the more likely catalyst for the emergence of the democratic corporation is a fully Hegelian one: the growth of human reason. 'Real social change, when it comes' declares Ellerman,

> is driven by ideas and principles, not simply 'efficiency considerations'. Absolute government as well as slavery sagged after centuries of inefficiency, but it was their illegitimacy in the light of first principles that drove the democratic revolutions and the abolition of slavery in the eighteenth and nineteenth centuries. Thus we have focused on the basic principles that drive toward economic democracy.[32]

Ellerman acknowledges that the worker-owned democratic corporation leaves many social questions unanswered. This can only be one part of a strategy to open up both civil society and the state – what

Held has termed 'the process of *double democratization*'.[33] Worker-ownership schemes do not address significant areas of contemporary politics, such as 'civil and military nuclear policy, environmental and sexual rights – they also neglect that growing number of citizens outside the active working population'.[34] We shall examine Hegel's proposals for democratic reform below.

Hegel's rational state after the fall of communism

The rise of union power in the so-called golden age of capitalism that followed the Second World War arguably helped to achieve a highly circumscribed version of Hegel's rational state in Western democracies. In the social-market countries – Germany and its European Union neighbours, and Scandinavia – where capital and labour are co-partners in government, these gains have been consolidated. Hutton notes that in Germany, 'capital and labour are represented by all-encompassing self-governing organisations which are allowed to manage wages and industrial relations'. Stable finance and ownership structures are 'matched by a welfare system – the *socialstaat* – which offers a high degree of social protection, the visible expression of social solidarity'. Labour–capital partnership in German corporations and government has encouraged blending 'academic education with workplace experience': one of the goals of communism, according to Marx's *Critique of the Gotha Program*. Workers' education and status have been supported through the corporation, as Hegel recommended. 'Over 70 per cent of German employees are technically qualified compared with 30 per cent in the UK and the status of *handwerke* (craftsman) and *meister* (craftsmaster) is deeply etched in German culture.'[35]

The sphere of social rights outside the market has widened in most advanced capitalist countries, reducing people's dependence on bourgeois market relations. 'To the degree to which housing, basic diet, clothing, health care, education, childcare, electricity, water, sanitation, transportation and access to cultural and recreational activities are guaranteed,' says McNally, 'the realm of "bourgeois right" contracts.'[36]

Still, Western capitalist democracy, whether in Germany, Scandinavia, Britain or the USA, bears only a slight resemblance to Hegel's ideal. Hegel's electoral prescription, for example, appears to be a non-starter. As we shall see below, his concept of parliamentary representation assumes voting based on work groups and corporate communities. Elections at the national and regional levels would be structured around the individual's place of work, and his or her local neighbourhood. These proposals are similar to Macpherson's 'pyramidal councils system as a model of participatory democracy', put forward twenty years ago in *The Life and Times of Liberal Democracy*. 'Nothing but a pyramidal system', Macpherson explains, 'will incorporate any direct democracy into a nation-wide structure of government, and some significant amount of direct democracy is required for anything that can be called participatory democracy.'[37]

In contrast to Hegel's vision of labour democracy, workers possess very narrow rights within the corporation which offers limited communal orientation. In the UK and North America especially, the past twenty years of union-busting, downsizing, contracting-out and globalization have severely weakened the already tenuous position of workers. Similarly, with unemployment rates in Western Europe reaching double digit levels, the European social market is under attack. 'The spread of the dogma of restrictive fiscal policy', notes Ethan Kapstein, 'is undermining the bargain struck with workers in every industrial country. States are basically telling their workers that they can no longer afford the postwar deal and must minimize their obligations.'[38] Workers' democratic clout is confined to an atomized electoral system, but corporations and the wealthy possess overpowering direct influence in government.

Under the screen of the 'globalization thesis' – which asserts that national governments are irrelevant compared to 'world market forces' and the 'internal decisions of transnational corporations'[39] – capitalist elites are signing away the sovereign rights of nation states.[40] 'Globalization arguments', contends John Ralston Saul in the 1995 Massey Lectures, 'insist on the unregulable nature of all social policy in a new world without economic borders. This is manifestly untrue. A series of international binding [free trade] agreements of great complexity have been signed over the last few years.' Saul opines that agreements on 'job equity and social standards', such as those enforced by the European Community, could easily be brought forward on a regional basis. 'What is described as the impossibility of international social regulation is actually the unwillingness of the corporate elites to enter into such negotiations.'[41]

Hegel's discussion of the dog days of guilds and corporations in the late feudal era is reminiscent of our age of transnational corporate power and declining social responsibility: '[W]hat happened was that each corporation – not looking to the whole but merely to itself, since the authority of the state was insufficient – amassed all the rights it could lay its hands on, disregarding the rights of other corporations.'[42] The result was a backlash against the corporations. 'For the state to be able to subsist, it was therefore necessary for the corporations to be deprived of power and prestige, and so they fell into decay.' According to Hegel, 'the revolutions of recent times' – meaning the French Revolution and its progeny throughout Europe – were aimed at recovering rights which the state had given over, one by one, to private hands. '[T]he right of reason has been asserted over against the form of private right ... this explains the people's struggle against the magnates in our states.' Before the Revolution of 1789, corporations and associations of civil society took advantage of the 'weakness of the state to secure privileges for themselves'. 'There were classes and individuals', writes Hegel, 'who possessed as purely private rights, rights belonging to the state, especially in regard to taxes (e.g. freedom from taxation) and jurisdiction.'[43] (We have our own contemporary examples of this: the press lord Rupert Murdoch has been quoted as saying, 'So much to spend money on ... that giving extra to the tax man is seen as a waste.'[44]) According to Hegel, public rights monopolized by corporations and individuals must be retrieved, even if this demands toppling the old regime by force.

> The state must not allow the purposes of the state based on need [the external state] to take root within it, but must constantly draw them back within its substance; its attitude to them is merely negative. If a corporation adopts an attitude counter to the universal purpose of the state, if what is private seeks to use the state merely for particular purposes, then the state appears as a coercive power .... The state's right of coercion enters into play when the state departs in any respect from what is ideal.[45]

The 'state of freedom' that Hegel asserts over against the external state of civil society represents the rational element present in the spirit and culture of a people. For Hegel, the French Revolution symbolized victory of the ideal state over the corrupt old regime.[46] The social state embodies the corporate spirit of solidarity and community that is lost in civil society and which must be retrieved. 'The proper strength of states resides in their [internal] communities', says Hegel. And the best way to rally this strength is through a system of popular democracy. In one of the most remarkable statements on democracy in the history of philosophy, Hegel makes this brilliantly clear.

> For some time now, organization has always been directed from above, and efforts have been devoted for the most part to this kind of organization despite the fact that the lower level of the masses as a whole can easily be left in a more or less disorganized state. Yet it is extremely important that the masses should be organized, because only then do they constitute a power or a force; otherwise they are merely an aggregate, a collection of scattered atoms. Legitimate power is to be found only when the particular spheres are organized.[47]

One possible source of this corporate spirit, as I have suggested, is the struggle of the working class for freedom within the democratic corporation. Another source is the universal class of public servants, which opposes the exercise of arbitrary self-interest in civil society. In Hegel's ideal state these springs of freedom are given objective embodiment in the constitutional structure of government.

As noted in chapter 7, the constitution of Hegel's state of freedom outwardly resembles the familiar outlines of the liberal democratic state. Yet the Hegelian state – unlike Marx's communism or Fukuyama's liberal democracy – never grows free of contradictions. The confrontation between civil society and the ideal state, between the forces of private interest and those of the public good, is a permanent feature of the human condition. According to Hegel, the threat posed by rapacious private interests is required precisely to 'give life' to the community and to reawaken the need for universality.[48] Even the democratic corporation must be kept under the surveillance of the state. Otherwise it would slip its lead and become as dangerous to the commonweal as any other degenerate corporate order.

> It was a particular defect of earlier corporations that the officials themselves chose their successors; this gave rise to an aristocracy, which afforded an example of the particular interest that was taken into account in making the choice. But as members of a whole, corporations must in turn be subordinate to higher authorities.[49]

Market-socialist thinkers take a similar position. Many fear that workplace democracy may come into conflict with a more general public interest. Within the corporation itself there will always be struggles around ownership, interests, competing groups and personalities. The state, in particular, poses an ominous danger to the citizenry – the possibility of a dictatorship based on knowledge – that must be fought against. I deal further with these issues below.

Leadership

There are three main elements in Hegel's rational state. First is the sovereign and ministers of cabinet; second is the executive or civil service; the legislature makes up the third.

Hegel's ideal state is a constitutional monarchy, but, as Avineri points out, Hegel's sovereign is divested 'of any real power by making the Crown the symbol of self-determination'.[50] Fukuyama observes that the role played by Hegel's monarch is not unlike that of any democratic leader.[51] Allen W. Wood goes further, claiming, rightly I think,

> that the Hegelian constitutional monarch differs from most heads of state with which we are more familiar in having less actual power than they do. Real power in the Hegelian state is supposed to lie with a professional governing class, under the watchful eye of a representative states assembly with the power to recall any particular ministry and replace it with another.[52]

The Crown, for Hegel, represents the democratic power exercised by the nation's citizens, and on that account has no real power of its own. Accordingly, his discussion of monarchy is a veiled criticism of it at that time. 'In a mature constitution,' declares Hegel in his Heidelberg lectures, 'the individuality of the monarch becomes unimportant owing to the state's being organized in a rational, stable manner, and it is in this very insignificance of the person of the ruler that the strength and rationality of the constitution reside.'[53] We saw in chapter 4 that in his unpublished *The German Constitution* Hegel equates an elected chief of state with a constitutional monarch; and in an early version of the *Philosophy of Right* (written before the Karlsbad Decrees) Hegel accepts popular sovereignty as a legitimate means to choose a nation's leader. Similarly, by downgrading the decision-making capacities of the sovereign, and suggesting that the monarch may be incompetent in most of the fields he or she is required to make decisions about, Hegel leaves the question of leadership wide open to a democratic alternative. 'The person of the monarch', says Hegel, tongue firmly in cheek, 'may involve numerous chance attributes, so he must be a simple person, not answerable for anything [particular].'[54] Obviously, any number of recently elected democratic leaders in the Western world could fill Hegel's requirements. The leader does not even have to be a morally exemplary figure. The bedroom carousing of a Kennedy would not have surprised Hegel (though I think he would have been appalled by the amount of power wielded by him and other American presidents).

> Debauchery on the part of the monarch can also have no effect on the whole for the further reason in particular that he can easily gratify all passions; and the position of the one extreme, the sovereign, is as simple as that of the other extreme, the man of the soil.[55]

Žižek proposes an interesting parallel between Hegel's monarch and democratic leadership. Following Lacan, he contends that 'the locus of Power' in modern democracies 'becomes *an empty place*; what was before the anguish of interregnum, a period of transition to be surmounted as soon as possible – the fact that "the throne is empty" – is now the only "normal state"'. The empty throne becomes the antidote to Jacobin terror. 'The "monarch" is nothing but a positivization, a materialization of the *distance* separating the locus of power from those who exert it . . . The vicious circle of Terror – of democrats cutting off each other's heads indefinitely – is thus interrupted.'[56] Žižek is overly sanguine, however; democratic leaders can be victims of terror, perhaps because they enjoy more power than envisaged by Hegel's constitutional proposals. The 1960s assassinations of President John F. Kennedy and his brother Bobby Kennedy; Chilean President Salvador Allende's death in 1973; the murder in 1986 of Swedish Prime Minister Olaf Palme; the shooting of Israeli leader Yitzhak Rabin in 1995, and the 1994 killing of Luis Donaldo Colosio, presidential candidate of Mexico's ruling Institutional Revolutionary Party (PRI), to name only six such victims, all raise questions about the immunity of democratic leadership from terror.

Because an orderly succession to power followed each of these assassinations (with the exception of Dr Allende's), they bear witness to a key feature of democratic leadership: it avoids anarchy in the state, another lesson Hegel learned from the French Revolution. 'All French constitutions [after 1789] had the defect that they lacked the subjective unity, the apex, which came necessarily into being in the form of imperial and then royal power.' As a result, before Napoleon and the restoration of the Bourbons, France was caught in a constant duel between the legislative and the executive powers, with frightful results.

THE STATE IN TIME

Hegel concludes in the following excerpt from the Heidelberg lectures that leadership must be based on the democratic principle (what Hegel calls, the 'rational'), not dictatorship or absolute monarchy. This was the flaw that ultimately toppled Napoleon and the Bourbons. At the outset of the Revolution, writes Hegel,

> the legislative power prevailed over the royal power, and the king was sentenced and executed by the legislative power. Then the Committee of Public Safety rose to the top, and the very top of the pinnacle was Robespierre. This point of unity centered in an individual, to whom the legislative power was slavishly subservient, performing deeds that attracted universal amazement. A wholly republican constitution was drafted, for the legislative body had collapsed. However, this democratic constitution could not take effect because of its inner nullity, and the Directory's constitution came into being. But the basic evil remained notwithstanding, in that the legislative power was quite independent of the Directory, which was surrounded by a great show of pomp and might. The inevitable struggle ensued, each side making it a point of duty to save the state; however, the power that was at the head of the army, the executive power, was the stronger. The apex of power was then reestablished by Bonaparte, first as consul, then as emperor; but because in so doing he did injury to the rational, the apex he established was overthrown despite the external power at its disposal.[57]

Hegel's sovereign is protected from the consequences of decision-making in government. These are borne by the monarch's council of ministers, who lead the public service and 'are answerable for the decisions of the executive'. As in many democratic systems today, the leader selects his or her ministers, and has the power of dismissal. Similarly, the monarch's decisions on which ministers to select, or to sack, is guided by the reception these alternatives are likely to receive in parliament.[58] Ministerial councils advise the monarch, and the appropriate minister 'has to sign the sovereign's decision and is answerable for it'. Hegel cautions that the state 'is organized as an inwardly organic system' to ensure that rational decisions are taken. 'A monarch at the head of a state that has no rational constitution extends his caprice over the whole and is capable of ruining everything. That what is necessary by virtue of the concept – that this *exists* must inspire the confidence of the people.' Hegel's description of the relationship between sovereign and ministers is reminiscent of the one between minister and bureaucrat in the British TV comedy series, *Yes Minister!*

> Since ... the ministers have to deal with the person of the monarch, have to explain to him the whys and wherefores and persuade him, and accordingly have to adopt themselves to the personality of the monarch in order to bring their plans into effect, they must particularly avoid making him obstinate, and must flatter him by attributing all merit to the monarch, rather than to themselves who have done all the preliminary work ... All personal willing must remain hidden from sight.[59]

Hegel refers to the experience of the French Revolution to explain why the hiring and firing of cabinet ministers must be the sovereign's prerogative. 'Should it not be the case that ministries can be appointed and dismissed by the monarch, we would have a directory, and they would carry everything into effect, or else sovereign and ministry would be in hostile opposition to one another.' This situation would lead to factional infighting, 'and the supreme power of the state would be dragged down into particularity, into faction'. Hegel turns to British and French parliamentary administrations to underline the precarious nature of a ministerial position.

> [G]iven the extent of the business and the interests [he has to bear in mind], an incompetent minister will not remain in office for long. The mass of the nation repudiates the incompetence of ministers and stands firm against them. The main guarantee of competence in ministers is their answerability to parliament, to which they have to indicate clearly what they intend. So a minister's position is the most dangerous in the state, for he has to defend himself against the monarch, against his colleagues, against public opinion, and against parliament. The French and English ministers are necessarily our examples here. Men who maintain their position as ministers, and show themselves good at the job, merit the highest respect.[60]

The universal class and the corporation

The second element of Hegel's state is the executive power – the bureaucracy or universal class. This aspect of Hegel's theory of politics, as we shall see, drew heated criticism from Marx. Indeed, in our own market-orientated period, Hegel's view of the public service may be the least palatable component of his outlook. It exposes him to charges of élitism, such as David Held levels against Schumpeter's 'technocratic vision' of democracy, which in some ways is similar to Hegel's. 'In

Schumpeter's democratic system,' writes Held, '. . . the role of ordinary citizens is not only highly delimited, but it is frequently portrayed as an unwanted infringement on the smooth functioning of "public" decision-making.'[61]

For Hegel, the role of the executive is chiefly to offer universal services, and keep corporations in civil society from violating community interests. It does this through provision of social infrastructure, for example; or, as with the courts, through application of rules and regulations and enforcement of law. It is responsible for maintaining the physical health of citizens, and also has the task of educating members of civil society to a more civilized mode of life. Comprising 'a major part of the . . . educated middle class',[62] the universal class does not support itself, but relies on taxes levied by the state on other groups in civil society.

While discussing the public service in the Heidelberg lectures, Hegel emphasizes autonomy and self-government for the various organizations within civil society. 'Particular concerns as such are in the first place the particular property, aims, and interests of the individual local communities, guilds, estates, and corporations, and are administered by these bodies themselves as a matter of right.' Democracy is a pivotal consideration. '[T]he fact that the particular spheres are necessarily self-governed constitutes the democratic principle in a monarchy.' Hegel fully realizes that the democratic setup he calls for lies far in the future. He thunders against the suppression of democracy by arbitrary authority. 'Nowadays governments have relieved the citizens of all these cares for a universal. But this is the democratic principle, that the individuals should share in the government of local communities, corporations, and guilds, which have within themselves the form of the universal.'[63]

As mentioned in chapter 6, posts within self-governed corporations and communities in civil society are filled by a mixture of popular elections and appointments by the Crown. Hegel advises that self-government within the corporations must be designed so that directors and managers, elected by the members, 'must have an authority over against those by whom they are chosen. There must be a specific provision making them independent of the local community, etc.' Leadership in the corporations 'must then be confirmed . . . by senior officials, so as to confer . . . the seal of authority'.[64]

Interestingly, while Ellerman acknowledges the problem of authority within the democratic worker-owned firm, as discussed above, he is not concerned with difficulties that might arise at the interface between state and corporation.[65] Similarly, Macpherson's concept of 'pyramidal participatory democracy' concerns only the upward relationship of citizens with the state – the mechanisms of representation from bottom to top. Hegel, however, is also anxious that the interests of the whole society be represented within the corporation. Rogue firms and corporate groups must be subject to state discipline. Accordingly, Hegel constructs a model which allows societal influence to percolate through to the level of the corporation. This is achieved 'by the efforts of agents of the executive, the state officials, and the higher authorities, who are constituted essentially on a departmental basis and form a pyramid at the apex of which stands the ministries'. It is all very well to ensure the democratic principle for particular interests, but not at the expense of the whole.

> The essential point in regard to the organization of governmental authorities is that on the one hand civic life should be governed in a concrete manner from below where it is concrete, but that on the other hand the business of the community should be divided into its abstract branches looked after by special authorities as different centres [of administration] but converging again in the supreme executive power to form a concrete means of supervision.[66]

Regarding government organization, Hegel strongly favours the British ministerial model, with ministries divided into several departments, even though this system has 'the disadvantage of delay'. In its favour, the departmental model 'has . . . tradition, and upholds a cut-and-dried definite mode of acting, since the personality of the individual involved makes no difference, has no influence on the course of the whole'. Hegel makes one of his few references to the US presidential system, noting that it is perilous to make cabinet secretaries and departments operate entirely under the prerogative of the supreme chief. This arrangement

> gives undue scope to caprice and personality, and there is undue delay until the new president has worked himself in; there can be no uniformity here. Only in the case of danger to the state may it be necessary to transfer more power to a single individual, but never in peacetime.[67]

Appointment to the bureaucracy is geared entirely 'to proof of ability' so that the state becomes a major source of upward mobility for talented and interested citizens. Hegel observes that 'the genesis of present-day higher education' lies in the requirement that the government be served by highly qualified individuals from all classes: 'the possibility of participating in the service of the state is open to every citizen and is not confined exclusively to individual classes or conferred by birth'. This necessitates a nation-wide system of publicly provided education. 'Not all can take part in the universal activity of government, but all must have the possibility of doing so, and must be given the right to do so by education directed to that end.' Entrance to the public service is controlled by 'a system of examinations in order to demonstrate ability'. A major qualification of candidates for government service is concern for the interests of the whole society, and respect for the constitution of the state. Bureaucrats and court officials must have job security; they may be dismissed from their posts 'not by arbitrary decision, but solely as the result of a formal judgement'.[68] Dismissal is a serious matter since '[i]ndividuals devote themselves to the service of the state and pin to it their spiritual existence . . . and their existence . . . as pertaining to their needs'.[69]

The civil service forms an autonomous corporate body, with its own rules and hierarchical arrangements. 'Civil servants are answerable in the first place to their superior authorities, whose essential concern it must be to maintain the authority of government, represented as it is by civil servants, and whose members are drawn from within the same particular class.'[70] Here Hegel's vision conforms with Schumpeter's, who insists on a 'well-trained bureaucracy' capable of instructing 'the politicians who head the ministries'. Schumpeter avers that bureaucrats must necessarily control appointments, promotions and tenure within the public service, 'in spite of all the clamor that is sure to arise whenever politicians and the public feel themselves crossed by it as they frequently must'.[71]

A large part of the universal class consists of teachers, 'who apply themselves to the various fields of knowledge for the greatest good of the community'. This is perhaps the most important occupation in civil society (like other groups, the universal class belongs to both civil society and the state; what separates it from other classes is the part it plays in government), and Hegel faults Germany for not adequately rewarding its educators.

It is honorable for a state if, in order to support the universal class and in particular develop knowledge, it confers on individuals who devote their whole lives exclusively to this purpose certain privileges and independence of means. Instead of this it was the custom in Germany to give privileges to the nobility, who abandoned themselves to the most shameful passions at the expense of their few vassals.[72]

Civil servants must have their rights enshrined in the constitution to protect their independence from powerful interests in civil society. Hegel, however, is no blind supporter of bureaucrats. Without a democratic counter-balance, public officials may become ruthless and authoritarian, as was the case in communist states before 1989. 'Conflict arises in that the government authorities like to keep the civil authorities in their place, and their vanity and particularity come into play in this connection.'[73] Safeguards must be installed to prevent 'one of the greatest ills that can befall states' – a dictatorship based on knowledge.[74] Here Hegel sounds an alarm later echoed by Weber, who worried about an 'iron cage' of bureaucracy that would stifle the democratic impulse in capitalist society.[75] Hegel observes that the rise of the modern state involved replacement of the power of the feudal hierarchy with that of the educated middle class. This is a mixed blessing. On one hand, '[t]he educated middle class constitutes the people's consciousness of freedom and right, the developed consciousness of right is to be found in the middle class'. On the other hand, 'if this class does not have the interests of the citizens at heart, it is like a net thrown over the citizens in order to oppress them, particularly as the whole class forms a whole since its interests are one and the same'.

> Alienated from the people, officials become, by reason of their skill, themselves the object of people's fear; even the way they talk strikes the ears of citizens as gibberish, a kind of thieves' slang . . . Officials must therefore accustom themselves to a popular approach, to popular language, and seek to overcome the difficulties this occasions them.[76]

Hegel's warnings about the danger of a straddling, self-regarding bureaucracy unimpeded by democratic procedures place him beside, rather than against, Marx. Marx, however, appeared unaware of this identity in their views. He took it for granted that Hegel was an unabashed defender of oppressive bureaucracy. In his 1843 *Critique of Hegel's 'Philosophy of Right'*, Marx suggests acidly that 'Hegel gives an empirical description of the bureaucracy partly as it actually is, and partly according to the opinion which it has of itself.' Marx complains of the 'crass materialism' of the bureaucrat, 'the materialism of passive obedience, of trust in authority, the mechanism of an ossified and formulistic behaviour, of fixed principles, conceptions and traditions'.[77] Sounding like one of today's New Right critics of 'rent-seeking bureaucrats',[78] Marx contends that '[a]s far as the individual bureaucrat is concerned, the end of the state becomes his private end; a pursuit of higher posts, the building of a career'. Tellingly, Hegel makes almost the same critique in the Heidelberg lectures – though his comments are framed within an overall theory of bureaucracy:

> If, in the mind of the official, his remuneration is the principal thing and he and his family exist for that alone, he easily comes to see his post as existing for his own sake, not that he is there for the sake of the citizens, and he believes his only duties are to his superior, who can promote him.[79]

For Marx, the requirement that knowledgeable bureaucrats run the state is a sham, since in an ideal society every responsible citizen would possess appropriate qualifications for governing.

> In a rational state, taking an examination belongs more properly to becoming a shoe-maker than an executive civil servant, because shoe-making is a skill without which one can be a good citizen of the state, a social man; but the necessary state knowledge is a condition without which a person in the state lives outside the state, is cut off from himself, is deprived of air. The examination is nothing other than a masonic right, the legal recognition of the privileged knowledge of state citizenship.[80]

Marx is not interested in a reformed bureaucracy, since a truly free civil society would not need a state. Accordingly, he pays little attention to Hegel's recommendations, detailed below, for a democratically accountable public service. As I have suggested, Marx's one-sided perspective on bureaucracy – and, indeed, that held today by a broad spectrum of the left – conforms to the New Right outlook on the state. Hegel is no less sensitive than Marx (and Weber) to the limitations and hazards of bureaucratic rule. But while Marx expected bureaucracy to be abolished in a truly universal society, Hegel recognized the state apparatus as a necessary, and welcome, counterweight to market power.

Censorship forced Hegel to mask his criticism of bureaucratic authoritarianism in the published version of the *Philosophy of Right* (though even here Hegel's criticism of bureaucracy, while muted, can still be discerned – Marx could have found it had he looked for it!).

But in his Heidelberg lectures, Hegel pours abuse on the untrammelled power of the educated middle class over the people.

> The privileged position this education confers on the middle class may enable it to impress the sovereign and oppress the citizens, although it is not something innate like nobility but something acquired. This undue power of the middle class is commonly the essential ill affecting our states.[81]

The role of the police is especially problematic. '[P]olice supervision must go no further than is necessary, though it is for the most part not possible to determine where necessity here begins.' Hegel mocks Fichte's crime-fighting proposal to have all citizens carry identity papers: '[S]uch a state becomes a world of galley slaves, where each is supposed to keep his fellows under constant supervision.' Police officers must be prevented, wherever possible, from invading the privacy of individuals. House searches, for example, should be rare, 'for what the family does within the home must be unobserved'. 'Secret police', Hegel opines, 'would be best' since 'it is repugnant to see policemen everywhere . . . people ought not to see that they are exercising supervision even though such supervision is necessary. But the purpose of what is hidden is [in this event] that public life should be free.' Hegel was no admirer of police methods. 'Police are hated because they [have to] proceed in such a petty fashion and have such petty things to do.' Nor was he an unabashed cheerleader for this branch of the universal class. '[A] good police force should not be noticed at all, and since it is not seen doing anything, it gains no praise either.'[82]

Perhaps thinking of his own (and Hölderlin's) encounters with repressive police authority (discussed in chapter 5), Hegel makes some scathing observations regarding police use of civilians working undercover to catch criminals. 'These people, or police spies, hunt around, without being officials, or out of subjective interest, and they seek themselves to make criminals or to impute crimes falsely.' He cites the example of three Irish labourers in London who 'were made counterfeiters without knowing what they were doing, and were then arrested'. Such practices 'can give rise to the abyss of depravity'.[83] Hegel is pointing to a key problem of our own age. Through widescale use of spies, the police may become a captive agency of the criminal underworld.

The strange universe slowly being revealed by release of documents relating to the assassination of John F. Kennedy suggests that 'the abyss of depravity' Hegel feared may now be an integral feature of modern liberal democracies. Peter Dale Scott's important study, *Deep Politics and the Death of JFK*, shows that 'lone assassin' Lee Harvey Oswald was working undercover for several US government agencies prior to the shooting of the president. It seems likely that Oswald was framed for the murder while the real assassins, perhaps acting for a coalition of Kennedy's political enemies, escaped detection. To explain the Kennedy shooting – and other examples of political corruption, such as infiltration by the Mafia of the central apparatus of the Italian state – Scott constructs a theory of deep politics, which he contrasts with traditional conspiracy theory. The latter assumes 'a single objective and/or control point', while deep political analysis is 'the study of "all those political practices and arrangements, deliberate or not, which are usually repressed rather than acknowledged"'. Scott adds that a *deep political system or process* is one which habitually resorts to decision-making and enforcement procedures outside as well as inside those publicly sanctioned by law and society. In popular terms, collusive secrecy and law-breaking are part of how the deep political system works.' Citing 'the mechanics of accommodation', Scott criticizes mainstream political science which claims that 'law enforcement and the underworld are opposed to each other; the former struggling to gain control of the latter'. A deep political analysis, however,

> notes that in practice these efforts at control lead to the use of criminal informants; and this practice, continued over a long period of time, turns informants into double agents with status within the police as well as the mob. The protection of informants and their crimes encourages favors, payoffs, and eventually systemic corruption. The phenomenon of 'organized crime' arises: entire criminal structures that come to be tolerated by the police because of their usefulness in informing on lesser criminals. In time one may arrive at the kind of police–crime symbiosis familiar from Chicago, where the controlling hand may be more with the mob than with the police department it has now corrupted.[84]

Earlier, I mentioned David Held's concept of 'a double-sided process of democracy', which is 'concerned on the one hand with *re-*form of state power and, on the other hand, with the restructuring of civil society'.[85] Hegel, I think, advocates a very similar process. We have already examined his blueprint for the democratic corporation. This would place power in the hands of those governed by the corporation, and would also provide points of entry for representatives of government into corporate decision-making. Equally urgent for Hegel is a democratic restructuring of the state itself. One aspect of this, discussed above, is the integration of the Crown into an organic system to avoid arbitrary rule. Another key element is reform of the civil service.

For Hegel, a central justification of hierarchy is that it provides a means for those affected by arbitrary decisions to obtain redress. Through hierarchy in the civil service,

> the power of government officials, which impinges directly on the citizens, is in the first place limited primarily to supervising, advising and taking formal decisions, and civil servants are obliged to become genuine officials of the state, i.e., officials of the citizenry as well as officials of the sovereign.

Nevertheless, hierarchy in itself cannot solve the problem of an intractable bureaucracy. '[I]t is not enough to rely on the junior official's being answerable to the senior officials as a safeguard against oppression, for the interests of junior and senior officials vis à vis the citizenry coincide.'[86]

Hegel calls for open, democratic processes in government. This does not mean requiring civil servants to submit even more written reports to their superiors.

> [T]he written word in itself is lifeless and indefinite, and there are far too many special reports for the senior officers to be able to examine and appraise them, so there is precious little protection for the citizen who has to complain about officials who are then judged in secret.

Citizens must be able to appeal 'first, to the nearest responsible official, then to the senior official, and, if they get no satisfaction from that quarter, to the estates assembly [parliament]'. A free press is also required to enforce the right of citizens to a fair hearing. Private property in the corporations must, above all, be administered by corporate officials so that government appointees have only a small role to play in civil society. The less bureaucrats interfere with corporations, the more they 'become true officials of the state'. Hegel acknowledges that his reform programme means 'organizing [the civil service] from the bottom up, and all other plans are of no avail'.[87]

More than 150 years later, Hegel's reformed bureaucracy remains a distant hope in most advanced capitalist democracies. Governments hide behind 'cabinet secrecy', or declare certain matters out of bounds because of 'national security'. Perpetrators of police violence or officials responsible for incompetent criminal investigations are often beyond the public's reach. Governments frequently take decisions regarding, for example, the environment or social welfare without public consultation, or guarantees for affected groups. We are still a long way from bureaucrats who are, in Hegel's words, 'genuine officials of the state, i.e., officials of the citizenry as well as the sovereign'.[88]

Prospects for Hegel's universal class

Since the Second World War, the universal class in advanced capitalist nations has attained a prominence that might have surprised even Hegel. In many countries it makes up perhaps a third of the labour force. Yet Hegel's concept has been generally ignored, and is seen by commentators as a peculiarity of his nineteenth-century outlook. As we have seen, Marx ridiculed it and substituted the proletariat as his own version of the universal class. Francis Fukuyama's influential *The End of History and the Last Man* barely mentions it, even though Fukuyama himself, a former deputy director of the US State Department's Policy Planning Staff, is a prominent member of the universal class in the USA. This reticence is not unusual. Most members of Hegel's universal class are unaware of the distinct character of their place in the class structure. Alvin Gouldner – one of a handful of social scientists who take Hegel's concept seriously – observes that most nineteenth- and twentieth-century revolutionaries, starting with Marx himself, sprang from the educated middle class. For Gouldner, classical Marxism represents the disguised ideology of Hegel's universal class (which includes the bulk of the educated middle class) since its members are usually the ones thrust into power by revolution. The leadership of the Russian Communist Party offers a telling illustration.

> There is no doubt that the Old Bolsheviks consisted overwhelmingly of intellectuals, who were middle class in origin, well-travelled, and who read broadly and wrote extensively. The average member of the early Politburo undoubtedly wrote more books than the average economics professor. Even Stalin wrote several books which, he saw to it, had numerous readers. The early Bolsheviks were dominated by intellectuals who evidently believed in the rule, publish or perish. Stalin later taught them another rule, publish *and* perish.[89]

Marxist revolutionaries have a built-in bias against recognizing their own universal-class affiliations, since they are self-proclaimed representatives of the working class. Only Lenin – in his world-shaking 'What is to be done?' – dared to spell out the connection between Marxism and the intelligentsia.[90] 'The theory of socialism', says Lenin, 'grew out of the philosophic, historical, and economic theories elaborated by educated representatives of the propertied classes, by intellectuals. By their social status the founders of modern scientific socialism, Marx and Engels, belonged to the bourgeois intelligentsia.'[91] More generally, the unpopularity of the universal class as a theoretical construct is connected to the dislike people in civil society – including those on the left as well as the right – have for a public authority that interferes with their own conduct. In civil society, advises Hegel, 'each posits his interest as the sole end and lets it stand opposed to the interest of another class; the public authority then has to act as a moderating factor and seek to maintain equilibrium between all'.[92] Additionally, the universal class must always suffer the opprobrium visited on it by resentful taxpayers. Over the past twenty years, public anger against the universal class has been whipped up by multinational corporations and the wealthy, who seek, for obvious reasons, to limit the size and power of government.

Free-market dogma advises radical downsizing of state bureaucracy, as supposedly already experienced by many large corporations. Clamour for reduced government is especially loud in the USA. David Gordon's *Fat and Mean* documents, however, that the top-heavy bureaucratic structure of American corporations has grown over the 1990s while millions of workers have been laid off. Massive corporate bureaucracies are associated, notes Gordon, with conflictual labour–management relations. Squads of bosses are needed to wield the stick against recalcitrant workers. This is true of the USA, along with Canada and the United Kingdom, which have bloated, highly paid corporate bureaucracies, and the worst record of labour relations in the Western world.[93] Countries with comparatively small and efficient business bureaucracies, such as Sweden and Germany – which also enjoy a large and active public service – experience fairly co-operative relations between workers and capital.

History shows that efforts to restrict the growth of the state are unlikely to succeed for long. 'The bureaucracies of Europe', relates Schumpeter, are the product of a long development that started with the *ministeriales* of medieval magnates (originally serfs selected for administrative and military purposes who thereby acquired the status of petty nobles) and went on through the centuries until the powerful engine emerged which we behold today. It cannot be created in a hurry. It cannot be 'hired' with money. But it grows everywhere, whatever the political method a nation may adopt. Its expansion is the one certain thing about our future.[94]

Pierson's careful study of the welfare state under Reagan and Thatcher shows that New Right attempts to reduce government have not had much success. 'Despite the aggressive efforts of retrenchment advocates,' Paul Pierson counsels, 'the welfare state remains largely intact ... [A]ny attempt to understand the politics of welfare state retrenchment must start from a recognition that social policy remains the most resilient component of postwar domestic policy.' The right-wing offensive has badly hurt the poor, and stifled attempts to address new social problems. Nevertheless, public approval for welfare-state programmes has soared since the 1970s; and citizens' resistance to state cutbacks has inflicted considerable political damage upon right-wing parties and governments. 'The maturation of social programs has produced a new network of organized interests – the consumers and providers of social services – that are well placed to defend the welfare state.' Perhaps most important, the case for welfare-state services is very strong. There are simply no efficient private-sector replacements for public programmes such as health, childcare, work safety, and environmental regulation.[95] Robert Kuttner's devastating attack on the free-market model, *Everything For Sale*, reaches a similar conclusion:

> In markets where the consumer is not effectively sovereign (telecommunications, public utilities, banking, airlines, pure food and drugs), or where the reliance on market verdicts would lead to socially intolerable outcomes (health care, pollution, education, gross inequality of income, the buying of office or purchase of professions), a recourse purely to ineffectual market discipline would leave both consumer and society worse off than the alternative of a mix of market forces and regulatory interventions.[96]

Without an activist public service, poverty, pollution and other social ills would become unmanageable. In order to deal with rising social discontent, states would have to resort to arbitrary measures and restriction of political freedom. Such actions, designed to protect the powerful, would jeopardize economic life in civil society.[97]

How realistic is Hegel's picture of the universal class as a principal force for good in civil society, 'the universal element in the social condition itself'? As discussed above, Hegel has few illusions about the state bureaucracy. He understands its capacity for corruption and naked self-interest. 'All too frequently the character of authorities and officials is compounded of pride, sordidness, and dishonesty.'[98] Alvin Gouldner's New Class differs in important respects from Hegel's universal class. Gouldner's concept embraces the entire educated middle class, whereas Hegel's refers to the bureaucracy alone. Nevertheless, Gouldner's assessment of the New Class as a 'flawed universal class' is remarkably similar to Hegel's evaluation of public servants. 'The paradox of the New Class', says Gouldner, 'is that it is both emancipatory *and* elitist . . . Even as it subverts old inequities, the New Class silently inaugurates a new hierarchy of the knowing, the knowledgeable, the reflexive and insightful.' In spite of its élitism, says Gouldner, 'the New Class is the most progressive force in modern society and is a center of whatever human emancipation is possible in the foreseeable future'.[99]

Habermas quarrels with the Hegelian idea that 'exponents of the state apparatus' are a leading element in social-reform projects. Instead, he suggests that the educated middle class – Gouldner's New Class – is the source of radical change. Habermas notes that issues such as nuclear disarmament, the ecological threat posed by industry, or the impoverishment of the Third World, were not initially raised by government bureaucrats. 'Instead they were broached by intellectuals, concerned citizens, radical professionals, self-proclaimed "advocates" and the like.'[100] There is much truth in this. But Habermas ignores several important factors in his analysis of the roots of social change. As Gouldner accepts, the New Class is characterized by its close connection to the state. This was especially clear in the former communist societies, but equally valid 'under capitalism' where 'the educated have already begun to make the state apparatus their special property'.[101] The vital core of the educated middle class invariably consists of those with close relations with the state, such as teachers, social workers, nurses or city planners. Even those not directly employed in government service often have strong links with the state. Hence, the initial success of Reaganite efforts in 'defunding the left' by reducing the flow of funds to 'groups with an interest in domestic policy'.[102]

Habermas overlooks the inclination of public servants to secrecy, anonymity, and (ostensible) aversion to leadership. This is not a group that desires publicity or self-display since these are inimical to its own survival. What Hegel says about the sovereign's ministers also applies more generally to state functionaries: 'All personal willing must remain hidden from sight.'[103] Conditions associated by critics with the bureaucracy, such as poor service and inadequate public facilities, are often the result of funding and supply decisions by politicians. Similarly, the low profile of state officials in social-protest movements may be a direct consequence of the hostile attitude of concerned government ministers. Despite these factors, activist public servants are not uncommon. Frequently, the data and terms of debate around controversial issues are provided by reports of public servants, whether these are officially published or leaked to the press. Bureaucrats working behind the scenes are often the source of revelations about government malfeasance. Abrupt changes in government policy brought about by popular protest are invariably planned and directed, in consultation with citizens, by capable civil servants aware of the issues and possible remedies involved.

A dramatic recent illustration of Hegel's universal class as an active promoter of social justice – 'the mainstay of the state as far as integrity ... and intelligence are concerned'[104] – is the anti-Mafia movement in Italy in the 1980s and 1990s which severely weakened the Cosa Nostra. Alexander Stille notes that '[t]he war against the mafia in Sicily is not a local problem of law and order but . . . the struggle for national unity and democracy in Italy'. High state officials who dared to challenge Mafia rule were principal targets for execution, becoming, in Mafia parlance, 'excellent cadavers'. Ignoring the considerable risk to their lives, two intrepid state magistrates, Giovanni Falcone and Paola Borsellino, followed the trail of deception and murder that ultimately led to the office of the former Prime Minister himself, Guilio Andreotti. Along the way politicians and officials from every political party were implicated. When both Falcone and Borsellino were assassinated by the Mafia in the summer of 1992, Italians reacted with outrage. Operation Clean Hands (1992–4), a massive bribery investigation, started after Borsellino's death by Judge Antonio de Pietro, brought the fall of the First Italian Republic, with one-third of parliament under indictment. 'For the first time,' Stille writes, 'investigators had the reserves, the tools and the organizational structures they needed to attack the mafia in a coordinated, global manner.'[105]

The legislature

The most acute problem faced by modern liberal democracies is the dominance of wealth and corporate interests in politics. The institutions of Hegel's ideal state are designed to avoid this quandary: 'the legislature must not be in the hands of those, who, guided by their interests, oppose ... mature concepts of right, because this would prevent the constitution from ever developing'.[106] The legislature consists of representatives from various classes and corporations whose duty is to protect the constituencies they represent from the application by the state 'of universal rules, which may be very oppressive for particular spheres and individuals'. Far from favouring elite rule, Hegel cautions that change cannot be imposed from above. '[I]nsight into what is better must rise up from below, and must have permeated the lowest as well as the upper strata.'[107]

Hegel's state follows the standard liberal democratic model (especially that of British parliamentary democracy) by including two houses or chambers of parliament. This set-up guarantees that decisions are not made too quickly on 'the mood of the moment which can attach to any decision by a numerical majority'.[108] In addition it moves opposition away from direct confrontation with the government. Issues are fought out between the two halves of the legislature rather than between the government and the people's representatives. House sessions are open to all citizens so that, as in Britain, the full weight of public opinion can be exerted on parliamentary representatives. Contrary to standard commentary – which tends to regard Hegel as an opponent of British democratic traditions – he is a qualified admirer of the Westminster system: 'How vastly more advanced the English people are than the German', Hegel enthuses. 'How false and silly is the judgment one usually hears [in Germany] ... by contrast with the judgment of the English.'[109] But Hegel was also aware that the unreformed British constitution was badly flawed, and compromised by widespread bribery.[110]

Open parliamentary debate must be bolstered by freedom of the press and '[likewise the possibility] that other individuals from the general public should have their say publicly as they please, and the possibility for all to participate directly'.[111] Press freedom, 'judicial proceedings involving jury courts' ('so that all can know how and by whom they are being judged'[112]), and open debate in parliament are part of a universal effort to educate the public in democratic governance. 'When a people obtains this education ... having regard to the self-consciousness of its freedom and its right, this provides the root of all public virtues.'[113]

The first or upper house consists of individuals appointed from the nobility. The lower chamber is made up of elected representatives from democratic corporations, and – as in the British system – ministers of government, who are required to defend publicly the administration's policies. Hegel favours party democracy, with at least two parties in the assembly. The governing party has the most members in the house, and forms the cabinet; 'but the opposition must necessarily be there as well'.[114] Some of Hegel's constitutional proposals suggest that he was trying to avoid prosecution for sedition. They also register the radical departure of his ideal state from the norms of liberal democracy.

Hegel clearly outlines principles that underlie elections to the lower house. He emphasizes that democracy is the product of working people. 'The principle of labor is the precondition for democracy.'[115] Accordingly, property qualifications are absent ('no actual citizen is excluded, regardless of means'[116]), and citizens of both sexes are eligible to vote.[117] Yet he appears to bend to the mood of his time, which dealt severely with advocates of popular democracy. 'It goes without saying', he intones, 'that day laborers, servants, etc., are not allowed to vote, but are excluded as not being members of an association.' But Hegel affirms that the fundamental right of everyone in civil society, regardless of social class, is to belong to a corporation. No one can be excluded, whatever their occupation. The right to vote rests not with single persons as in modern liberal democracies, whether they are day labourers, servants or anyone else – but with corporations: 'it is no longer left to the chance patriotism of individuals'.[118]

Seen in the light of his commitment to democracy, Hegel's inclusion of aristocracy in the ruling circles of the ideal state is a shocking concession to the despotic governments of his own time. It is also at variance with his contention that, as in England, the agricultural class tends to disappear as a unique class grouping in civil society.[119] In fact, Hegel's discussion of the unique qualifications of landowners for a parliamentary role directly (even comically) contradicts his own account of the backward character of the 'innocent' agricultural mind. This class would seem exactly the one that Hegel was trying to exclude from the state of freedom. Oddly, Hegel refers to the landowning class as the 'universal class' while discussing the make-up of the first house.[120] Elsewhere, however, he clearly equates universal class membership with being a civil servant.

In fact, Hegel was concealing his most radical proposal for the structure of the ideal state: the exclusion of the wealthy from the upper house. The first chamber, he writes, has no place 'for the pursuit of abstract profit, for cunning or guile'. Capitalists need not apply. 'Even large-scale traders, though they disregard petty gains and their business involves them in universal matters, are always after profits, albeit on a larger scale, and seek to accumulate wealth.' Landowners can take their place in the first house, but they must be angels first. Hegel suggests impossible qualifications for the parliamentary nobility.

> A nobility of this kind must have no privileges, as in England; and the exercise of certain trades, and also the right to dispose of landed estate, must be forbidden to it. It has to accept the sacrifice of renouncing the general civil right of doing whatever does not adversely affect the rights of another.[121]

What Hegel means to do, I think, is to reserve the seats in the upper house for elected representatives of the universal class. As Hegel makes clear, members of the universal class are infinitely more qualified than landowners (even eviscerated ones) for a part in government. '[T]here is no longer any room for a nobility that lacks all recognized employment and is proud of the fact, nor must it take precedence over the middle class in offices of state.'[122] The legislature reflects the clash of public and private worlds, in a dialectical movement made up of three political groupings and two legislative chambers. On one side is the government, and its majority of elected corporate representatives; on the other, the opposition party from the corporations. In the middle, comprising the upper house, is the universal class, which represents its own democratic corporate interest.

> It is usually thought that civil servants ought not to be members of an estates assembly on the grounds that they are on the side of government; but government, as the unity of the whole, is the foremost thing that has to be preserved. As for civil servants, whose corporation must itself have rights and who cannot simply be dismissed, they are not unduly dependent on government. Yet they are for the most part the best educated, who were at universities, and bring with them into the assembly this mentality trained for office.[123]

Prospects for left-Hegelian politics

Hegel's proposal (as I interpret it) for an upper house consisting of public servants appears today rather curious, even dangerous. It represents Hegel's (perhaps impractical) solution to a pivotal conflict in civil society: the extreme divergence of interest between an acquisitive business class, organized in corporations (which include both capitalists and workers), and the universal class, concerned with the welfare of the whole society. So far this conflict has not been resolved, or even adequately confronted, in modern liberal democracies. On the contrary, the best cards are in the hands of the ruling capitalist class, which dominates government in most countries (whether or not social democrats are in power). In the USA, the Senate performs some of the duties of Hegel's upper house, but it is organized around regional interests, and is, perhaps, even more susceptible than the House of Representatives to the dictates of wealth. Canada retains the British tradition of an upper house, but hereditary peers have been replaced with appointees of the ruling party, who are usually retired or defeated members of parliament. Tony Blair may replace Britain's House of Lords with an appointment system similar to Canada's, though, as Robin Blackburn observes, this is 'not a prospect to enthuse those outside the charmed circle'. Blackburn proposes, instead, 'a new democratic mandate for the second chamber, representing society in some different yet complementary way to that supplied by the House of Commons'.[124] Unless such a new system can sidestep the dynamic of wealth that rules elections in Britain, however, the fundamental conflict Hegel marks out between state and civil society will remain.

In more optimistic times for the left, before the onslaught of financial markets and corporate capital that has marked politics during the past two decades, Alvin Gouldner, who died in 1980, forecast the demise of 'the old moneyed class' and the irresistible ascent of the New Class, based on knowledge and culture rather than financial wealth. He defined his 'neo-Hegelian sociology' in terms that conform to my own interpretation of Hegel's social theory.

> It is *left* Hegelianism in that it holds that knowledge and knowledge systems are important in shaping social outcomes, but, far from seeing these as disembodied eternal essences, views them as the ideology of special classes; and while ready to believe that knowledge is one of the best hopes we have for a humane social reconstruction,

also sees our knowledge systems as historically shaped forces that embody limits and, indeed, pathologies.

Gouldner predicted that *détente* between East and West would threaten Communist Party rule, and 'result in a worldwide intensification of technological development and competition'. While both the Communist Party apparatus and the old Western bourgeoisie were dying, according to Gouldner, the Communists were likely to be the first to go since 'party officials and bureaucrats were even more of an obstacle to New Class technical ambitions than the old class of propertied capitalists in the west'. The moneyed class was dangerously weak, declared Gouldner, although he admitted that this condition 'is no sudden, new debility . . . The old class . . . has never been greatly beloved; its grip on society has never been matched by a *legitimacy* of equal force. Indeed, it was *born* with a "legitimation crisis".' In the USA (the world leader of the old class) the Vietnam War and Watergate challenged people's faith in big business and government. This accentuated the historic feebleness of the bourgeoisie: it hands over management of violence to the military, itself part of the New Class. Similarly, the development of culture is a monopoly of paid intellectuals, rather than the wealthy.[125]

As Gouldner anticipated, the popularity of US big business with the public has continued to decline, and more Americans than ever are alienated from government. 'In 1992, just 38 percent of eligible citizens cast ballots for president . . . The voting rate of poor and working-class voters is below 20 percent. That gives the affluent approximately three effective votes for every one of the poor's.'[126] The American sociologist marvelled at the proportion of the globe that was then outside the market system and increasingly under New Class control. 'A new social system', he enthused, 'has been established in a huge land block ranging from Berlin to Vladivostok and the Eastern Islands of China . . . this land mass includes one out of every three persons on earth . . . And the old class is firmly excluded from the territory.'[127] Twenty years later, most of the former socialist world is capital's oyster.

Perhaps Gouldner underestimated the determination of the old moneyed class, and its ability to fight back. Certainly, he was aware of the source of its power, the creation of a privatized and depoliticized social existence for a mass market of consumers, 'that seems for the moment to compensate for their often "pointless" lives'. In the years after Gouldner's death, the old class enjoyed a striking resurgence, and government – the major instrument of the New Class – suffered a humiliating series of defeats.[128] Russia and other states in the former Soviet Union have experienced the defeat of the New Class, and the transformation of the *nomenclatura* into capitalists, mainly with the help of 'Mafia-like groups'. But there is at least one major confirmation of Gouldner's analysis: the countries of Central East Europe (the Czech Republic, Hungary and Poland) are distinguished (so far) by the absence of a capitalist class. Instead they are dominated by a 'power elite' that 'exercises power principally on the basis of knowledge, expertise and the capacity to manipulate symbols, in short, "cultural capital"'.[129]

At the conclusion of his Heidelberg lectures, Hegel extends an assessment almost identical to Gouldner's estimate of the New Class. 'Rationality', he declares, 'is to be found in the middle class, which is the intellectual estate.' The best hopes for humanity rest with the social class of knowledge and culture.

> The people are a material extreme; to say that the people will what is good means that they do not want to be oppressed, and that they want to give as little as possible and get as much enjoyment as possible. It is through the middle class that the wishes of the people are laid before the sovereign.[130]

Hegel laments that the culture of spirit, the life of religion, art and philosophy, which should be the end of the ideal state, are neglected by the bourgeois order. 'Knowing is the highest way in which reason is real, and this reality must come about in a people. There must be one class in the people that devotes itself to it.' Instead the state was 'regarded as merely attending to the protection of its citizens'. There were no universal institutions dedicated to the 'absolute concerns of the people'. In the Middle Ages the monasteries devoted to knowledge 'shut themselves off from the world [and] were of no benefit to the universal interest since they only looked after themselves'. The same situation exists under capitalism,[131] where 'the universities and academies of learning have taken the place of the monasteries'. Rather than deal with the real concerns of ordinary individuals, the intellectual classes 'bury themselves so deeply' in the spheres of knowledge 'as to lose themselves, as happened for instance in Egypt'. Hegel advocates that '[i]n its institutions the state must be a temple of reason. This is how philosophical cognition must comprehend the state; and even if individuals cannot know it in this way, at least they have the impression that the state is something rational.'[132]

A growing realization in the 1990s about the limits of markets, and the failure of what Galbraith has called 'the culture of contentment', may lead to a renewal of government, and improved fortunes for the universal class – and also for the majority of people, who have been left out of the dominant system. We may have a long way to go before Hegel's conception of the state as 'the temple of reason' is a universal insight. But the owl of Minerva may be finally taking flight. 'The central requirement,' writes Galbraith, 'cannot be escaped: almost every action that would remedy and reassure involves the relationship between the citizen and the state.' Central to such efforts would be the recovery of respect for the public service. 'If public servants are widely publicised as inept and incompetent, so, quite possibly, some of them become. The people who serve well are those who are hailed for serving well.'[133]

A vigorous Keynesian movement among economists, especially in the USA, also promises recovery for the (left-Hegelian) idea of the state. Free-market economics contains a powerful justification for the privileges of wealth, 'for it appears to legitimize such arrangements as natural and unimprovable. Keynes proves that they are not – and invites the state to make good the shortcomings.'[134] Robert Heilbroner and William Milberg explain that the critical problems of poverty and environmental degradation facing capitalism dictate 'the need for expanded public intervention', and a new form of economics that regards 'itself as a discipline that follows in the wake of sociology and politics rather than proudly leading the way for them'. Instead, as Hegel would say, of intellectuals burying themselves so deeply in knowledge that they lose themselves, they should take part in incorporating a creative vision of politics 'into the agenda of a society that wishes itself to be governed by its own choices, not by blind obedience'. Heilbroner and Milberg admit that 'the popular view in America today is clearly in favor of a delegitimation of the public sector, not its enhancement'.[135] Yet this may change, and the impetus for such change will have to come from below – as indeed it has already in Europe, where, despite the difficulties of the left, a social democratic tide has uprooted conservative regimes in the UK, Italy and France. What is good, says Hegel, is what relieves the oppression of the people and offers them the most enjoyment for the least personal cost. If Hegel is right, the good will be found eventually not in markets, but in public service.

Notes

Introduction

[1] David Hoffman, 'Banditry threatens to subvert the state', *The Guardian Weekly* (15 June 1997).
[2] Federico Varese, 'Is Sicily the future of Russia? Private property and the rise of the Russian Mafia', *Archives of European Sociology*, 35 (1994), 258.
[3] Seymour F. Hersh, 'The wild East', *The Atlantic Monthly*, 273 (6) (June 1994), 76.
[4] Karl Marx, *Capital: A Critique of Political Economy*, vol.1 (trans. Ben Fowkes) (Harmondsworth, Penguin Books, 1976), p.103.
[5] Louis Althusser, *Politics and History: Montesquieu, Rousseau, Hegel and Marx* (London, NLB, 1972), p.164.
[6] See Tom Mayer, *Analytical Marxism* (Thousand Oaks, CA, Sage Publications, 1994).
[7] See Patricia Jagentowicz Mills (ed.), *Feminist Interpretations of Hegel* (University Park, PA, Pennsylvania State University Press, 1996).
[8] Terry Eagleton, *The Illusions of Postmodernism* (London, Routledge, 1997).
[9] Errol E. Harris, *The Spirit of Hegel* (Atlantic Highlands, NJ, Humanities Press, 1993), p.51.
[10] Richard Sieburth, introduction to Friedrich Hölderlin, *Hymns and Fragments* (trans. Richard Sieburth) (Princeton, Princeton University Press, 1984), p.xvi.
[11] Asa Briggs, *Marx in London* (London, British Broadcasting Corporation, 1982), p.10.
[12] S. S. Prawer, *Marx and World Literature* (Oxford, Oxford University Press, 1976), p.378.
[13] Jerrold Seigel, *Marx's Fate: The Shape of a Life* (Princeton, Princeton University Press, 1978).
[14] Terrell Carver, 'Hegel and Marx: reflections on the narrative', paper delivered at the Hegel-Marx Conference, Nottingham Trent University, 24–5 March 1997, pp.1, 3.
[15] Shlomo Avineri, 'Feature book review: the discovery of Hegel's early lectures on the philosophy of right', *The Owl of Minerva*, 16 (2) (Spring 1985), 200, 201.
[16] Leon Harold Craig, *The War Lover: A Study of Plato's Republic* (Toronto, University of Toronto Press, 1994), p.xx.

1 Marx's Relationship with Hegel

[1] Kevin Anderson, *Lenin, Hegel, and Western Marxism: A Critical Study* (Chicago, University of Illinois Press, 1996), p.5.
[2] See, for example, *Grundrisse: Foundations of the Critique of Political Economy* (trans. Martin Nicolaus) (Harmondsworth, Penguin Books, 1973), p.151; and Jerrold Seigel, *Marx's Fate: The Shape of a Life* (Princeton, Princeton University Press, 1978), p.371.
[3] Karl Marx, Preface to *A Contribution to the Critique of Political Economy* (ed. Lewis S. Feuer) (New York, Doubleday and Company, 1959), pp.42–6.
[4] Seigel, *Marx's Fate*, p.373.
[5] Karl Marx, 'Postface to the Second Addition', of *Capital: A Critique of Political Economy*, vol.1 (trans. Ben Fowkes) (Harmondsworth, Penguin Books, 1976), p.102.
[6] Ibid.
[7] Ibid.
[8] 'Marx may not have seen this', writes Ian Fraser, 'but his "own" dialectic clearly parallels that of Hegel ... the dialectic of Hegel *is* the dialectic of Marx.' 'Two of a kind: Hegel, Marx, dialectic and form', *Capital and Class*, 61 (Spring 1997), 81–106, p.103.
[9] G. W. F. Hegel, *Hegel: The Letters* (trans. Clark Butler and Christiane Seiler) (Bloomington, University of Indiana Press, 1984), p.711.
[10] Stephen Houlgate, *Freedom, Truth and History: An Introduction to Hegel's Philosophy* (London, Routledge, 1991), p.1.
[11] Theodor W. Adorno, *Hegel: Three Studies* (trans. Shierry Weber Nicholsen) (Cambridge, MA, The MIT Press, 1994), p.89.
[12] Terrell Carver, 'Reading Marx: life and works', in Terrell Carver (ed.) *The Cambridge Companion to Marx* (Cambridge, Cambridge University Press, 1991), p.14.
[13] Tom Mayer, *Analytical Marxism* (Thousand Oaks, CA, Sage Publishing, 1994), p.1.
[14] Douglas Kellner, 'The obsolescence of Marxism?', pp.3–30, in Bernd Magus and Stephen Cullenberg (eds.), *Whither Marxism? Global Crises in International Perspective* (New York, Routledge, 1995), pp.5, 9, 11.
[15] Quoted in Hegel, *Letters*, p.711.
[16] Quoted in Georg Lukács, *The Young Hegel: Studies in the Relations between Dialectics and Economics* (London, Merlin Press, 1975), p.267.
[17] Marx, 'Postface to the Second Addition' of *Capital*, p.102.
[18] Charles Taylor, *Hegel* (Cambridge, Cambridge University Press, 1975), p.72.
[19] Perry Anderson, *Considerations on Western Marxism* (London, NLB, 1976), p.61.
[20] Arpad Kadarkay, *Georg Lukács: Life, Thought, and Politics* (Cambridge, MA, Basil Blackwell, 1991), p.353.

NOTES

[21] Lukács, *Young Hegel*, p.41.
[22] Ibid., pp.87, 176.
[23] Ibid., p.335.
[24] Ibid., p.511.
[25] Ibid., p.197.
[26] Friedrich Engels, *Anti-Dühring: Herr Eugen Dühring's Revolution in Science* (Moscow, Progress Publishers, 1969), p.43.
[27] Terrell Carver, *Marx and Engels: The Intellectual Relationship* (Brighton, Wheatsheaf Books Ltd., 1983), p.157.
[28] Dillard Hunley, *The Life and Thought of Friedrich Engels: A Reinterpretation* (New Haven, CT, Yale University Press, 1991).
[29] Randall Collins, *Three Sociological Traditions* (Oxford, Oxford University Press, 1985), p.60.
[30] Tom Rockmore, *Before and After Hegel: A Historical Introduction to his Thought* (Berkeley, University of California Press, 1993), p.152.
[31] Marx, quoted in Hunley, *Friedrich Engels*, p.1.
[32] Arnold Ruge, quoted ibid., p.14.
[33] George Lichtheim, *The Concept of Ideology and Other Essays* (New York, Vintage Books, 1967), p.36; see also Lichtheim's *Lukács* (London, Fontana, 1970), p.135.
[34] Terrell Carver, *Friedrich Engels: His Life and Thought* (London, Macmillan Press Ltd., 1989), p.247.
[35] David Lamb, 'Hegelian-Marxist millenarianism', *History of European Ideas*, 8 (3) (1987), 271.
[36] Friedrich Engels, *Ludwig Feuerbach and the End of Classical German Philosophy*, in Karl Marx and Frederick Engels, *Selected Works in Three Volumes*, vol.3 (Moscow, Progress Publishers, 1970), pp.340–1.
[37] Engels, *Ludwig Feuerbach*, pp.341–2.
[38] Ibid., p.340.
[39] G. W. F. Hegel, *Philosophy of Mind: Being Part Three of the Encyclopaedia of the Philosophical Sciences* (Oxford, Oxford University Press, 1971), §482, p.239.
[40] James H. Cone, *Martin and Malcolm and America: A Dream or a Nightmare?* (Maryknoll, NY, Orbis Books, 1991), p.133.
[41] Francis Fukuyama, *The End of History and the Last Man* (New York, The Free Press, 1992), p.145.
[42] Hegel, *Philosophy of Mind*, §433A, p.174.
[43] George Ritzer, *The McDonaldization of Society*, revised edn. (Thousand Oaks, CA, Pine Forge Press, 1994), p.9.
[44] G. W. F. Hegel, *Elements of the Philosophy of Right* (ed. Allen W. Wood, trans. H. B. Nisbet) (Cambridge, Cambridge University Press, 1991), §21, p.52.
[45] Henry Mintzberg, 'Managing government, governing management', *Harvard Business Review*, 74 (3) (May–June 1996), 77.
[46] Engels, *Ludwig Feuerbach*, p.367.

47 Ibid., p.362.
48 Hegel, *Philosophy of Right*, p.20.
49 Engels, *Ludwig Feuerbach*, p.338.
50 Hegel, quoted in Allen W. Wood, 'Editorial notes', to Hegel, *Philosophy of Right*, p.390.
51 Engels, *Ludwig Feuerbach*, p.338.
52 Jadwiga Staniszkis (*The Dynamics of Breakthrough in Eastern Europe* (Berkeley, University of California Press, 1991), pp.244–6) offers a fascinating comparison of the East European transition with the French Revolution. Writing in 1991, she predicts that the emergence in Western Europe of left Christianity as a reaction to the rise of liberal capitalism in the first half of the nineteenth century may be duplicated in post-communist Eastern Europe. '[G]rowing hostility toward economic liberalism', she writes, will be matched with 'the populist image of Christ . . . This can shift the reform movement from an objective of "liberty" to "equality/fraternity" themes.'
53 G. W. F. Hegel, *Lectures on the History of Philosophy*, vol.2 (trans. E. S. Haldane and Frances H. Simpson) (London, Routledge and Kegan Paul, 1955), pp.97–8.
54 Andrew G. Walder, 'The quiet revolution from within: economic reform as a source of political decline', in A. G. Walder (ed.), *The Waning of the Communist State: Economic Origins of Political Decline in China and Hungary* (Berkeley, University of California Press, 1995), p.18.
55 Hegel, *History of Philosophy*, p.98.
56 Katherine Verdery, *What Was Socialism, and What Comes Next?* (Princeton, Princeton University Press, 1996), p.10.
57 Hegel, *History of Philosophy*, p.98.
58 For a critical overview of China's reform movement, see Richard Smith, 'Creative destruction: capitalist development and China's environment', *New Left Review*, 222 (March–April 1997).
59 Hegel, *History of Philosophy*, p.98.
60 See, for example, Verdery, *What Was Socialism?*, p.31.
61 Ibid., p.1.
62 Hegel, *History of Philosophy*, p.98.
63 Ibid.
64 James Petras and Steven Vieux, 'Bosnia and the revival of U.S. hegemony', *New Left Review*, 218 (July–August 1996), 10, 11.
65 Ibid., p.12.
66 Hegel, *History of Philosophy*, p.98.
67 Richard Hudelson, *The Rise and Fall of Communism* (Boulder, CO, Westview, 1993), p.147.
68 Noam Chomsky, 'U.S. policy: the passion for free markets', *Z Magazine*, 10 (5) (May 1997), 30.
69 Noam Chomsky, *Perspectives on Power: Reflections on Human Nature and the Social Order* (Montreal, Black Rose Books, 1997), p.81.

[70] Engels, *Ludwig Feuerbach*, p.339.
[71] Verdery, *What Was Socialism?*, p.32.
[72] Ibid., pp.32, 33, 37.
[73] Engels, *Ludwig Feuerbach*, p.339.
[74] Theodor Adorno, *Minima Moralia: Reflections from Damaged Life* (trans. E. F. N. Jephcott) (London, New Left Books, 1974), p.198.
[75] Adorno, *Three Studies*, p.40.
[76] Lamb, 'Hegelian-Marxist millenarianism', p.273.
[77] Engels, *Ludwig Feuerbach*, p.362.
[78] Ibid., p.347.
[79] Georg Lukács, *History and Class Consciousness* (Cambridge, MA, The MIT Press, 1971), pp.131–3.
[80] G. W. F. Hegel, *Logic: Being Part One of the Encyclopaedia of the Philosophical Sciences* (trans. William Wallace) (Oxford, Oxford University Press, 1975), §41Z, p.71.
[81] Quoted by E. L. Doctorow, 'Mythologizing the bomb', *The Nation*, 261 (5) (August 1995), 149.
[82] Hegel, *Philosophy of Mind*, §396, p.59.
[83] G. W. F. Hegel, *The Philosophy of History* (trans. J. Sibree) (New York, Dover Publications Inc., 1956), p.21.
[84] E. L. Doctorow, 'Hiroshima', *The Nation* (7 August 1995).
[85] Hegel, *Philosophy of History*, p.313.

2 Dialectics of Youth and Maturity

[1] Quoted in Richard Cockett, *Thinking the Unthinkable* (London, HarperCollins Publishers, 1994), pp.84, 82.
[2] Jerry Ravetz, 'Last of the great believers', *Radical Philosophy*, 70 (March–April 1995), 5.
[3] Karl Popper, *The Open Society and its Enemies*, vol.2. *The High Tide of Prophesy: Hegel, Marx and the Aftermath* (London, Routledge & Kegan Paul, 1977), p.29.
[4] Ravetz, 'Last of the great believers', p.5.
[5] Robin Blackburn, 'Popper and the New Left', *Radical Philosophy*, 70 (March–April 1995), 8.
[6] Dillard Hunley, *The Life and Thought of Friedrich Engels: A Reinterpretation* (New Haven, CT, Yale University Press, 1991), p.37.
[7] Quoted in Gareth Steadman Jones, 'The Marxism of the early Lukács', *New Left Review*, 70 (November–December 1971), 63.
[8] Georg Lukács, *The Young Hegel* (London, The Merlin Press, 1975), pp.102, 101. Lukács's evidence for Hegel's psychological crisis is slim, as we shall see below.

9. Steadman Jones, 'Marxism of the early Lukács', p.65.
10. Arpad Kadarkay, *Georg Lukács: Life, Thought, and Politics* (Cambridge, MA, Basil Blackwell, 1991), pp.352–3.
11. Lukács, *Young Hegel*, pp.71, 72.
12. Ibid., pp.98–9.
13. Herbert Marcuse, *Reason and Revolution: Hegel and the Rise of Social Theory*, 2nd edn. (Boston, Beacon Press, 1973), 169.
14. Shlomo Avineri, *Hegel's Theory of the Modern State* (Cambridge, Cambridge University Press, 1972), 107.
15. James Schmidt, 'Recent Hegel literature (Part I)', *Telos* (1975), 236.
16. Raymond Plant, *Hegel: An Introduction*, 2nd edn. (Oxford, Basil Blackwell, 1984), 186.
17. Michael O. Hardimon, *Hegel's Social Philosophy: The Project of Reconciliation* (Cambridge, Cambridge University Press, 1994).
18. Joseph McCarney, 'The true realm of freedom: Marxist philosophy after communism', *New Left Review*, 189 (1991), 37.
19. Quoted in Warren Montag, 'A process without a subject or goal(s)', in Antonio Callari, Stephen Cullenberg, and Carole Biewener (eds.), *Marxism in the Postmodern Age: Confronting the New World Order* (New York, The Guilford Press, 1995), 57.
20. Louis Althusser, *For Marx* (trans. Ben Brewster) (London, Allen Lane, The Penguin Press, 1969), p.239.
21. Louis Althusser, *Politics and History: Montesquieu, Rousseau, Hegel and Marx* (trans. Ben Brewster) (London, NLB, 1972), p.166.
22. *For Marx*, p.73.
23. E. P. Thompson, *The Poverty of Theory* (London, The Merlin Press, 1978), p.304.
24. Michael Kelly, *Modern French Marxism* (Oxford, Basil Blackwell, 1982), p.120.
25. Louis Althusser, *Lenin and Philosophy and Other Essays* (London, NLB, 1971), pp.90–1.
26. Althusser, *For Marx*, p.74.
27. John Boswell, *The Kindness of Strangers: The Abandonment of Children in Western Europe from Late Antiquity to the Renaissance* (New York, Pantheon Books, 1988), p.30.
28. G. W. F. Hegel, *The Philosophy of Mind: Being Part Three of the Encyclopaedia of the Philosophical Sciences* (trans. William Wallace) (Oxford, Oxford University Press, 1971), pp.56–7.
29. Ibid., p.59.
30. Ibid., p.61.
31. Ibid.
32. Erik H. Erikson, *Childhood and Society*, 2nd edn. (New York, Norton, 1963).
33. Hegel, *Philosophy of Mind*, p.62.
34. Ibid.

NOTES

[35] Ibid.
[36] H. S. Harris, *Hegel's Development: Toward the Sunlight*, pp.259–60. Harris agrees that Hegel experienced 'hypochondria', while in Berne, but this 'is a peculiarly intellectual experience, rather than a psychological condition in any ordinary sense. It is the feeling – which has certainly afflicted every author if not every man – that although one knows where one wants to go, one does not quite know how to get there' (p.265).
[37] Ibid., pp.115–16.
[38] Ibid., p.62.
[39] G. W. F. Hegel, *Logic: Being Part One of the Encyclopaedia of the Philosophical Sciences* (trans. William Wallace) (Oxford, Oxford University Press, 1975), p.276.
[40] Hegel, *Philosophy of Mind*, p.63.
[41] Ibid.
[42] Ibid., p.64.
[43] Ibid.
[44] G. W. F. Hegel, *The Letters* (trans. Clark Butler and Christiane Seiler) (Bloomington, University of Indiana Press, 1984), p.64.
[45] G. W. F. Hegel, 'Preface' to *Elements of the Philosophy of Right* (ed. Allen W. Wood, trans. H. B. Nisbet) (Cambridge, Cambridge University Press, 1991), p.32.
[46] Karl Marx, *The Economic and Philosophical Manuscripts of 1844* (ed. Dirk J. Struik, trans. Martin Milligan) (New York, International Publishers, 1964), p.174.
[47] Karl Marx and Friedrich Engels, *Selected Works*, vol.1 (Moscow, Progress Publishers, 1969), p.13.

3 Hegel's Development, 1770–1801

[1] H. S. Harris, *Hegel's Development: Toward the Sunlight* (Oxford, Oxford University Press, 1972), p.2.
[2] Daniel Berthold-Bond, *Hegel's Theory of Madness* (Albany, NY, State University of New York Press, 1995), p.59.
[3] G. W. F. Hegel, *The Letters* (trans. Clark Butler and Christiane Seiler) (Bloomington, Indiana University Press, 1984), p.408.
[4] Harris, *Hegel's Development*, p.2.
[5] Hegel, *Letters*, p.434.
[6] Quoted in Clark Butler, 'Commentary', in Hegel, *Letters*, p.433.
[7] Hegel, *Letters*, p.438.
[8] Ibid., p.271.
[9] Clark Butler, 'Commentary', in Hegel, *Letters*, pp.17–18.

10. Laurence Dickey, *Religion, Economics, and the Politics of Spirit, 1770–1807* (Cambridge, Cambridge University Press, 1987).
11. Christoph Jamme, 'Hegel and Hölderlin', *Clio*, 15 (4) (1986), 365.
12. Harris, *Hegel's Development*, p.420.
13. Z. A. Pelczynski, 'An introductory essay', to *Hegel's Political Writings* (trans. T. M. Knox) (Oxford, Oxford University Press, 1964), p.9.
14. W. Walsh, 'Kant as seen by Hegel', *Idealism Past and Present* (ed. G. Vesey) (Cambridge, Cambridge University Press, 1982).
15. Harris, *Hegel's Development*, p.62.
16. William Doyle, *The Oxford History of the French Revolution* (Oxford, Oxford University Press, 1989), p.285.
17. Harris, *Hegel's Development*, p.156.
18. Clark Butler, 'Commentary', in Hegel, *Letters*, p.47.
19. Hegel, *Letters*, p.46.
20. Alan Olson, *Hegel and the Spirit: Philosophy as Pneumatology* (Princeton, Princeton University Press, 1992), p.58.
21. G. W. F. Hegel, *Three Essays, 1793–1795: The Tübingen Essay, Berne Fragments, The Life of Jesus* (ed. and trans. with introduction and notes by Peter Fuss and John Dobbins) (Notre Dame, IN, University of Notre Dame, 1984), pp.77–8.
22. Ibid., pp.91–2.
23. Ibid., p.91.
24. Olson, *Hegel and the Spirit*, p.58.
25. G. W. F. Hegel, *Early Theological Writings* (trans. T. M. Knox) (Philadelphia, University of Philadelphia Press, 1948), 278.
26. Ibid., p.281.
27. Jamme, 'Hegel and Hölderlin', p.363.
28. Olson, *Hegel and the Spirit*, p.64.
29. Ibid., p.63.
30. Hegel, *Early Theological Writings*, p.217.
31. Olson, *Hegel and the Spirit*, p.68.
32. Jamme, 'Hegel and Hölderlin', p.365.
33. Harris, *Hegel's Development*, p.253.
34. G. W. F. Hegel, 'Earliest system-programme of German idealism', trans. in Harris, *Hegel's Development*, pp.510, 511.
35. Ibid., p.512.
36. Stephen Bungay, *Beauty and Truth: A Study of Hegel's Aesthetics* (Oxford, Oxford University Press, 1984), p.vi.
37. Allen W. Wood, *Hegel's Ethical Thought* (Cambridge, Cambridge University Press, 1990), p.xiv.
38. Hegel, *Letters*, p.145.
39. Hegel, 'System-programme', pp.510–11.

40 Michael O. Hardimon, *Hegel's Social Philosophy: The Project of Reconciliation* (Cambridge, Cambridge University Press, 1994), p.248.
41 G. W. F. Hegel, *Lectures on Natural Right and Political Science: The First Philosophy of Right* (trans. J. Michael Stewart and Peter C. Hodgson) (Berkeley, University of California Press, 1995), §146, pp.269, 270.
42 George Armstrong Kelly, *Hegel's Retreat From Eleusis* (Princeton, Princeton University Press, 1978), pp.208–9.
43 G. W. F. Hegel, *Elements of the Philosophy of Right* (ed. Allen W. Wood, trans. H. B. Nisbet) (Cambridge, Cambridge University Press, 1991), §157, p.198.
44 David MacGregor, *Hegel, Marx and the English State* (Toronto, University of Toronto Press, 1996).
45 Thomas Paine, *Rights of Man* (Harmondsworth, Penguin Books, 1984), p.195.

4 Hegel and Tom Paine in the Age of Revolution

1 John Keane, *Tom Paine: A Political Life* (Boston, Little, Brown and Company, 1996), p.xiii.
2 Francis Fukuyama, *The End of History and the Last Man* (New York, The Free Presss, 1992), p.65
3 Richard Sakwa, 'The Hegelian triumph', *The Times Higher Education Supplement* (12 July 1991), 15.
4 Perry Anderson, *A Zone of Engagement* (London, Verso, 1992), p.283.
5 Heinrich Heine, quoted in Georg Lukács, *The Young Hegel* (London, Merlin Press, 1975), p.462.
6 Keane, *Tom Paine*, p.304.
7 H. S. Harris, *Hegel's Development: Towards the Sunlight* (Oxford, Oxford University Press, 1972), p.416.
8 Keane, *Tom Paine*, p.307.
9 Harris, *Hegel's Development*, p.433.
10 G. W. F. Hegel, *Lectures on the Philosophy of World History: Introduction* (trans. H. B. Nisbet) (Cambridge, Cambridge University Press, 1980).
11 Z. A. Pelczynski, 'An introductory essay', *Hegel's Political Writings* (trans. T. M. Knox) (Oxford, Oxford University Press, 1964), p.55.
12 Thomas Paine, *Rights of Man* (Harmondsworth, Penguin Books, 1984), p.55.
13 Keane, *Tom Paine*, p.287.
14 Pelczynski, 'Introductory essay', p.37.
15 Keane, *Tom Paine*, pp.396–7.
16 Thomas Paine, *Political Writings*, ed. Bruce Kuklick (Cambridge, Cambridge University Press, 1989), p.211.
17 Ibid., p.125.
18 Paine, *Rights of Man*, pp.211–12.

[19] G. W. F. Hegel, *Elements of the Philosophy of Right* (ed. Allen W. Wood, trans. H. B. Nisbet) (Cambridge, Cambridge University Press, 1991), §333, p.368.
[20] Keane, *Tom Paine*, p.117. See also Keane's essays on this topic in John Keane (ed.), *Civil Society and the State* (London, Verso, 1988), and John Keane, *Democracy and Civil Society* (London, Verso, 1988).
[21] Paine, *Political Writings*, p.197.
[22] Lewis P. Hinchman, 'The origins of human rights: a Hegelian perspective', *The Western Political Quarterly*, 37 (1) (March 1984), 18.
[23] Hegel, *Political Writings*, p.190.
[24] Hegel, *Philosophy of Right*, §185, p.123
[25] Paine, *Rights of Man*, p.198.
[26] Hegel, *Philosophy of Right*, §183, p.123.
[27] Pelczynski, 'Introductory essay', to Hegel, *Political Writings*, p.72.
[28] John Keane, 'Despotism and democracy', in Keane (ed.), *Civil Society*, p.50.
[29] Hegel, *Political Writings*, pp.162–3.
[30] Schiller quoted in Allen W. Wood, 'Editorial notes', to *Philosophy of Right*, p.442.
[31] Paine, *Rights of Man*, p.71.
[32] Fukuyama, *End of History*, p.350.
[33] Paine, *Rights of Man*, p.220.
[34] Keane, *Tom Paine*, pp.107, 111.
[35] Ibid., p.121.
[36] Douglas Moggach, 'Bruno Bauer's political critique, 1840–1841', *The Owl of Minerva*, 27 (2) (Spring 1996), 140.
[37] Hegel, *Political Writings*, p.217.
[38] Hegel, *Philosophy of World History: Introduction*, pp.163–70.
[39] Randall Collins, *Weberian Sociological Theory* (Cambridge, Cambridge University Press, 1986), p.2.
[40] Hegel, *Philosophy of World History: Introduction*, pp.166, 163.
[41] Ibid., pp.163–4, 165.
[42] Ibid., p.165.
[43] Peter Windgate, *The Penguin Medical Encyclopedia* (Harmondsworth, Penguin Books, 1976).
[44] Hegel, *Philosophy of World History: Introduction*, pp.165–6.
[45] Ibid., p.167.
[46] Ibid.
[47] Ibid.
[48] Ibid., p.168.
[49] Alexis de Tocqueville, *Democracy in America*, vol.1 (New York, Alfred A. Knopf, 1980), p.355.
[50] G. W. F. Hegel, *Lectures on Natural Right and Political Science: The First Philosophy of Right* (trans. J. Michael Stewart and Peter C. Hodgson) (Berkeley, University of California Press, 1995), p.97.

NOTES

51 Hegel, *Philosophy of World History: Introduction*, p.168.
52 Ibid.
53 Ibid., pp.169–70.
54 Ibid., p.168.
55 Ibid., pp.170–1.
56 James Petras and Morris Morley, *Empire or Republic? American Global Power and Domestic Decay* (New York, Routledge, 1995), p.139.
57 Thomas I. Palley, 'The forces making for an economic collapse', *The Atlantic Monthly* (July 1996), 44–5.
58 Hegel, *Philosophy of World History: Introduction*, p.172.
59 Hegel's assessment of the USA has not gone out-of-date. In a recent interview with US novelist Norman Mailer, Christopher Hitchens observes that 'a lot of non-Americans think that the United States is ... an insecure country that's been lucky in war, ... always trying to prove itself – that it has a macho problem'. Asked by Hitchens 'if America was a person, would it be male or female?' Mailer responds, 'this is a male country, it's an insecure country but that's understandable. We simply don't have the cultural tradition of the European countries ... And you know we do have this big energy here. But we're a country without standards, we're kind of ... there's a seven letter word that begins with A to describe the kind of country we are.' (Christopher Hitchens, 'Interview with Norman Mailer', *New Left Review*, 222 (March–April 1997), 119.)
60 Colonel Harry G. Summers, Jr., 'How to become the world's policeman', *New York Times Magazine* (19 May 1991), 43, 44.
61 Hegel, *Philosophy of World History: Introduction*, p.158.
62 John McMurtry, Letter to the Editor, *Globe and Mail*, 25 May 1991.
63 Hegel, *Philosophy of World History: Introduction*, pp.70–1.
64 Keane, *Tom Paine*, p.376.
65 G. W. F. Hegel, *Phenomenology of Spirit* (trans. A. V. Miller) (Oxford, Oxford University Press, 1977), p.360.
66 Robert Wokler disagrees with Hegel's account of Rousseau's social theory. Hegel misperceived Rousseau's general will as 'the union of individuals within the state as a mere contract of particulars, whose indeterminacy and arbitrariness made impossible the really concrete union of wills upon which the establishment of a genuine political community depends'. However, notes Wokler, 'Rousseau's vision of the moral personality of the state, as outlined in the *Contrat social*, entailed much the same dimension of political solidarity and self-recognition as part of a greater whole that were embraced in his [Hegel's] account of ethical life. He did not perceive that Rousseau shared with him a notion of community that transcended the arbitrariness of the individual will in civil society.' ('The French revolutionary roots of political modernity in Hegel's philosophy, or the enlightment at dusk', *Bulletin of the Hegel Society of Great Britain*, 35 (Autumn/Winter 1995), 84–6.)
67 Paine, *Rights of Man*, p.93.

[68] Wokler, 'French revolutionary roots', p.84.
[69] Hegel, *Phenomenology of Spirit*, p.360.
[70] Ibid.
[71] Paine, *Rights of Man*, p.162.
[72] Friedrich Schiller, *On the Aesthetic Education of Man* (ed. and trans. Elizabeth M. Wilkinson and L. A. Willoughby) (Oxford, Oxford University Press, 1967), pp.11, 23.
[73] Paine, *Rights of Man*, p.218.

5 Revolution, Despotism and Censorship, 1801–1831

[1] G. W. F. Hegel, *Hegel: The Letters* (ed. Clark Butler, trans. Clark Butler and Christiane Seiler) (Bloomington, University of Indiana Press, 1984), p.114.
[2] Ibid., p.398.
[3] Ibid., pp.140, 141.
[4] Ibid., p.151.
[5] Ibid., p.167.
[6] Clark Butler, 'Commentary', in Hegel, *Letters*, p.171.
[7] Ibid., p.301.
[8] Terry Pinkard, personal communication to the author, 12 September 1996; see also *Georg Wilhelm Hegel in Nuernberg: 1808–1816* (Nuremberg, Selvstverlag der Stadt Bibliothek Nuernberg, 1966).
[9] Hegel, *Letters*, p.307.
[10] Jacques D'Hondt, *Hegel in his Time* (trans. John Burbidge) (Peterborough, Ontario, Broadview Press, 1988), p.68.
[11] John Edward Toews, *Hegelianism: The Path Toward Dialectical Humanism. 1805–1841* (Cambridge, Cambridge University Press, 1985), p.114.
[12] Clark Butler, 'Commentary', in Hegel, *Letters*, p.378.
[13] Christoph Jamme, 'Hegel and Hölderlin', *Clio*, 15 (4) (1986), 375, 360.
[14] Hegel, *Letters*, p.66.
[15] Ibid.
[16] Richard Sieburth, 'Introduction' to Friedrich Hölderlin, *Hymns and Fragments* (trans. Richard Sieburth) (Princeton, Princeton University Press, 1984), p.6.
[17] Ibid., p.24.
[18] Alan Olson, *Hegel and the Spirit: Philosophy as Pneumatology* (Princeton, Princeton University Press, 1992), p.69.
[19] Sieburth, 'Introduction', to Hölderlin, *Hymns and Fragments*, p.10.
[20] Ibid., p.36.
[21] Hegel, *Letters*, p.64.
[22] Sieburth, 'Introduction', to Hölderlin, *Hymns and Fragments*, p.33.
[23] Hölderlin, *Hymns and Fragments*, p.245.
[24] Hegel, *Letters*, pp.46, 289–90.

[25] H. S. Harris, preface, to D'Hondt, *Hegel in his Time*, p.ii.
[26] Hegel, *Letters*, p.641.
[27] Harris, preface, D'Hondt, *Hegel in his Time*, p.vii.
[28] D'Hondt, *Hegel in his Time*, pp.2–3.
[29] Diether Raff, *A History of Germany: From the Medieval Empire to the Present* (trans. Bruce Little) (New York, Berg Publishers, 1988), pp.59–60.
[30] Hegel, *Letters*, p.69.
[31] Ibid., p.470.
[32] Clark Butler, 'Commentary', in Hegel, *Letters*, pp.445, 448.
[33] D'Hondt, *Hegel in his Time*, p.129.
[34] Hegel, *Letters*, p.467.
[35] D'Hondt, *Hegel in his Time*, p.135.
[36] Hegel, *Letters*, pp.639–40.
[37] Quoted in D'Hondt, *Hegel in his Time*, p.172.
[38] Ibid., p.176.
[39] Hal Draper, *The Marx–Engels Chronicle: A Day-by-Day Chronology of Marx and Engels' Life and Activity* (New York, Schocken Books, 1985), pp.5–7.
[40] All quotations in this paragraph are from Michael H. Hoffheimer, *Eduard Gans and the Hegelian Philosophy of Law* (Boston, Kluwer Academic Publishers, 1995), pp.7, 8.
[41] Toews, *Hegelianism*, p.228.
[42] Ibid., p.229.
[43] Victor Keegan, *The Guardian Weekly* (28 July 1996), 13.
[44] Norbert Waszek, 'Eduard Gans on poverty: between Hegel and Saint-Simon', *The Owl of Minerva*, 18 (2) (1987), 172–3.
[45] Ibid., pp.178, 177.
[46] Hegel, *Letters*, p.667.
[47] Jonathan Beecher, *Charles Fourier: The Visionary and his World* (Berkeley, University of California Press, 1986), p.403.
[48] Butler, 'Commentary', Hegel, *Letters*, p.667.
[49] G. W. F. Hegel, *Lectures on Natural Right and Political Science: The First Philosophy of Right* (trans. J. Michael Stewart and Peter C. Hodgson) (Berkeley, University of California Press, 1995), §147, p.272.
[50] Butler, 'Commentary', in Hegel, *Letters*, p.669.
[51] See chapter 2 in David MacGregor, *Hegel, Marx and the English State* (Toronto, University of Toronto Press, 1996).
[52] Butler, 'Commentary', in Hegel, *Letters*, p.676.
[53] Hoffheimer, *Eduard Gans*, pp.11–12.
[54] Eduard Gans, 'Preface to *Hegel's Philosophy of History* (1837), translated by J. Sibree (1857)', in Hoffheimer, *Eduard Gans*, p.104.
[55] Eduard Gans, 'Preface to Hegel's *Philosophy of Law* (1833)', in Hoffheimer, *Eduard Gans*, p.89.
[56] D'Hondt, *Hegel in his Time*, pp.191, 192, 195.

6 Property and the Corporation

1. George Soros, 'The capitalist threat', *The Atlantic Monthly* (February 1997) 45.
2. Shlomo Avineri, *The Social and Political Thought of Karl Marx* (Cambridge, Cambridge University Press, 1968), p.8.
3. Ibid., pp.189, 196.
4. Isaac Deutscher, *Marxism in Our Time* (ed. Tamara Deutscher) (London, Jonathan Cape, 1972), p.23.
5. R. N. Berki, *The Genesis of Marxism: Four Lectures* (London, J. M. Dent & Sons, 1988), p.141.
6. Louis Dupré, *Marx's Social Critique of Culture* (New Haven, CT, Yale University Press, 1983), p.205.
7. Berki, *Genesis of Marxism*, p.142.
8. Karl Marx, *Capital: A Critique of Political Economy*, vol.1 (trans. Ben Fowkes) (Harmondsworth, Penguin Books, 1976), p.929.
9. Quoted in Richard N. Hunt, *The Political Ideas of Marx and Engels*, vol.2. *Classical Marxism, 1850–1895* (Pittsburgh, University of Pittsburgh Press, 1984), p.223.
10. Avineri, *Social and Political Thought*, p.51.
11. Jürgen Habermas, 'What does socialism mean today? The revolutions of recuperation and the need for new thinking', in Robin Blackburn (ed.), *After the Fall: The Failure of Communism and the Future of Socialism* (London, Verso), p.38.
12. See my *Hegel, Marx, and the English State* (Toronto, University of Toronto Press, 1996).
13. R. N. Berki, *Insight and Vision: The Problem of Communism in Marx's Thought* (London, J. M. Dent & Sons, 1983), p.147.
14. Isaac Deutscher, *The Prophet Unarmed, Trotsky 1921–1929*, vol.2 (New York, Vintage Books, 1965), pp.347, 436.
15. Perry Anderson, *A Zone of Engagement* (London, Verso, 1992), p.374.
16. Quoted in Alex de Jonge, *Stalin and the Shaping of the Soviet Union* (Glasgow, William Collins, 1986), p.202.
17. Henry Mintzberg, 'Managing government, governing management', *Harvard Business Review*, 74 (3) (May–June 1996), 75.
18. 'It is... somewhat paradoxical to note that... the views of the New Right and their critics on the left... share a vision of reducing arbitrary power and regulatory capacity [of government] to its lowest possible extent.' David Held, *Models of Democracy*, 2nd edn. (Stanford, Stanford University Press, 1997), p.298.
19. Christopher Pierson, *The Modern State* (London, Routledge, 1995), p.81.
20. Mintzberg, 'Managing government', p.81.
21. Avineri, *Social and Political Thought*, p.109.
22. G. W. F. Hegel, *Political Writings* (ed. Z. A. Pelczynski) (Cambridge, Cambridge University Press, 1964), pp.190, 178, 194.

NOTES

23 Joseph McCarney, 'The true realm of freedom: Marxist philosophy after communism', *New Left Review*, 189 (September–October 1991), 33.
24 Ibid., pp.33, 35.
25 Richard Sakwa, 'The Hegelian triumph', *The Times Higher Education Supplement* (12 July 1991), 15.
26 Karl Marx, 'Critique of the Gotha Program', in Lewis S. Feuer (ed.), *Marx and Engels: Basic Writings on Politics and Philosophy* (Garden City, NY, Doubleday & Company, Inc., 1959), p.119.
27 Berki, *Insight and Vision*, p.158.
28 G. W. F. Hegel, *Elements of the Philosophy of Right* (ed. Allen W. Wood, trans. H. B. Nisbet) (Cambridge, Cambridge University Press, 1991), §237, p.263.
29 Katherine Verdery, *What Was Socialism and What Comes Next?* (Princeton, Princeton University Press, 1996), p.24.
30 Ibid., p.25.
31 Berki, *Insight and Vision*, p.160.
32 Quoted in Verdery, *What Was Socialism?*, p.vii.
33 G. W. F. Hegel, *Lectures on Natural Right and Political Science: The First Philosophy of Right* (trans. J. Michael Stewart and Peter C. Hodgson) (Berkeley, University of California Press, 1995), §17, p.66.
34 Ibid., §§98, 144, pp.172, 265.
35 C. B. Macpherson, *Property: Mainstream and Critical Positions* (Toronto, University of Toronto Press, 1983).
36 G. W. F. Hegel, *Phenomenology of Spirit* (trans. A. V. Miller) (Oxford, Oxford University Press, 1977), pp.448–9.
37 Hegel, *Lectures on Natural Right and Political Science*, §§95, 20, pp.169, 69.
38 Ibid., §21, pp.69–70.
39 G. Heiman, 'The sources and significance of Hegel's corporate doctrine', in Z. A. Pelczynski (ed.), *Hegel's Political Philosophy: Problems and Perspectives* (Cambridge, Cambridge University Press, 1971), p.116.
40 William Greider, *Who Will Tell the People?: The Betrayal of American Democracy* (New York, Simon & Schuster, 1993), p.401.
41 Allen W. Wood, *Hegel's Ethical Thought* (Cambridge, Cambridge University Press, 1990), p.103.
42 Hegel, *Philosophy of Right*, §§46, 270, pp.77, 296.
43 Hegel, *Lectures on Natural Right and Political Science*, §119, p.213.
44 Quoted in Allen W. Wood, 'Editorial Notes', to Hegel, *Philosophy of Right*, p.453.
45 Hegel, *Lectures on Natural Right and Political Science*, p.183.
46 Ibid., §104, p.183.
47 William Greider, *One World, Ready or Not* (New York, Simon & Schuster, 1997), p.229.
48 Marx, *Capital*, p.926.
49 Greider, *One World*, p.35.

50 For example, George Armstrong Kelly, *Hegel's Retreat From Eleusis* (Princeton, Princeton University Press, 1978), p.113.
51 Peter Singer, *Hegel* (Oxford, Oxford University Press, 1980), p.38.
52 Asher Horowitz and Gad Horowitz, *'Everywhere they are in Chains': Political Theory from Rousseau to Marx* (Scarborough, Ontario, Nelson Canada, 1988), p.132. For a comparison between Burke's and Hegel's views on popular sovereignty, see J.-F. Suter, 'Burke, Hegel, and the French Revolution', in Pelczynski (ed.), *Hegel's Political Philosophy*.
53 Steven B. Smith, *Hegel's Critique of Liberalism: Rights in Context* (Chicago, The University of Chicago Press, 1989), p.144.
54 Norbert Waszek, 'Eduard Gans on poverty: between Hegel and Saint-Simon', *The Owl of Minerva*, 18 (2) (Spring 1987), 175, 177.
55 Heiman, 'Sources and significance', p.125.
56 Stephen Houlgate, *Freedom, Truth and History: An Introduction to Hegel's Philosophy* (London, Routledge, 1991), p.116.
57 Hegel, *Lectures on Natural Right and Political Science*, §104, p.183.
58 Marx, 'Critique of the Gotha Program', p.119.
59 Smith, *Hegel's Critique of Liberalism*, p.143.
60 Hegel, *Lectures on Natural Right and Political Science*, §107, pp.186–7.
61 Hegel, *Phenomenology of Spirit*, p.360.
62 Verdery, *What Was Socialism?*, p.229.
63 De Jonge, *Stalin and the Shaping of the Soviet Union*, p.357.
64 Smith, *Hegel's Critique of Liberalism*, p.223.
65 Quoted ibid., p.225.
66 Hegel, *Lectures on Natural Right and Political Science*, §119, p.212.
67 Anderson, *Zone of Engagement*, p.287.
68 Hegel, *Lectures on Natural Right and Political Science*, §120, p.214.
69 Ibid., §141, pp.261–2.
70 Ibid., §141, p.262.
71 Ibid., §141, p.261.
72 Harry Brod, *Hegel's Philosophy of Politics, Idealism, Identity and Modernity* (Boulder, CO, Westview Press, 1992), p.143.
73 Hegel, *Lectures on Natural Right and Political Science*, §§143, 144, pp.263–4.
74 Ibid., §145, p.268.
75 Mintzberg, 'Managing government', pp.76, 83.
76 Howard Kainz, *G. W. F. Hegel: The Philosophical System* (Toronto, Prentice Hall International, 1996), p.148.
77 Hegel, *Lectures on Natural Right and Political Science*, §153, p.285.
78 Heiman, 'Sources and significance', p.131.
79 Hegel, *Lectures on Natural Right and Political Science*, §121, p.219.
80 Kainz, *Hegel*, p.148.
81 Hegel, *Lectures on Natural Right and Political Science*, §121, p.218.
82 Hegel, *Political Writings*, p.206.

[83] Helen Irving, 'Guilds, corporations and socialist theory', *Economy and Society*, 15 (1) (February 1986), 127.
[84] Antony Black, *Guilds and Civil Society in European Political Thought from the Twelfth Century to the Present* (Ithaca, NY, Cornell University Press, 1984), pp.131–2.
[85] Quoted ibid., p.133.
[86] Hegel, *Lectures on Natural Right and Political Science*, §121, pp.218–19.
[87] Smith, *Hegel's Critique of Liberalism*, p.144.
[88] Black, *Guilds and Civil Society*, pp.202, 237, 241.
[89] David Held, *Models of Democracy*, 2nd edn. (Stanford, CA, Stanford University Press, 1996), pp.253–4.
[90] Joe Hermer, 'Keeping Oshawa beautiful: policing the loiterer in public nuisance by-law 72–94', in *Canadian Journal of Law and Society*, vol. 12, no. 1 (Spring 1997), p.192.
[91] Hegel, *Lectures on Natural Right and Political Science*, §121, p.218.
[92] Wood, *Hegel's Ethical Thought*, p.242.
[93] Hegel, *Philosophy of Right*, §252, p.271.
[94] Houlgate, *Freedom, Truth and History*, p.119.
[95] See his 'Hegel on work, ownership and citizenship', in Pelczynski (ed.), *State and Civil Society*, p.194. See also Heiman, 'Sources and significance', p.123.
[96] Hegel, *Lectures on Natural Right and Political Science*, §§118, 106, pp.209, 185–6.
[97] Ibid., §120, pp.215–16.
[98] Greider, *One World*, pp.24–5.
[99] Ibid., p.25.
[100] Ibid.
[101] Marx, *Capital*, p.929.

7 Labour and Civil Society

[1] Shlomo Avineri, *The Social and Political Thought of Karl Marx* (Cambridge, Cambridge University Press, 1969), p.221.
[2] We shall see that Habermas's ideal society is not a Hegelian one. Jürgen Habermas, *Between Facts and Norms: Contributions to a Discourse Theory of Law and Democracy* (trans. William Rehg) (Cambridge, MA, The MIT Press, 1996), p.xli.
[3] Francis Fukuyama, *The End of History and the Last Man* (New York, The Free Press, 1992), pp.206, 64.
[4] Ibid., p.46.
[5] Ibid., p.325.
[6] Joseph McCarney, 'Shaping ends: reflections on Fukuyama', *New Left Review*, 202 (November–December 1993), 46.

7 Ibid., p.49.
8 Ibid., p.52.
9 Jürgen Habermas, quoted in Mikael Carleheden and Rene Gabriels, 'An interview with Jürgen Habermas', *Theory, Culture and Society*, 13 (3) (1996), 7.
10 Habermas, *Between Facts and Norms*, p.xli.
11 Habermas, 'What does socialism mean today? The revolutions of recuperation and the need for new thinking', in Robin Blackburn (ed.), *After the Fall: The Failure of Communism and the Future of Socialism* (London, Verso), pp.24–46.
12 For an excellent critique of Marx's vision of politics under communism, see David Held, *Models of Democracy*, 2nd edn. (Stanford, Stanford University Press, 1996), pp.151–4.
13 Habermas, 'What does socialism mean today?', p.34.
14 Alex Callinicos, *The Revenge of History: Marxism and the East European Revolutions* (University Park, PA, The Pennsylvania State University Press, 1991), p.130.
15 Ibid.
16 In a critique of Callinicos, David Held notes that 'Marxism has consistently underestimated the significance of the liberal preoccupation with how to secure freedom of criticism and action, i.e. choice and diversity, in the face of political power' (*Models of Democracy*, pp.287–8).
17 Steven B. Smith, *Hegel's Critique of Liberalism: Rights in Context* (Chicago, University of Chicago Press, 1989), p.238.
18 Lewis P. Hinchman, 'The origins of human rights: a Hegelian perspective', *The Western Political Quarterly*, 37 (1) (March 1984), 16.
19 Ibid., p.15.
20 Some of the ideas in this discussion emerged from a conversation with Joe Hermer.
21 Shlomo Avineri, 'Labor, alienation, and social classes in Hegel's Realphilosophie', *Philosophy and Public Affairs*, 1 (1971–2), 100.
22 Hinchman, 'Origins of human rights', p.24.
23 G. W. F. Hegel, *Lectures on Natural Right and Political Science: The First Philosophy of Right* (trans. J. Michael Stewart and Peter C. Hodgson) (Berkeley, University of California Press, 1995), p.174.
24 Ibid., p.162.
25 Ibid., pp.167–8.
26 Ibid., p.169.
27 Ibid., p.170.
28 Ibid., pp.175, 176–7.
29 Ibid., pp.181–2.
30 Ibid., pp.183–4.
31 Ibid., pp.183–4, 177.
32 William Greider, *One World, Ready or Not* (New York, Simon & Schuster, 1997), p.28.

NOTES

33 Ibid., pp.28–9, 39.
34 Doug Henwood, 'A jobless future?', *Left Business Observer*, 75 (16 December 1996), 7.
35 Hegel, *Lectures on Natural Right and Political Science*, p.179.
36 'Preface to the First German Edition' of *The Poverty of Philosophy* (Moscow, Progress Publishers, n.d.), p.11.
37 Habermas, 'What does socialism mean today?', p.35.
38 Ibid., pp.34–5.
39 Ibid., p.35.
40 *Lectures on Natural Right*, §119, p.210.
41 Ibid., §120, p.214.
42 *Political Writings*, p.242.
43 Ibid.
44 Hinchman, 'Origins of human rights', p.27.
45 See M. J. Petry, 'Propaganda and analysis: the background to Hegel's article on the English Reform Bill', in Z. A. Pelczynski (ed.), *The State and Civil Society: Studies in Hegel's Political Philosophy* (Cambridge, Cambridge University Press, 1984), p.298.
46 Alan Ryan, *Property and Political Theory* (Oxford, Blackwell, 1984).
47 Ibid., p.123.
48 Ibid., pp.123–4.
49 Ibid., pp.125–7.
50 Robert A. Dahl, *A Preface to Economic Democracy* (Cambridge, Polity Press, 1985), p.75.
51 *Philosophy of Right*, §57, pp.86–8.
52 Ryan, *Property and Political Theory*, p.131.
53 *Property* (Minneapolis, Minn., University of Minnesota Press, 1987), p.117.
54 Jeremy Waldron, *The Right to Private Property* (Oxford, Clarendon Press, 1988).
55 '[F]or Waldron, defence of the right to private property is anything but a defence of the status quo. The right of *everyone* to private property, allied to the general background right to subsistence, is likely to justify serious curtailment of some of the rights of existing property-holders, substantial redistribution of existing assets, an extensive role for the state in guaranteeing welfare and redistribution, further restrictions upon the right of inheritance, a fairly frontal assault on the claims of corporate capital and at least the possibility of some form of citizen's basic income.' Christopher Pierson, *Socialism after Communism: The New Market Socialism* (Cambridge, Polity Press, 1995), p.155.
56 Waldron, *Right to Private Property*, pp.374, 389.
57 *Lectures on Natural Right*, §31, p.80.
58 *Philosophy of Right*, §57, p.87.
59 David P. Ellerman, *Property and Contract in Economics: The Case for Economic Democracy* (Cambridge, MA, Blackwell Publishers, 1992), p.103.
60 Hegel's distinction between possession and use is mentioned in Stephen R.

Munzer's encyclopaedic *A Theory of Property* (Cambridge, Cambridge University Press, 1990), p.69, but not understood. 'The contemporary reader', Munzer declares, 'will rightly be intolerant of obscurities in Hegel's discussion and skeptical of the sharp separation between possession and use.'
[61] *Philosophy of Right*, §62, p.90.
[62] *Lectures on Natural Right*, p.70.
[63] Ibid., p.73.
[64] Daniel Berthold-Bond, *Hegel's Theory of Madness* (Albany, NJ, State University of New York Press, 1995), p.41.
[65] David MacGregor, *Hegel, Marx and the English State* (Toronto, University of Toronto Press, 1996), pp.157–84; *The Communist Ideal in Hegel and Marx* (Toronto, University of Toronto Press, 1990), pp.190–2.
[66] *Philosophy of Right*, §62, p.91.
[67] Ibid., §62, pp.91–2.
[68] Allen W. Wood, 'Editorial notes', in G. W. F. Hegel, *Elements of the Philosophy of Right* (Cambridge, Cambridge University Press, 1991), p.411.
[69] Ellerman notes the similarity between feudal rights and those of capital over labour in *The Democratic Worker-Owned Firm: A New Model for the East and West* (Boston, Unwin Hyman, 1990), p.121. He observes that under feudalism '[t]he ownership of land was equated with political sovereignty over the people on the land. The landlord was Lord of the land. By substituting capital for land, that interpretation of pre-democratic political government becomes one of the intellectual origins for the Fundamental Myth which interprets governance rights over workers as part of the "ownership of the means of production".'
[70] J. J. Rousseau, *The Social Contract* (trans. Maurice Cranston) (Harmondsworth, Penguin Books, 1968), p.54.
[71] *Philosophy of Right*, §57, p.87.
[72] Ellerman, *Property and Contract in Economics*, p.57.
[73] Ibid., p.56.
[74] Ibid., p.57.
[75] Ellerman, *Democratic Worker-Owned Firm*, p.18.
[76] Karl Marx, *Capital*, vol.1 (trans. S. Moore and E. Aveling) (New York, Modern Library, 1906), p.830, quoted in Ellerman, *Democratic Worker-Owned Firm*, p.19.
[77] Ellerman, *Democratic Worker-Owned Firm*, p.19.
[78] *Property and Contract in Economics*, p.259.
[79] Ibid., pp.156–7.
[80] *Lectures on Natural Right*, pp.79–80.
[81] *Philosophy of Right*, §76, pp.106–7.
[82] *Labour and Contract in Economics*, p.59.
[83] *Lectures on Natural Right*, pp.180–1.
[84] Ibid., pp.87, 183.
[85] Ibid., pp.180–4.

NOTES

[86] Noam Chomsky reminds us that the flow of big-business propaganda supporting class distinctions based on privilege is 'surely one of the central themes of modern history'. This is especially true in the 'American business community, which is unusual for its quite high level of class consciousness and dedication to class warfare, quite openly expressed by business leaders'. *Perspectives on Power: Reflections on Human Nature and the Social Order* (Montreal, Black Rose Books, 1997), p.226.

[87] *Lectures on Natural Right*, §108, p.189.

[88] Ibid., p.184.

[89] Karl Marx, *The Revolutions of 1848* (ed. David Fernbach) (Harmondsworth, Penguin Books, 1973), p.76.

[90] I discuss the connection between Hegel, Hodgskin and Marx in *Hegel, Marx and the English State*, pp.139–42.

[91] Ellerman, *Property and Contract in Economics*, p.59.

[92] Ryan, *Property and Political Theory*, pp.161, 167.

[93] *The Marx–Engels Reader*, 2nd edn., ed. Robert C. Tucker (New York, W. W. Norton & Co., 1978), pp.484–5.

[94] Ryan, *Property*, p.124.

[95] Lawrence Wilde, *Modern European Socialism* (Aldershot, Dartmouth, 1994), p.144.

[96] Ellerman, *Democratic Worker-Owned Firm*, p.22.

[97] Pierson, *Socialism after Communism*, p.80.

[98] Andrew G. Walder, 'The quiet revolution from within', in Andrew G. Walder (ed.), *The Waning of the Communist State: Economic Origins of Political Decline in China and Hungary* (Berkeley, University of California Press, 1995), pp.8–9.

[99] Ellerman, *Democratic Worker-Owned Firm*, p.32.

[100] *Between Facts and Norms*, p.489.

[101] Ibid., p.45.

[102] Ibid., p.366.

[103] Ibid., pp.366–7.

[104] Ibid., pp.368–9, 371.

[105] Ibid., p.372.

[106] Ibid., pp.373–4, 379.

[107] Ibid., 380–1.

[108] Will Hutton, *The State We're In* (London, Jonathan Cape, 1995), p.37.

[109] Barry Yeoman, 'The *real* state takeover: lobbyists new weapon to thwart local government controls', *The Nation*, 264 (7) (24 February 1997), 21–4.

[110] G. Heiman, 'The sources and significance of Hegel's corporate doctrine', in Z. A. Pelczynski (ed.), *Hegel's Political Philosophy: Problems and Perspectives* (Cambridge, Cambridge University Press, 1971), p.126.

[111] *Lectures on Natural Right*, §153, p.285.

[112] *Between Facts and Norms*, p.373.

[113] According to Hegel's political theory, writes Allen W. Wood, '[w]e cannot actualize subjective freedom as citizens of the state unless we can participate in the formation of public opinion through the give and take of free discussion'. *Hegel's Ethical Thought* (Cambridge, Cambridge University Press, 1990), p.52.

[114] *Lectures on Natural Right*, §155, p.288.

[115] *Philosophy of Right*, §317, p.353.

[116] Ibid., §290, p.331.

[117] Antony Black, *Guilds and Civil Society in European Thought From the Twelfth Century to the Present* (Ithaca, NY, Cornell University Press, 1984), p.241.

[118] *Between Facts and Norms*, p.381.

8 The State in Time

[1] Ian Fraser makes claims similar to mine about the relationship of Hegel and Marx. See his *Hegel, Marx and the Concept of Need* (Edinburgh, Edinburgh University Press, forthcoming). Fraser's contributions also include 'Two of a kind: Hegel, Marx, dialectic and form', *Capital and Class*, 61 (1996); 'Speculations on poverty in Hegel's *Philosophy of Right*', *Journal of the International Society for the Study of European Ideas*, 1 (7) 1996, pp.2069–82; and 'Hegel and modern need theory', I. Hampsher Monk and J. Stanyer (eds.), *Contemporary Political Studies* (Belfast, Political Studies Association of the UK, 1996), pp.424–32.

[2] Will Hutton, *The State We're In* (London, Jonathan Cape, 1995), p.238.

[3] G. W. F. Hegel, *Lectures on Natural Right and Political Science: The First Philsophy of Spirit* (trans. J. Michael Stewart and Peter C. Hodgson) (Berkeley, University of California Press, 1995), §158, p.295.

[4] Ibid., §146, p.269.

[5] Raya Dunayevskaya, 'The dialectics of liberation today', *News and Letters* (June 1997), 5.

[6] Slavoj Žižek, *For They Know Not What They Do: Enjoyment as a Political Factor* (London, Verso, 1991), p.271.

[7] As we shall see, this is not exclusively an Hegelian-Marxist expectation. Robert Heilbroner, for example, makes a similar forecast from the perspective of liberal economics. The systemic problems of capitalism, he writes, 'must be addressed by political will. In one form or another – and there are many avenues of address – the undesired dynamics of the economic sphere must be contained, redressed, or redirected by the only agency capable of asserting a counterforce to that of the economic sphere. It is the government.' *Twenty-First Century Capitalism* (Concord, Ontario, House of Anansi Press Ltd., 1992), p.109.

[8] David Held, *Models of Democracy*, 2nd edn. (Stanford, Stanford University Press, 1996), p.286.

[9] Noel Thompson, *The Market and its Critics: Socialist Political Economy in*

NOTES

Nineteenth Century Britain (London, Routledge, 1988). Thompson argues, however, that the prevailing tide in nineteenth-century British radical political economy went against the market, with 'disastrous' consequences 'for the subsequent evolution of socialist economic thinking' (p.285).

[10] 'The term "market socialism" has been used recently by Raymond Plant, David Miller and Julian LeGrand who have developed many of the themes of the liberal egalitarian tradition, in particular reconciling the principles of social justice with those of market allocation.' Andrew Gamble and Gavin Kelly, 'The new politics of ownership', *New Left Review*, 220 (1996), 77. Plant is also a leading commentator on Hegel.

[11] Christopher Pierson, *Socialism after Communism: The New Market Socialism* (Cambridge, Polity Press, 1995), pp.84, 104.

[12] Pierson registers severe doubts about the market-socialist proposal to jettison the state. '[A] system of market *socialism* will be heavily dependent upon the management of the social and economic framework of the market by the state. Handing over powers to an unreformed civil society would have little appeal to socialists. Markets (along with many other institutions in civil society) will need to be *patrolled*, not necessarily by the state, but almost certainly under the final jurisdiction of the state.' (Ibid., p.207).

[13] Gamble and Kelly, 'New politics of ownership', p.96.

[14] David McNally, *Against the Market: Political Economy, Market Socialism and the Marxist Critique* (London and New York, Verso, 1993), pp.183, 221, 195.

[15] *Socialism after Communism*, p.208.

[16] Ibid., p.115.

[17] Ibid., p.122.

[18] Marx quoted ibid., p.150.

[19] Ibid., p.153.

[20] Gamble and Kelly, 'New politics of ownership', p.75.

[21] Ibid., p.95.

[22] Ibid., p.97.

[23] David Ellerman, *The Democratic Worker-Owned Firm: A New Model for East and West* (Boston, Unwin Hyman, 1990), p.48.

[24] This principle is not readily understood by all, as evidenced by David Held's contention in *Models of Democracy* that true corporate democracy would entail 'that companies, while pursuing strategic objectives, must operate within a framework which does not violate the requirement to treat their employees and customers as free and equal persons' (p.329). To equate employees and customers in a discussion of corporate governance suggests that Held is not certain of the actual meaning of democracy – that is, the involvement of the governed in the organization of governance. A company's 'customers' in this regard are not 'equal' to its employees. You may use Colgate toothpaste daily but this does not mean your life is affected by the company to the same extent as that of one of its

employees. Held makes a similar error when he equates citizens with 'consumers' of the services of 'government institutions' (p.317).
25 Ellerman, *Democratic Worker-Owned Firm*, p.59.
26 'The number of workers who own stock in their companies grew from about 6.5 million in 1983 to approximately 14 million, with shares worth almost $300 billion, in 1993.' Roger Alcaly, 'Reinventing the corporation', *New York Review of Books*, 44 (6) (10 April 1997).
27 Firms with ESOPs are a little more likely than non-ESOP firms to embrace worker participation in management. Alcaly estimates that 10 per cent of US companies have adopted 'a new kind of corporate culture in which the interests of managers, shareholders, and workers are closely and deliberately linked'. However, not all of these firms have ESOPs. (Ibid., 8).
28 Ibid.
29 An ESOP, explains Roger Alcaly, is 'a pension plan that requires a majority of its assets to be invested in the stock of the sponsoring company, and is allowed to borrow money (to use "leverage") to do so'. ESOPs have been encouraged in the US through generous tax savings provisions. (Ibid., p.10).
30 Ellerman, *Democratic Worker-Owned Firm*, p.213.
31 Alcaly, 'Reinventing the corporation', 11.
32 *Democratic Worker-Owned Firm*, p.211.
33 *Models of Democracy*, p.316.
34 Christopher Pierson, *Beyond the Welfare State? The New Political Economy of Welfare* (Cambridge, Polity Press, 1991), p.214.
35 Hutton, *The State We're In*, p.286.
36 *Against the Market*, p.196.
37 C. B. Macpherson, *The Life and Times of Liberal Democracy* (Oxford, Oxford University Press, 1977), pp.109–15.
38 Ethan Kapstein, 'Workers and the world economy', *Foreign Affairs*, 75 (3) (May-June 1996), 17.
39 Paul Hirst and Grahame Thompson, *Globalization in Question* (Cambridge, Polity Press, 1996), p.185.
40 According to the 1995 United Nations report on global investment, no fewer than 374 pieces of legislation were introduced by national governments throughout the world, between 1991 and 1994, which had to do with investment by corporations. Some 369 of these legislative initiatives were designed to eliminate regulations on corporate practices. In other words, 98.7 per cent of the legislation brought forward by national governments in this area was aimed at providing transnational corporations with a free environment in which to 'transcend national boundaries'. Tony Clarke, *Silent Coup: The Big Business Takeover of Canada* (Toronto, James Lorimer & Company, Ltd., 1997), p.43.
41 John Ralston Saul, *The Unconscious Civilization* (Concord, Ontario, House of Anansi Press Ltd., 1995), p.178.
42 Hegel, *Lectures on Natural Right*, §121, p.219.

NOTES

43 Ibid., §125, pp.224–5.
44 *Guardian Weekly* (28 July 1996), 14.
45 Hegel, *Lectures on Natural Right*, §128, p.227.
46 Ibid., §146, p.270.
47 *Elements of the Philosophy of Right*, §290A, p.331.
48 *Lectures on Natural Right*, §128, p.228.
49 *Lectures on Natural Right*, §142, p.263.
50 Shlomo Avineri, *Hegel's Theory of the Modern State* (Cambridge, Cambridge University Press, 1972), p.187.
51 Francis Fukuyama, *The End of History and the Last Man* (New York, The Free Press, 1992), p.350.
52 Allen W. Wood, *Hegel's Ethical Theory* (Cambridge, Cambridge University Press, 1990), p.282.
53 Hegel, *Lectures on Natural Right*, §138, pp.251–2.
54 Ibid., §104, p.258.
55 Ibid., §140, p.257.
56 *For They Know Not What They Do*, pp.267, 269.
57 Hegel, *Lectures on Natural Right*, §133, p.238.
58 Ibid., §140, p.259.
59 Ibid., §140, pp.257–8.
60 Ibid., §140, pp.258–9.
61 Held, *Models of Democracy*, p.198.
62 Hegel, *Lectures on Natural Right*, §145, p.267.
63 Ibid., §141, pp.260–1.
64 Ibid., §142, pp.262–3.
65 Ellerman, *Democratic Worker-Owned Firm*, pp.141–4.
66 Hegel, *Lectures on Natural Right*, §143, p.263.
67 Ibid., §143, p.264.
68 Ibid., §144, p.265.
69 Ibid., §144, pp.265–6.
70 Ibid., §145, p.267.
71 Joseph A. Schumpeter, *Capitalism, Socialism and Democracy*, 3rd edn. (New York, Harper & Row Publishers, 1950), p.293.
72 Hegel, *Lectures on Natural Right*, §105, p.185.
73 Ibid., §143, p.264.
74 Ibid., §145, p.267.
75 Weber 'was . . . animated by what he called the "iron cage of rationality." In Weber's view, bureaucracies are cages in the sense that people are trapped in them, their basic humanity denied. Weber feared most that these systems would grow more and more rational and that rational principles would come to dominate an accelerating number of sectors of society . . . Society would become nothing more than a seamless web of rationalized structures, there would be no escape.' George Ritzer, *The McDonaldization of Society: An Investigation into*

the *Changing Character of Contemporary Social Life*, rev. edn. (Thousand Oaks, CA, Pine Forge Press, 1996), p.21. Hegel conjured an almost identical image to describe the effects of bureaucratic rule: 'a net thrown over the citizens in order to oppress them'. (*Lectures on Natural Right and Political Science*, §145, p.269.)
76 Hegel, *Lectures on Natural Right*, §146, p.269.
77 *Critique of Hegel's 'Philosophy of Right'* (trans. Annette John and Joseph O'Malley) (Cambridge, Cambridge University Press, 1970), pp.45, 47.
78 A central premiss of New Right theory 'was the ubiquity of rent-seeking in politics, whether by organized interest groups, politicians or bureaucrats. A "rent" ... is an excess profit – a presumptively illicit return that would be competed away in a free market. By analogy, a political "rent" is a benefit that a rational voter would not willingly confer but that a wily interest group or bureaucrat is able to extract from a naive or disorganized electorate.' Robert Kuttner, *Everything for Sale: The Virtues and Limits of Markets* (New York, Knopf, 1997), p.335.
79 Hegel, *Lectures on Natural Right*, §145, p.269.
80 Marx, *Critique of Hegel's 'Philosophy of Right'*, p.47.
81 Hegel, *Lectures on Natural Right*, §145, pp.267–8.
82 Ibid., §119, p.212.
83 Ibid., §119, p.212.
84 Peter Dale Scott, *Deep Politics and the Death of JFK*, rev. paperback edn. (Berkeley, University of California Press, 1996), pp.xi–xii.
85 Held, *Models of Democracy*, p.316.
86 Hegel, *Lectures on Natural Right*, §145, pp.267–8.
87 Ibid., §145, pp.268–9.
88 Ibid., §145, p.267.
89 *The Future of Intellectuals and the Rise of the New Class* (New York, Continuum, 1979), p.54.
90 See Alvin Gouldner's fascinating remarks on this subject in *Against Fragmentation: The Origins of Marxism and the Sociology of Intellectuals* (New York, Oxford University Press, 1985), pp.16–17, 42–3.
91 V. I. Lenin, *What Is To Be Done?* in *Selected Works in Three Volumes*, vol.1 (Moscow, Progress Publishers, 1970), p.143.
92 *Lectures on Natural Right*, §117, p.208.
93 'In 1989,' writes Gordon, 'the relative size of the U.S. bureaucratic burden had reached more than three times the level in Japan and Germany and more than four times the percentage in Sweden.' *Fat and Mean: The Corporate Squeeze of Working Americans and the Myth of Managerial 'Downsizing'* (New York, The Free Press, 1997), p.44.
94 *Capitalism, Socialism and Democracy*, p.294.
95 Paul Pierson, *Dismantling the Welfare State? Reagan, Thatcher, and the Politics of Retrenchment* (Cambridge, Cambridge University Press, 1994), pp.179–82.
96 Kuttner, *Everything for Sale*, p.328.

NOTES

[97] Hegel, *Lectures on Natural Right*, §120, p.214.
[98] Ibid., §§105, 153, pp.184, 287.
[99] *Future of Intellectuals*, pp.83–4.
[100] *Between Facts and Norms: Contributions to a Discourse Theory of Law and Democracy* (Cambridge, MA, MIT Press, 1996), p.381.
[101] Gouldner, *Against Fragmentation*, p.36.
[102] Pierson, *Dismantling the Welfare State*, p.160.
[103] Hegel, *Lectures on Natural Right*, §140, p.258.
[104] *Philosophy of Right*, §297A, p.336.
[105] Alexander Stille, *Excellent Cadavers: The Mafia and the Death of the First Italian Republic* (New York, Pantheon Books, 1995), pp.13, 407. Stille's book is dedicated, in part, to the 'memory of Giovanni Falcone, Paola Borsellino and the many other courageous public servants who have died working in Sicily'.
[106] Hegel, *Lectures on Natural Right*, §146, p.271.
[107] Ibid., §§146, 149, pp.271, 277.
[108] Ibid., §151, p.280.
[109] Ibid., §154, p.288.
[110] Ibid., §149, p.276.
[111] Ibid., §155, pp.288–9.
[112] Ibid., §155, p.289.
[113] Ibid., §144, p.288.
[114] Ibid., §156, p.291.
[115] Ibid., §135, p.244.
[116] Ibid., §153, p.285.
[117] In *Hegel, Marx and the English State* (Toronto, University of Toronto Press, 1996), pp.133–6, I argue, contrary to received opinion, that women are included in Hegel's rational state and the corporation. For Hegel, women have the right to own property, and thus to enter the institutions of civil society and the state.
[118] Hegel, *Lectures on Natural Right*, §153, p.286.
[119] Ibid., §120, p.216.
[120] Ibid., §152, p.283.
[121] Ibid., §135, p.244.
[122] Ibid., §152, p.284.
[123] Ibid., §156, p.291.
[124] Robin Blackburn, 'Reflections on Blair's velvet revolution', *New Left Review*, 223 (May–June 1997), 9.
[125] *Future of Intellectuals*, pp.92, 91, 87.
[126] Kuttner, *Everything for Sale*, p.350.
[127] *Future of Intellectuals*, p.89.
[128] Paul Pierson sums up the relevant trends: 'Business interests were increasingly influential, and appeared eager to question the old social contract. The enhanced mobility of capital in an increasingly integrated world economy, combined with slack labor markets, strengthened the position of employers, while devaluing the

bargaining chips of unions (e.g., promises of wage restraint) and of the nation-state (effective demand management.' (*Dismantling the Welfare State?*, p.180).

[129] Gil Eyal, Iván Szelényi, and Eleanor Townsley, 'The theory of post-communist managerialism', *New Left Review*, 222 (March–April 1997), 61.

[130] Hegel, *Lectures on Natural Right*, §170, p.315.

[131] Denis Dutton, editor of the *Journal of Philosophy and Literature*, which sponsors an annual bad scholarly writing contest, observes: 'There have always been academics guilty of bad writing. But I'd have to say that gibberish is more widely written today than at any time since the physicians of the Middle Ages.' *The Guardian Weekly* (22 June 1997).

[132] Hegel, *Lectures on Natural Right*, §158, p.296.

[133] J. K. Galbraith, *The Culture of Contentment* (Boston, Houghton Mifflin Company, 1992), p.175.

[134] Hutton, *The State We're In*, p.247.

[135] Robert Heilbroner and William Milberg, *The Crisis of Vision in Modern Economic Thought* (Cambridge, Cambridge University Press, 1995), pp.120, 126, 127–8, 124.

Index

aboriginal peoples 77–8
Adorno, Theodor 5, 25–6, 34
  Minima Moralia 25–6
Alcaly, Roger 180
Altenstein, Baron von 94
Althusser, Louis xvi, 31, 37–40
  For Marx 37, 39
  Reading Capital 37
Althussius, Johannes
  Systematic Analysis of Politics 134
America, Latin 82, 151
  see also South America
American Revolution 18, 52, 74, 75–7, 130
Anderson, Perry 32, 64, 116, 130
Avineri, Shlomo xv, 113, 117–18, 146, 185
  Hegel's Theory of the Modern State 36

Bauer, Bruno 109
Berki, R. N. 114, 116, 120, 121
Berlin, University of 93–4, 103, 109, 114, 127
Berthold-Bond, Daniel 48
  Hegel's Theory of Madness 158
Black, Antony 173
  Guilds and Civil Society in European Political Thought 135
Blackburn, Robin 32, 205
  New Left Review 32
Blair, Tony 205
Blake, William 97
Bolsheviks 116, 197
Bosnia 22
Bray, John Francis 160

Briggs, Asa
  Marx in London xiii
Britain *see* United Kingdom
Brod, Harry 131
Bulgaria 19–20
Bungay, Stephen 58
bureaucracy 115, 117, 120, 124, 169, 188–202, 208
Burke, Edmund 127
  Reflections on the Revolution in France 67
Burschenschaften 93, 100, 101, 103
business *see* corporations, business
Butler, Clark 92

Callinicos, Alex 144–5
Canada 19, 76, 82, 83, 170–2, 198, 205
  Charter of Rights and Freedoms 146
  Harris, Mike (Premier of Ontario) 170–1
  Toronto, Ontario 171–2
Capital see Marx, Karl
capital, finance 139–40, 150
capitalism 105, 106, 112, 117–23, 125–6, 142, 167, 176, 181
  and fall of communism 24–5
  Hegel on 9, 69, 118–19, 124–5, 151–2, 154, 160
  Marx on 114–15, 144, 174
  global *see* globalization
  industrial 136, 138
  post-socialist 121–2, 179
Carlsbad *see* Karlsbad
Carové, Friedrich 101

Cart, J. J.
  Lettres Confidentielles 51, 66, 75, 102
Carver, Terrell xv, 5, 10, 12
Catholic Church 79, 90
Ceauşescu, Nicolae 21
censorship 104, 108, 112, 122
  and Hegel xv–xvi, 59, 60, 62, 64, 69, 89–91, 93, 99–103, 175, 193
Charles X, King of France 104, 107
child labour 81, 94, 138
Chile 186
China 20, 22–3
Christianity
  Hegel on xvii, 48, 52, 55–6, 57, 67–8, 102
  Paine on 67–8
Church, Catholic *see* Catholic Church
Church, Protestant 79
civil society 88, 105, 117, 151, 168–73, 195, 198, 199
  and equality 147–51
  Habermas on 168–73
  Hegel on 69–75, 79–80, 82, 106, 113–14, 124, 137–8, 147–51, 157–9, 164–5, 183, 189, 191–2, 200, 203
  Marx on 111, 114–15, 118, 128, 153, 193
  Paine on 69–74
  post-socialist 119
  and the state 68–75, 112, 180, 184
class, universal 188–205
  see also bureaucracy
class, working 105, 137, 184, 198
  see also labour; workers
class structure 115, 128, 205
  see also Hegel, G. W. F.; Marx, Karl
class struggle 106, 127, 138, 151–4, 177
Collins, Randall 10–11, 77
communism x–xi, xviii, 38, 141, 145, 151–2, 184
  fall of 18–23, 24, 143, 152, 168, 174, 176
  and property 113–25, 166
Communist Manifesto 9–10, 152, 165
Communist Party 197, 206
Congress of Vienna 23, 99
constitutional monarchy 76, 91, 185–8
corporation 179, 190
  see also civil society
corporation, democratic *see* democratic corporation
corporations, business 124, 136, 139, 172, 198
Cousin, Victor 99, 102, 108
  Introduction à la histoire de la philosophie 108
  translation of Plato's *Gorgias* 102
Croatia 22
Cuba 22–3, 82
Czechoslovakia 21, 22, 207

Dahl, Robert
  A Preface to Economic Democracy 156
deep politics 195
democracy 64, 111, 167, 186, 190, 205
  capitalist 181–2
  Hegel on 65, 74, 76, 86, 130–2, 144, 170–1, 183–4, 185, 189, 202–3
  labour 182
  Marx on 144, 153
democratic corporation 112, 125–40, 141, 151, 170, 178–81, 184
Deutscher, Isaac 114, 116
D'Hondt, Jacques 100, 102, 103, 110
dialectic, Hegelian 3–4, 5, 23–5
dialectical materialism 10
Dickey, Laurence 52
Dietz, K. I. 52
Dilthey, Wilhelm 95
Doctorow, E. L. 30
Dunayevskaya, Raya 175

INDEX

Eagleton, Terry xii
East Germany *see* German Democratic Republic
Ellerman, David 160–3, 166, 167, 179–80, 189–90
  The Democratic Worker-Owned Firm 179
Elster, Jon xi
employment contract *see* wage labour
'end of history' thesis xii, xviii, 130, 141, 142–3
  see also Fukuyama, Francis
Engels, Friedrich xi, xiv, 1, 9–15, 104, 198
  Anti-Dühring 10
  on communism 152
  Communist Manifesto (with Karl Marx) 9–10, 152, 165
  Dialectics of Nature 10
  on freedom 18, 25
  on French Revolution 18, 23
  The German Ideology (with Karl Marx) 9
  on Hegel 10–18
  The Holy Family (with Karl Marx) 9
  Ludwig Feuerbach and the End of Classical German Philosophy xvi, 1, 11, 12, 14, 17, 23, 25, 31, 32–3
  Marx, relationship with xv, 9, 11
  on Marx and Hegel *see Ludwig Feuerbach and the End of Classical German Philosophy*
  on Schelling 11
  'Socialism: utopian or scientific' 104
  on world war 33
environment, concerns about 123–4, 170, 181, 199, 200
equality 147–51
ESOP (Employee Stock Ownership Plan) 179, 180
ethnic separatism 153–4
Europe, Eastern 23–4, 150, 207
Europe, Western 22, 150, 181, 182

Factory Acts 138
feminism xi, 14, 170
Ferguson, Adam 53, 69, 70–1, 89
  The History of Civil Society 70–1
Feuerbach, Ludwig 6, 39, 109
  see also Engels, Friedrich
Fichte, Johann 39, 53, 73–4, 90, 93, 194
finance capital *see* capital, finance
Forster, Georg xvii, 65
Fourier, Charles 104, 107
France 90, 208
Frederick William III, Emperor of Germany and King of Prussia 13, 100, 109
free trade 182
freedom
  Engels on 18, 25
  of expression *see* censorship
  Habermas on 168–9
  Hegel on 14–17, 45–7, 66, 115, 130–1, 137–8, 151, 153–4, 157, 176–7, 183–4, 202–3
  Marx on 118, 137, 144, 166
  Paine on 85
French Revolution 51–2, 90, 97–8, 116, 136, 145
  Engels and 18, 23
  Hegel and 8, 46, 65, 74, 82, 93, 175, 183, 186–8
  Paine and 75–6, 85, 87
Fukuyama, Francis xii, xviii, 14, 25, 32, 63, 74, 141, 143, 184, 185
  The End of History and the Last Man 142, 197
  see also 'end of history' thesis

Galbraith, John Kenneth 208
Gamble, Andrew 177–9
  'The New Politics of Ownership' (with Gavin Kelly) 178
Gans, Eduard xvii, 14, 103–7, 109–11, 114–15, 122, 127, 134, 140
  Lectures on the Philosophy of History, preface to 110

Marx, influence on 103–4, 106, 112–13, 127, 151–2
  on poverty 103–7
German Democratic Republic 20–1
Germany 20–1, 22, 69, 78, 154, 181, 191–2, 198
  censorship in xv–xvi, 59, 60, 62, 64, 69, 89–91, 93, 95–103, 112, 113, 122, 175, 193
  Nazi period 154
Gibbon, Edward
  Decline and Fall of the Roman Empire 53
globalization, economic 24–5, 36, 106, 125–6, 138–9, 182
Goethe, Johann Wolfgang von 3, 5, 101
Gorbachev, Mikhail 20, 21, 24
Gordon, David
  Fat and Mean 198
Gouldner, Alvin 197, 200, 205–6
Gramsci, Antonio xi
Greider, William 124, 125–6, 139, 140, 150
guilds 134–6, 172, 182–3

Habermas, Jürgen xviii, 115, 141, 142, 143, 144, 152–3, 167–8, 200–1
  on civil society 168–73
  on freedom 168–9
Hallische Jahrbücher 11, 109
Hardenberg, Karl August, Fürst von 94, 100
Hardimon, Michael O. 37, 60
Harris, Errol E. xii
Harris, H. S. 44, 57
Hayek, F. A.
  The Road to Serfdom 36
Hegel, Georg Wilhelm Friedrich x, xiii
  on America 76–85, 190
  on aristocracy 192, 203–4
  in Berlin 93–4, 109
  on bureaucracy 115, 188–97, 203–5
  on capitalism 9, 69, 118–19, 124–5, 151–2, 154, 160
  and censorship xv–xvi, 59, 60, 62, 64, 69, 89–91, 93, 99–103, 175, 193
  on Christ 48, 52, 55–6, 57, 67–8, 102
  and Christianity 48, 54–7, 67–8, 159
  on civil service *see* bureaucracy
  on civil society 69–75, 79–80, 82, 106, 113–14, 124, 137–8, 147–51, 157–9, 164–5, 183, 189, 191–2, 200, 203
  on class 128–9, 137, 144, 151–4, 163–5, 167, 188–97, 203–4
  on community *see* class; democratic corporation
  on constitutional monarchy 76, 185–8, 189, 196, 202
  on corporations 182–3, 189, 196, 203, 205
  death of 109
  on democracy 65, 74, 76, 86, 130–2, 144, 170–1, 183–4, 185, 189, 202–3
  on democratic corporation 125–40, 144, 159, 167, 195–6
  dialectics of 5, 6, 23
  'Difference between Fichte's System of Philosophy and Schelling's' 54
  'The earliest system-programme of German idealism' 57–62
  education of 51–4
  on education 91–2, 122–3, 190–1
  Encyclopaedia of the Philosophical Sciences 41, 93
    Logic 3
    Philosophy of Mind 14, 41, 93, 97
    Philosophy of Nature 93
  'The English Reform Bill' 61, 108
  family life of 48–51
  on feudal rights 159–60

INDEX

on freedom 14–17, 45–7, 66, 115, 130–1, 137–8, 151, 153–4, 157, 176–7, 183–4, 202–3
on French Revolution 8, 46, 65, 74, 82, 93, 175, 183, 186–8
Geist, concept of 6–7
on geography 77–8
The German Constitution 71, 73, 76, 118, 185
on Germany 153–4, 202
and Goethe 4–6
and Greece, ancient 8, 14–15, 35, 54, 62, 67
guilds *see* corporations
Heidelberg lectures xvi, 93, 112, 147, 158, 171, 185, 187, 189, 193–4, 207
see also Lectures on . . .
Hölderlin, relationship with xii–xiii, xvii, 44, 48, 52, 53, 54, 56–7, 62, 65, 87–8, 95–8
on hypochondria as alienation 44
ideal state *see* constitutional monarchy
on idealism, concept of 3, 25, 27, 91–2
on individual, role of 131, 146, 154, 165, 183
and property 114, 155, 178
on insanity 158–61
see also Berthold-Bond, Daniel
on labour 145–7, 160–8
Lectures on Natural Right and Political Science xv, 81, 93, 122, 127, 156
Lectures on the History of Philosophy 18, 75
Lectures on the Philosophy of History 16, 110
on life, stages of 41–7
'Life of Jesus' 52, 55, 58, 102
on love, concept of 56–7
Marx, influence on xi, 1–30, 112–22
on Napoleon 90–1, 93, 186–7
on nobility *see* aristocracy

on North America 76–85, 190
in Nuremberg 91–2
On the Orbits of the Planets 54
Paine, influence of 64–88, 89, 91, 130, 134
parliamentary democracy *see* democracy
Phenomenology of Spirit 7, 8, 9, 14, 46, 49, 85, 90, 99, 107, 113, 116, 123, 129, 143, 145
Philosophy of Right xv, 3, 9, 17, 47, 59, 61, 64–5, 70–6, 89, 93, 94, 108, 110, 112, 120, 122, 143, 156–8, 172–3, 185, 193
poetic expression of 53, 58–9, 61–2
and police 59, 64, 69, 91, 97–8, 100–2, 194
'The Positivity of Christianity' 55
on possession, concept of 156, 157
on poverty 105–6, 112, 118, 124–6, 130, 165
on property 81, 111, 113–25, 140, 146, 154–68, 172, 199
labour theory of 157–62
rights 80, 137, 154–7, 162–8, 178
and state 79, 153, 196, 199
on Protestantism 81
and racism 78
on rational state *see* state, rational
on rationality 17–18, 66, 148, 183, 187, 207
see also understanding consciousness
on reality 17–18
on reason 29, 66, 87, 114
on recognition, concept of 143, 145–6, 154
on reconciliation, concept of 107–11, 143
on republican government 76, 81
on revolutions 60–1, 113, 175, 183, 187, 188

Science of Logic 2, 3, 9, 92
on slavery 78, 156, 157, 162
'The Spirit of Christianity and its Fate' 55–6, 95
on state, characteristics of 60–1, 70–5, 81, 152, 174, 183
on state, ideal *see* constitutional monarchy
on state, rational 144, 145, 152, 185–97
on taxes 73, 80
on truth 12–13, 25–6, 28–9
on understanding consciousness, concept of 15–16, 26, 72, 79
at University of Berlin 93–4, 101, 107, 109
at University of Heidelberg 92–3, 99
see also Heidelberg lectures
at University of Jena 90
on wealth 122, 164–5
on will 15, 86, 113, 158–9, 165
Hegelians, Young 6, 11, 12
Heilbroner, Robert 208
Heiman, G. 170
Heine, Heinrich 64
Held, David 175, 181, 188–9, 195
Henning, Leopold von 101
Henrich, Dieter 95
Henwood, Doug 150
Hinchman, Lewis 146–7, 154
Hiroshima 26–30
Hobson, J. A. 36
Hodgskin, Thomas 152, 155, 160, 176
Labour Defended Against the Claims of Capital 166
Hoffheimer, Michael 109
Hölderlin, Friedrich xii–xiii, 44, 53, 54, 56–7, 62, 87–8, 97–9, 103, 112, 115, 194
Empedokles 95
Hegel, influence on 48, 52–4, 65, 87
Hyperion 96
madness of 95–8
Houlgate, Stephen 128, 137
Hudelson, Richard 23

Hungary 19, 20, 207
Hunley, Dillard 10, 33
Husák, Gustav 21
Hutton, Will 174

idealism 5, 14, 25–6
see also Hegel, G. W. F.
indigenous peoples *see* aboriginal peoples
individual, role of 114, 151
see also Hegel, G. W. F.
intelligentsia 197–8, 200, 207–8
Isidore of Seville 41, 43
Italy 153
anti-Mafia campaign in 5, 201

Jacobins 53, 65, 75, 85–7, 98, 116, 186
Jamme, Christopher 51
'Hegel and Hölderlin' 56
Jonge, Alex de 129–30
Judaism 103
July Revolution 104, 107, 108, 109

Kadarkay, Arpad 34–7
Kainz, Howard 133
Kant, Immanuel 28, 39, 70, 159
Religion within the Limits of Reason 53
Kapstein, Ethan 182
Karlsbad Decrees xvi, 64, 76, 81, 93, 100, 104, 122, 185
Keane, John 63, 65, 70, 73, 85
Kellner, Douglas 5
Kelly, Gavin 177–9
'The New Politics of Ownership' (with Andrew Gamble) 178
Kelly, George Armstrong 61
Kelly, Michael 40
Kennedy, John F., assassination of 186, 194–5
Keynes, John Maynard 105, 208
King, Martin Luther 14
Kinnel, Galway 28
Kojève, Alexandre xi, 142
Korea, North 22
Kotzebue, August von 93, 100, 101

INDEX

Kuttner, Robert
Everything for Sale 199

labour 145–51, 160–8, 198
  specialization of 148–9
  and technology 150
  wage labour 119, 137, 167
  see also class, working; Hegel, G. W. F.; unions, trade; workers
labour, child *see* child labour
Lacan, Jacques 186
Lamb, David 12, 25
Latin America 82, 151
  see also South America
leadership 185–8
legislature 202–6
Lenin, V. I. ix, xi, 2, 36, 113, 116
  'What is to be done?' 198
Lichtheim, George
  'The concept of ideology' 11–12
Locke, John 160
Louis XVI, King of France 66, 75–6
Louis Philippe, King of France 107
Lukács, Georg xi, 1, 7–9, 31, 33–7, 60
  on Hegel's concept of reconciliation 34–7, 60, 107
  History and Class Consciousness 7, 28
  The Young Hegel xvi, 7–9, 12, 33–4

MacGregor, David
  Hegel, Marx, and the English State 94, 108
Macpherson, C. B. 123, 182, 190
  The Life and Times of Liberal Democracy 182
Mafia *see* Italy
Marcuse, Herbert xi, 7
  Reason and Revolution: Hegel and the Rise of Social Theory 35, 107
market socialism 175–8, 184
market structures 169, 199, 208
Marx, Karl x, xvii, 110–11, 112–22, 137, 140, 143–5, 161, 163, 165–6, 198
  on bureaucracy 188, 192–3
  Capital xiii, xiv, xvi, 2, 11, 116, 126, 152, 155, 178
  on capitalism 114–15, 144, 174
  on civil society 111, 114–15, 118, 128, 153, 193
  Civil War in France 116
  on class 128, 129, 137, 138, 144, 151–3
  on communism x, 114–22, 141, 151, 166, 181
  Communist Manifesto (with Engels) 9–10, 142, 152, 165–6
  A Contribution to the Critique of Political Economy xvi, 2
  Critique of Hegel's 'Philosophy of Right' 192
  Critique of the Gotha Programme 40, 119, 120, 121, 181
  on democracy 144, 153
  dialectical method 2–3
  Economic and Philosophical Manuscripts of 1844 8, 39, 47, 120
  and Engels, Friedrich xv, 9, 11
  in England xiii–xiv, xv
  on freedom 118, 137, 144, 166
  Gans, Eduard, influence of 112–13, 127, 151–2
  The German Ideology (with Engels) 9, 38, 115
  Grundrisse 2
  Hegel, G. W. F., influence of xi, xiv, xv, 1–30, 103–4, 109, 112–22
  The Holy Family (with Engels) 9
  labour theories of 166
  Notes on Wagner 40
  on praxis, concept of 27, 28
  on proletariat 137, 144, 165, 197
  on property 115–22, 127, 166, 178
  on revolutions 113, 115

surplus value, theory of 152, 163
Theses on Feuerbach, 37, 47
union, workers' 144, 165
at University of Berlin 103, 114, 127
materialism, dialectical 10
materialism, historical 38
McCarney, Joseph 37, 118–19, 143
McMurtry, John 84
McNally, David 177
media, mass 169–70, 171
Mexico 78, 82
Milberg, William 208
Mintzberg, Henry 16, 117, 132
Moggach, Douglas 76
monarchy, constitutional *see* constitutional monarchy
Morley, Morris 83
multinational corporations *see* corporations, business

Nagasaki 27, 29–30
Napoleon Bonaparte xii, 23, 30, 85, 90–1, 92–3, 186–7
Nazis *see under* Germany
neo-conservatism xi, 83, 117, 135–6, 176, 178–9, 193, 199
neo-liberalism *see* neo-conservatism
New Right *see* neo-conservatism
Niethammer, Friedrich Immanuel 91, 94, 99, 100–1
Nietzsche, Friedrich 130
non-governmental organizations 132, 168–9, 171
North America 77–85, 182
North American Free Trade Agreement (NAFTA) 82
not-for-profit organizations *see* non-governmental organizations

Olson, Alan, 97
The Spirit of Hegel 56
Oswald, Friedrich (pseudonym) *see* Engels, Friedrich
Owen, Robert 104

Paine, Tom xvii, 63, 100, 111, 131
The Age of Reason 67
on Christianity 67–8
on civil society 69–74
Common Sense 70–1, 75
and the French Revolution 75–6, 85, 87
Hegel, G. W. F., influence on 64–88, 89, 91, 130, 134
Rights of Man 61, 63, 64–7, 68, 72–5, 77, 85–8
Palley, Thomas 83
Pays de Vaud *see* Vaud, Pays de
Pelczynski, Z. A. 66, 67
Petras, James 22, 83
Pierson, Chris 167, 177–8, 199
Socialism after Communism 176
Pietro, Antonio de 201
Pinkard, Terry 92
Plant, Raymond
Hegel: An Introduction 36
Pöggeler, Otto 95
Poland 19, 20, 153, 207
Popper, Karl 5, 32, 130
The Open Society and its Enemies 32, 36
possession *see* property
postmodernism xii
poverty
causes of 83, 105
in civil society 88
Gans, Eduard, on 103–7
Hegel, G. W. F., on 105–6, 112, 118, 124–6, 130, 165
present-day 150–1, 199, 200
solutions for 105–7
see also wealth
Prawer, S. S. xiv
praxis 27, 28
proletariat 173, 144, 165, 197
see also class; Marx, Karl
property xviii, 83, 104, 107, 141, 142, 147, 178–81
in bourgeois society 159–60
Hegel, G. W. F., on 79–81, 111, 113–25, 137, 140, 146, 153–68, 178, 196, 199
labour theory of 154–63, 166
Marx, Karl, on 115–22, 127, 166, 178
and privatization 112

rights 80, 137, 154–7, 162–8, 178
and state 79, 153, 196, 199
Protestant Church 79
Protestantism 81
public service *see* bureaucracy

rationality
and reason 15–16
and reality 17–18, 28
see also state, rational
Reagan, Ronald 135, 199, 200
reason 15–16, 104, 114, 180
recognition, Hegel's concept of 143
reconciliation xvi, 33–7, 60
republicanism 75–6, 84, 85
Revolution, American *see* American Revolution
revolution, communist 113–16, 119–20, 151
revolution, democratic 64, 65
Revolution, French *see* French Revolution
Revolution, July *see* July Revolution
Revolution, Russian *see* revolution, communist
revolution, socialist 105, 113
Ricardo, David 152, 163
Ritzer, George 15
Robespierre, M. M. I. 53, 75, 85–6, 116, 187
Rockmore, Tom 11
Roemer, Eric xi
Romania 21
Rousseau, Jean Jacques 70, 71, 86, 144, 160
Ruge, Arnold 11, 107, 109
Russell, Bertrand 5
Russia 116, 207
see also Soviet Union
Ryan, Alan 137, 155, 166–7

Saint-Simon, Henri de 104, 106–7
followers of 127, 152
Sakwa, Richard 63, 119
Sand, Karl 93, 100
Saul, John Ralston 182

Scandinavia 181, 186, 198
Schelling, Friedrich Wilhelm Joseph von 108
Engels, Friedrich, on 11
Hegel, G. W. F., and 47, 52, 53, 54, 90, 95–6, 98, 101
and Hölderlin, Friedrich 95–6
Schiller, Friedrich von 53, 73–4, 87, 140
Letters on the Aesthetic Education of Man 73
State of Freedom concept 87, 89
Schopenhauer, Arthur 4–5
Schumpeter, Joseph 188–9, 191, 198–9
Scott, Peter Dale
Deep Politics and the Death of JFK 195
separatism, ethnic *see* ethnic separatism
Serbs, Bosnian 22
Sibree, J. 110
Siegel, Jerrold 2
Marx's Fate xiv
Sinclair, Isaak von xi, xvii, 57, 65, 95, 97, 99, 110, 112
Singer, Peter 126–7
Sismondi, J.-C.-L. Simonde de 155
slavery 78, 80
Slovakia 21
Slovenia 22
Smith, Steven 53, 127, 128, 130, 135, 145
socialism 113–14, 142, 152, 167, 169, 175, 179
see also market socialism
society, civil *see* civil society
South America 77–9, 82
Soviet Union 23–4, 30, 84, 113–14, 116, 119, 121, 197, 207
dissolution of 20, 21, 24
and fall of communism 18, 19, 23–4, 30, 112
Perestroika in 20
and USA 30, 84
see also revolution, communist; Stalin

Stalin, Joseph 5, 9, 116, 129, 153, 197
state, ideal 183, 184
state, rational 151, 152, 175, 181–5
Sten, Jan 116
Steuart, Dugald 53, 69
Stille, Alexander 201
Stirner, Max 155
Storr, G. C. 52
Sweden 186, 198

Taylor, Charles 34, 52, 107
　Hegel 6–7
terror 186
　Paris Commune 116
Terror, Reign of 53, 69, 76, 85–7, 113, 129, 145, 186
Thatcher, Margaret 135, 170–1, 199
Thompson, Edward
　The Poverty of Theory 40
Thompson, William 160
Tocqueville, Alexis de
　Democracy in America 80
Toews, John 104
totalitarianism 145, 169
trade, free 82, 182
trade unions *see* unions, trade
truth, absolute 12–13, 25
Tucher, Gottlieb von 101

Ulrich, Karl 103
unions, trade 136, 139, 181
　Gans, Eduard, on 106–7
　Hegel, G. W. F., on 172
　see also corporations; labour
United Kingdom 117, 171, 198, 208
　governmental system of 190, 202
　labour in 181, 182, 198
United States of America 75–85, 88, 124, 136, 150–1, 180, 195, 206, 208
　American Revolution 18, 52, 74, 75–7, 130
　and communism, fall of 30, 117
　and Cuba 23
　destructive imperialism of 84

and Europe 22
Hegel, G. W. F., on 66, 76–85, 190
　leadership of 186, 205
　neo-conservatism in 197, 198
　and nuclear war 29–30
universal class *see* bureaucracy
USSR *see* Soviet Union

Vaud, Pays de 51–2, 66, 75
Verdery, Katherine 20, 21, 24, 121, 129
Vietnam 22
Vieux, Steve 22
voluntary organizations 168, 172

wage labour 119, 137, 162–8
　see also labour
Walder, Andrew G. 19
　The Waning of the Communist State 167
Waldron, Jeremy
　The Right to Private Property 156–7
Waszek, Norbert 106, 127
wealth 105, 122, 124, 174, 208
　see also Hegel, G. W. F.; poverty
Weber, Max 15, 192, 193
Weiss, Peter
　Hölderlin 98
welfare, social 181, 199
Wesselhöft, Robert 101
West Germany *see* Germany
Wilde, Lawrence 167
will 16, 86, 113
　see also Hegel, G. W. F.
Wokler, Robert 86
women's rights *see* feminism
Wood, Allen 58, 136, 159, 185
workers 141, 182, 198
　see also class, working; labour

Young Hegelians 6, 11, 12
Yugoslavia 21–2, 167

Zimmer, Ernst 96
Zizek, Slavoj 175, 186
Zwilling, Jakob 57